THE **SCIENCE** OF **HAPPINESS**

About the Author

STEFAN KLEIN, PhD, considered one of the most influential science writers in Europe, has written for Germany's leading newspapers and magazines. He was science editor of *Der Spiegel,* a leading German newsmagazine, from 1996–1999, a staff writer with *Geomagazine* from 1999–2000, and is now a freelance writer in Berlin. He has interviewed many of the world's most prominent scientists, including Antonio Damasio, Stephen Jay Gould, V. S. Ramachandran, Craig Venter, Ian Wilmut, and E. O. Wilson. In 1998 he won the Georg von Holtzbrink Prize for Scientific Journalism. He studied physics and philosophy at the universities of Munich and Grenoble and completed his PhD in biophysics in Freiburg. He is also the author of *The Diaries of the Creation.* He lives in Berlin and can be found online at www.stefanklein.info.

STEPHEN LEHMANN is a translator and the author of *Rudolf Serkin: A Life.*

STEFAN KLEIN, PhD

THE **SCIENCE** OF **HAPPINESS**

How Our Brains Make Us Happy—
and What We Can Do to Get Happier

TRANSLATED BY STEPHEN LEHMANN

MARLOWE & COMPANY
NEW YORK

THE SCIENCE OF HAPPINESS:
How Our Brains Make Us Happy—and What We Can Do to Get Happier
Copyright © 2002 by Stefan Klein
Translation copyright © 2006 by Avalon Publishing Group, Inc.

Published by
Marlowe & Company
An Imprint of Avalon Publishing Group, Incorporated
245 West 17th Street • 11th Floor
New York, NY 10011–5300

AVALON
publishing group incorporated

First published in Germany in 2002 by
Rowohlt Verlag GmbH, Rheinbeck bei Hamburg.

Library of Congress Cataloging-in-Publication Data
Klein, Stefan, 1965–
[Glücksformel. English]
The science of happiness : how our brains make us happy, and what we can
do to get happier / Stefan Klein ; translated by Stephen Lehmann.
p. cm.
Includes bibliographical references (p. 273) and index.
ISBN 1-56924-328-X (pbk.)
1. Happiness. I. Title.
BF575.H27K54 2006
152.4'2—dc22
2006002338

ISBN-13: 978-1-56924-328-2

9 8 7 6 5 4 3 2

Designed by Pauline Neuwirth, Neuwirth & Associates, Inc.

Printed in the United States of America

FOR ALEXANDRA

THE **SCIENCE** OF **HAPPINESS**

CONTENTS

INTRODUCTION

EVERYONE EXPERIENCES HAPPINESS differently. For one person it means running barefoot through the dewy grass, for another it's holding his baby in his arms. Sex can make people happy, as can a new outfit, a hotdog or Mozart's Concerto No. 13 for Piano and Orchestra. There are also people who find happiness in the very absence of all of this, as when a Zen monk experiences bliss by losing himself in emptiness.

What kind of feeling is happiness? Katherine Mansfield described a rapturous moment as being like a glowing slice of sun that one has suddenly swallowed. We all chase after this sensation, but it comes over us when we least expect it—only to disappear before we have a chance to enjoy it fully. Once again, there is no time left to look at happiness more closely and to uncover the rules that govern the game it plays with us.

In the spring of 2000, I visited the brain researcher Vilayanur

S. Ramachandran. This brilliant and eccentric Indian-born scientist had caused a stir with his theory of a "God module" in the brain. He'd also cured amputees of their phantom pains by having them look into a set of ingeniously arranged mirrors.[1] *Newsweek* named him a member of the "Century Club," one of the hundred most influential people to watch in the new century. We discussed people's lack of self-understanding, while he paced back and forth in his office among models of the brain, telescopes (he's an amateur astronomer) and statues of Hindu divinities: Ramachandran is a man who cannot sit still even for a moment. Suddenly he exclaimed in his melodious, Indian-inflected English, "And we don't even know yet what happiness is!"

That observation was the catalyst for this book. I wanted to know what happiness is. My own search for positive feelings certainly played a role in my hope that we could find happiness if we only knew where to look for it. I was also motivated by curiosity, which is an occupational disease of scientists and journalists—and I am both.

The deeper I dug into the subject, the more I read, the more I spoke with scientists, sages as well as ordinary people in Asia and in the West, the more convinced I became of a discovery that surprised even me: Ramachandran was wrong. We now know a great deal about what happiness is. Most of what we know, however, is very hard to find, scattered among countless scholarly articles, many of them difficult to learn about. There are other discoveries that have not even been published yet—to say nothing of new insights being gathered and described in a way that anyone can understand and put to use. That is what I hope to achieve with this book.

Perhaps you're surprised to read that happiness—this complex, seemingly divine feeling—can be scientifically researched. We see nothing strange in the study of *unhappiness*. Clinical psychologists have long attended to unpleasant feelings, and for the past two decades or so brain researchers have become increasingly knowledgeable about the origins of anger, fear, and depression. An entire industry that sells pills against pathological dejection profits from their discoveries, as, indeed, do countless patients. But for a long time happiness was more or less shrugged off.

This has changed only recently. Brain scientists have begun to direct their interest toward positive feelings, and they are making rapid and impressive progress. Much of what until relatively recently was still science fiction is reality in today's laboratories. New imaging techniques enable us to observe the brain as it thinks and feels. They allow us to see, for example, how joy arises in our brain when we think of someone we love. Molecular biology reveals what subsequently transpires within our ten trillion brain cells, and psychological experiments show how these internal changes affect our behavior. We are forming an understanding of the ways in which positive feelings come into being.

We are now beginning to answer questions that people have always asked themselves. Is happiness more than simply the opposite of unhappiness? Is it genetic? Does the feeling of anger pass if you vent it? Is it possible to prolong the good moments? Does money make people happy? Can we stay in love with the same person all our life? What is the greatest happiness?

Central to answering these questions are two fairly recent insights of brain research. One concerns the parts of the brain that produce a sense of well-being: our brains have a special circuitry for joy, pleasure, and euphoria—we have a happiness system. Just as we come into the world with a capacity for speech, we are also programmed for positive feelings. This discovery will shape our understanding of mankind as powerfully as Freud's theories of the deep unconscious did in the last century.

The other, still more surprising discovery is that the adult brain continues to change. Until a few years ago scientists believed that the brain, like bones, was fully grown by no later than the end of puberty. But exactly the opposite is true: the circuits in our brain are altered whenever we learn something, and new connections are forged in our network of nerve cells. Using the right microscopes, we can even see these transformations within the skull. After you have read this book, your brain will look different than it did when you started.

These changes are triggered by thoughts, but even more by emotions. This means that with the right exercises we can increase our capacity for happiness. Much as we can learn a foreign language, we can train our natural aptitude for positive feelings.

Fascinated by the discoveries of genetic research, we've tended for some time now to understand all our individual characteristics in terms of genes and chromosomes. It's easy for us to overlook the fact that we develop our genetic inheritance only in interaction with our day-to-day lives. Our happiness depends at least as much on our environment and our culture as on our genes, which is why this book considers not only the brain as a source of happiness but also the cultural influences and the daily occurrences that set these processes in motion.

The role culture plays in our perceptions of happiness is evident even in differences among languages. Sanskrit, the language of ancient India, for example, contains over a dozen words for as many different ways to express our English "happiness."[2] The other Western languages, too, lag well behind the abundance of positive sensations of which we are capable.

A study comparing American students and the inhabitants of a city in India provides persuasive evidence of the way in which these differences can play out. Both groups were shown a silent video in which certain gestures were demonstrated by two masters of Indian dance. These were accompanied by a random list of their meanings—joyful surprise, relaxed satisfaction after a completed task, or shy excitement. For the Indians this list consisted of a few appropriate words.[3] While the young

Americans had no difficulty in matching the correct description to the gestures of happiness, they lacked the specific vocabulary and required long circumlocutions to identify feelings for which the Indians needed only a few appropriate words. It seems, then, that our brains are capable of feelings that go more or less unrecognized in Western culture.

We pay a heavy price for this disregard of happiness. More than 25 percent of Americans suffer at least once in their lifetime from a psychological disturbance, and in the course of a year nearly one out of ten experiences a depression lasting several weeks.[4] Over thirty thousand people in the United States commit suicide every year. In other parts of the world, suicide rates are much lower.[5]

The incidence of serious depression is rising quickly—in the United States as in almost all industrial countries. Above all, this illness is affecting increasingly more children, adolescents, and young adults. Today the risk of depression for young people is three times higher than it was ten years ago.[6]

The mental suffering experienced in the industrialized countries is spreading to other parts of the world.[7] Within twenty years depression will affect more women throughout the world than any other illness, whether physical or mental. Only cardiac and circulatory illnesses will do more harm to men.[8] Depression is threatening to become the plague of the twenty-first century.

Far from everyone who is unhappy suffers from mental illness. Nonetheless, sadness is much more closely related to depression than was long assumed, for both result from similar processes in the brain. They're worth combating. The epidemic of depression shows how urgently we need a culture of happiness.

"Joy is the transition of mind into a state of perfection," according to the Dutch philosopher Baruch Spinoza. "Pain, on the other hand, is the transition to a lower state."

But joy affects the body at least as much as it does the mind. Unhappiness destroys the body. Happiness strengthens it.

New studies shed light on the connections between body and mind that scientists have long overlooked. Persistent fear and despondency endanger one's health because they cause stress. And stress increases the risk of dying of a heart attack or a stroke, to take only two examples. By contrast, someone who has learned to contain his dark moods and to fortify his sunny ones is also taking care of his body. Positive feelings counteract stress and its consequences for health. They even stimulate the immune system.

They increase mental productivity even more. In terms of the brain, thoughts and feelings are two sides of the same coin: happy people are more creative, and, as many studies show, they solve problems better and more quickly.[9] Happiness makes people smart, and not just momentarily, but permanently. Positive feelings stimulate growth in the nerve connections in the brain—happiness and new mental associations go together.

Finally, happy people are also nicer people. They are more aware and more likely to see the good in others. They are more likely to act altruistically, and they are more successful mediators in resolving conflict.[10]

Thus, happiness can be both one of life's goals and the means to a better life. Negative moods limit people, whereas positive feelings expand options. Happiness brings vitality.

In order to find happiness, you have to know what it is. This book will take you on a journey of discovery to positive feelings. You will learn many tips to help you apply new neuroscientific discoveries toward a happier life. But this isn't a self-help book in the usual sense. I want to explain causes, not to hand out easy answers, for each person's happiness is, after all, as unique as her personality. Our brains are built according to the same model, so we all experience pleasure and joy similarly, but what specifically triggers these feelings differs from one person to another. This is why generalized advice is of little use. In the end, everyone has to find her own way to happiness. This book is to be a kind of travel guide to make that journey possible.

In the first part of the book, you'll learn how happiness comes about and why nature invented positive feelings. At the center of these chapters is an account of how our brain can make us happy and bring negative emotions under control. Like muscles, these systems can be trained. The brain can reprogram itself, changing its structure not only through external experiences but also by learning about its own feelings. Surprisingly, many of the new scientific discoveries confirm age-old wisdom, which is why the first part of the book ends with a short comparison of the legacy of insights transmitted from ancient Greece and Rome as well as Eastern cultures.

The second part of the book explores the anatomy of the passions. The experience of pleasure, the joys of discovery, love, and sex have much in common, and yet they come about in different ways and serve different ends. These basic feelings are congenital and have developed over the course of millions of years. We can observe some of them in relatively simple creatures like mice and even bees. Passions are rooted so deeply within humans and animals that it is pointless to want to get rid of them, or even to change them. What is important is that we learn to live with them, living in such a way as to extract as much pleasure and as little pain as possible from evolution's programs. The last chapter of this section offers suggestions for making this possible.

Evolution has also equipped humans, unlike insects and rodents, with a highly developed cerebrum. We are built to steer our inborn drives, pleasures, and fears onto well-ordered pathways. The third part of this book deals with these accomplishments of consciousness and the means we have of putting them to use. Whether we see the famous glass as half full or half empty has much more influence on our feelings than do the actual contents of the glass. The ability to consciously steer our thoughts and feelings gives us a powerful tool against sadness and even depression. But the cerebrum enables us to do still more. Unlike animals, we can experience feelings of freedom, a sense of openness, receptivity, and oneness with the world. We can be in rapture over the play of light on the surface of the sea, and we can lose ourselves completely in an activity. Directed perception and concentration are the keys to such moments of euphoria. Possibly these mental states even explain how mystical experiences come about in people's minds.

An important source of happiness lies in the optimal development of our talents and potential. But no one lives for himself alone. For this reason the fourth and last part of this book looks at the conditions that must exist in society in order for citizens to engage—in the words of the Declaration of Independence—in "the pursuit of happiness." Where there is a sense of community, justice, and control over our own lives, the chances that an individual can lead a happy life are good.

The question, then, is how society as a whole, as well as every individual in it, can create a culture of happiness. Two thousand years ago, the sages sensed that it would be possible for people to increase their happiness. Today, thanks to the astonishingly productive field of neuroscience, there is no longer any doubt: we can learn to be happy.

PART ONE

HAPPINESS: WHAT IS IT?

1
THE SECRET OF SMILING

IN 1967, a young man from San Francisco named Paul Ekman went in search of a tribe that lived so far from "known civilization" that it might have been on another planet. Could there still be people on earth who had never been in contact with outsiders, who had no knowledge of writing or print, to say nothing of television? Ekman knew only that he didn't have much time, that within a few years the most remote jungle villages might be within reach of radio signals, roads, and airplanes.

At the time, Papua New Guinea was regarded as the end of the world, an island that one associated with headhunters and cannibals. But the thirty-three-year-old Ekman was fearless, and, all alone, he set out for the Stone Age. He wasn't really interested in exotic customs or in documenting still more examples of cultural strangeness for anthropological scholarship. Rather, he wanted to explore an area common to all humans: the secret of smiling.[1]

People's expectations for this endeavor were low. Colleagues warned that there was little to discover in the play of facial expression. A mother smiles at her baby, and the baby smiles back. That's that. When Ekman was setting out thirty years ago, no one dared question the assumption that humans come into the world as a blank page. A child was seen as an empty vessel to be filled with the knowledge and customs of its parents and environment. We learn our facial expressions in childhood, just as we learn everything else. Only Ekman thought otherwise. Wouldn't it be possible, he asked himself, for feelings to be present at birth? Do we perhaps have some kind of preinstalled switch for smiling? If this were true, everyone in the world would exhibit the same facial expressions at comparable moments. Hadn't Charles Darwin already suspected as much?

STONE AGE FACES

With his backpack filled with cameras, tape recorders, and photographs of faces, the young researcher hiked toward the New Guinea highlands, with a local guide leading the way. After a few weeks, they entered a region that no one of European descent had ever seen. It was inhabited by the South Fore, a tribe whose custom of eating the brains of deceased relatives had been prohibited only eight years earlier. They lived in huts constructed from woven grass and leaves and used tools carved from stone. The women wore grass skirts, while the men were clothed in tangas made from beef hide. They gave the scientist and his guide a friendly welcome.

Ekman sat down in the center of the small village and unpacked his tape recorders. Never had the people here seen a shiny box like this on which two circles turned, seemingly on their own. And suddenly they heard their own voices! Their mouths began to open, their cheekbones lifted, their eyes sparkled: they were smiling. Clearly they were excited by the surprise. In the background, Ekman's guide was filming the event—the first proof that people from the other end of the world smile just as we do.

From then on, the South Fore didn't leave Ekman's side for even a moment. They were surrounding him in eager anticipation of the day's entertainment before he woke up in the morning. Some days he chased after the children with a rubber knife so that his guide could photograph the frightened faces. On other days he showed portraits of Americans both cheerful and sad and through his guide asked the South Fore to identify the parent of a dying child. They pointed unanimously to the sad face—apparently they could understand the expressions on the faces of the foreign Americans with no difficulty. After a few weeks, Ekman asked his guide to arrange encounters in which one villager would meet another, as if spontaneously. The cameras recorded the happy smiles of greeting.

After four months in the jungle, Ekman returned to the United States and studied his photos. He no longer had any doubt: the faces of the South Fore showed exactly the same expressions as those of people in the Western world. Languages may differ from one nation to another, but faces, whether those of the South Fore of the New Guinea highlands or those of San Franciscans, express feelings in exactly the same way.

Scientists were excited and intrigued by this discovery. Some of them set out to disprove Ekman's theory. They went to the jungles of Borneo, to nomads in Iran, and to the most remote regions of the Soviet Union, only to return home empty-handed. It was the same story everywhere: culture has hardly any impact on the repertoire of human emotions. Some peoples may show feelings more openly, others less so, but joy and sadness, fear and anger, are feelings shared by everyone.

With this one discovery Ekman refuted two errors. First,

5

THE SCIENCE OF HAPPINESS

from now on it would be difficult to claim that children learn emotions from the people around them. If that were the case, there would have to be different kinds of smiles around the world, much as "joy" is "Freude" in Germany and "gaoxing" in China. But once it is established that facial expressions are the same everywhere, we know that basic emotions and the way in which our bodies express them are inborn.

Congenitally blind children, who are not able to copy facial expressions, smile spontaneously. This fact alone should have raised doubts in the minds of those who believed that joy was learned; even Charles Darwin had initiated a study in a home for the blind for his book *The Expression of Emotion in Man and Animals* (1872). But this work by the great evolutionary biologist was as good as forgotten, and belief in the learned acquisition of feelings was so unshakable that no scientist thought of following Darwin's suggestion and talking to a few teachers of the blind. Thus, Paul Ekman had to go to the South Seas. Science, too, can be prejudiced.[2]

There's another matter in which Ekman was even more influential. Filming the facial expressions of the South Fore, he showed that feelings can be the subject of scientific study. That was no small feat, for anyone concerned with emotions at the end of the 1960s was very much on the margins of academic psychology. The subjects deemed worthy of serious research were perception, thinking, and behavior. The examination of feelings unfolding inside people, seemingly hidden from sight, was left to philosophers and poets. But Ekman removed any doubts about the accessibility of private experience to science.

© PAUL EKMAN, 1995

This young man from the distant highlands of Papua New Guinea has never before seen someone from another tribe or nation, but the joy radiating from his face is familiar to us. Elementary feelings and the way we express them are inborn, which is why the language of smiling is understood worldwide. This photo comes from the psychologist Paul Ekman's research expedition.

GENUINE SMILES AND USEFUL SMILES

Encouraged by his success, the young researcher invented an entire system for translating expression of feeling into numbers and tables, as if dividing it into its constituent atoms. It takes forty-two muscles in the human face to create facial expressions. Ekman gave a number to each. "Nine," for example, meant wrinkling the nose, "fifteen," pressing the lips together. Now the researchers could record even the wildest grimaces on the computer.

With this tool, Ekman discovered nineteen different ways of smiling. Of these, eighteen are not genuine, though they are very useful, serving as masks when we don't wish to show others the entire truth about our feelings. There is a smile with which we show politeness after being embarrassed by a bad joke; a smile that conceals our fear; another that hides displeasure. Although all smiling engages the zygomatic muscle that stretches from the cheekbone to the upper lip and pulls up the corners of the mouth, the other muscle groups in the face orchestrate various false smiles. These make human interaction possible, but they have little to do with joy.

Only one kind of smile is genuine: not only do the corners of the mouth go up, but the eyes are slightly narrowed, small wrinkles appear in their corners ("crow's feet"), and the upper half of the cheeks rise. Only when the orbicularis oculi muscle contracts does the face show happiness. Ekman called this facial movement the Duchenne smile, in honor of the French physiologist Guillaume-Benjamin Duchenne, who in 1862 was the first to study the orbicularis oculi, the sphincter muscle that surrounds the entire eye,

With the help of his facial numbering system, Ekman could show that only the Duchenne smile expresses a true sense of contentment. When he showed subjects cheerful films, this smile—and almost never any other—frequently flitted across their faces. The more frequently the corners of their eyes crinkled into crow's feet, the more emphatic they were afterward about the pleasure the film gave them. But when they saw frightening scenes of fire victims or amputations, the Duchenne smile disappeared. The movement of the orbicularis oculi muscle, then, is an infallible sign of joy.[3]

Duchenne called these contractions the "sweet emotions of the soul." He already knew that we can control this muscle by force of will only with great difficulty, which is why most of us fail miserably when asked to "smile for the camera." So Duchenne used another method to help his experimental subjects smile: With thin wires he conducted an electric charge across their cheeks,[4] thereby stimulating the orbicularis oculi muscle so powerfully that his subjects showed a smile that was unnaturally cheerful. The photos of these experiments now hang in New York's Museum of Modern Art.

Only about ten percent of all people are able to control their facial muscles so well that without special training they can produce a Duchenne smile on command. This ability is probably congenital. Most of the rest of us have to learn to fake a real smile. A funny joke helps, or remembering a situation in which we felt especially good.

Even actors, and especially politicians, struggle with this problem. A cheaply produced soap opera shows how difficult it is to bring facial movements and feelings under control. Not for a second do we believe the actors' unskilled expressions of feeling. Among the more talented thespians, however, there are many who have been trained to control their facial muscles. Laurence Olivier, for example, was famous for knowing how each feeling had to look from the point of view of the spectator. But even some Hollywood stars never learn to control the features of their face, and it's for good reason that Steve McQueen and John Wayne made the unmovable poker face their trademark.

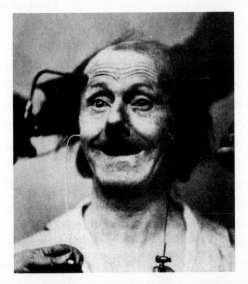

Using fine electric wires that he placed on the face of an experimental subject in 1862, the physiologist Guillaume-Benjamin Duchenne was able to stimulate an artificial smile. Weak currents stimulated the facial muscles of this old man in such a way that his expression shows a genuine smile: the corners are the mouth are turned upward, and the orbicularis oculi muscle contracts.

HAPPINESS ARISES FROM THE BODY

Has someone paid you a compliment, or sent you flowers, or have you enjoyed a particularly good meal? It is not only the face that shows positive feelings. Your body responds with excitement to whatever is giving you pleasure. This is worth paying attention to, because it becomes possible to be aware of many of the resulting changes.

When you are happy, the blood pulses somewhat faster in your veins. In most people, three to five heartbeats a minute distinguish happiness from their normal state. Because blood circulation improves, skin temperature rises by about a tenth of a degree centigrade. This stimulation causes skin to become somewhat damper, and skin conductance drops. Even your fingers tremble, though not in a jerky way. You'd notice this difference—which amounts to a tenth of a millimeter—only if you were trying to thread a needle. But perhaps you would be able to perceive the source of this trembling: the micromovements of the fingers that the scientists have measured is mirrored in the tension of the musculature of the shoulders, arms, and hands. When you feel good, these muscles relax and become more flexible.[5] In addition, since happiness also shifts our hormonal balance, changes take place that we don't feel directly—but more about this later.

Before you or the people around you become aware of the beginning of a smile, things have already happened in the face. The zygomatic muscle, which pulls the mouth upward, has tensed a bit. The orbicularis oculi muscle with its crow's feet has also contracted slightly. On the other hand, the corrugator supercilii muscle, which creates expressions of disgust, sadness, and fear by pulling up the eyebrows, is relaxed.

This is what happiness looks like. As with all feelings, it begins as much in the body as in the brain, because a sense of well-being happens only when the brain receives and interprets the necessary signs from the heart, the skin, and the muscles. Without our bodies, we would be incapable of happiness.

Initially, this might seem like a strange idea. Clearly, we owe some feelings of happiness—for example, when we eat or make love—to a sense of physical pleasure that is almost unalloyed. But what happens when we remember a good time with friends, or look forward to a vacation? In such moments of happiness our imagination seems to play the decisive role. But this is an illusion. Thoughts, memories, and hopes alone do not enable us to experience emotion. Only when they link with the right body signals can we experience joy, because it is from them that the brain constructs the perception of well-being. Try being happy with tense muscles and a cold sweat!

Thus, happiness arises at least as much from our bodies— arms and legs, heart and skin—as from our imagination and thinking. For this reason, we would be well advised to take our bodies much more seriously than we are accustomed to doing.

THE AUTONOMY OF POSITIVE FEELINGS

Positive feelings are linked to the body. This is why it is so difficult to feel or show happiness on command—an annoying fact that has to do with the architecture of the brain. There are nerves that are responsible for controlling the body and thus also for directing emotions over which our consciousness has no power. In order to understand this, we have to look more closely at how the human organism processes data.

Anatomy books usually show the nervous system of the body as a tree standing on its head and more or less rooted in the brain. Signaling pathways branch out ever more finely from the brain stem to the organs and limbs.

This may suggest the image of a unified structure that weaves all these pathways together, but that's not the way it is. In fact, the human nervous system is divided into two parts that work largely independently of one another: the voluntary and the autonomic nervous system. The voluntary (or somatic) nervous system directs most of the muscles that move our bones. The instruction to bend my index finger in order to continue typing this text follows these nerves. These commands issue from the cerebral cortex, that furrowed, gray dome directly under the top of the skull, where our wishes, imagination, and thoughts arise. The voluntary nervous system is in direct contact with this part of the brain.

The autonomic nervous system, on the other hand, originates on the other side of the brain. It begins in the brain stem, in the very first gray cells at neck level. Here reside the circuits that govern the basic functions of the organism. They direct waking and sleeping, control the heartbeat, and stimulate our genitals. The nerves of the involuntary nervous system barely lead to the skeletal muscles at all, but rather to the internal organs, the blood vessels, and all the way down to the tiny skin muscles that hold up each hair. This part of the nervous system causes us to blush when we're embarrassed, our hair to stand on end when we're afraid, and our pulse to race when we're in love.

Since, as its name suggests, we have no control over the autonomic nervous system, we can't simply decide to be happy. This part of the nervous system not only governs the orbicularis oculi muscle required for the genuine smile, it controls our heartbeat, circulation, and perspiration—all those unconscious movements of the body that the brain perceives in order to create positive feelings. This is why we can't change our emotions directly. We have to proceed more cleverly.

OUR BODIES KNOW MORE THAN WE DO

There's another reason why it wouldn't make sense for us to try to influence the autonomic nervous system. Because it governs those bodily functions that are essential to life, an incorrect decision could have fatal consequences. So the brain is programmed to prevent us from holding our breath for very long, or from making our heart stop.

The autonomic nervous system accomplishes most of its tasks in association with chemical transmitters called hormones. This gives the brain two ways of overseeing the organism: it sends electrical signals through the nervous system and chemical signals via the hormones. The brain itself can create hormones in the pituitary gland and secrete them into the bloodstream— something very practical, since this enables brain circuits to make direct contact with the organs rather than having to take a detour through the nerves. Transmitters help the brain to watch constantly over the level of substances in the body that are critical for survival and to intervene when necessary. In this way, the autonomic nervous system and hormones together keep the organism in optimal running order.

This automatic survival program has one other advantage: it prevents us from wasting too much attention on simple bodily functions. It leaves our head free for matters that we would seldom get to if we had to occupy ourselves with the question of whether our liver, for example, is producing enough enzymes to break down last night's alcohol.

We are aware of this system only when it becomes seriously imbalanced. Then our bodily reactions force us to act. If our blood sugar level gets too low, hunger torments us. If the alcohol doesn't disappear quickly enough from our blood after we've had a night on the town, our head pounds—a warning for the next time.

The control of our organism works like the user interface of a computer. Both place a protective shell around the complicated processes internal to the system, preventing us from getting near them. The only technical information that the user ever sees is the occasional error message, when the program can no longer help itself. Many unpleasant feelings correspond precisely to that message.

For this reason, the emotions themselves—and not only the processes that direct the body—are shielded from the will's direct influence. We can only control them indirectly by treating ourselves well—by changing our environment or our thoughts, or by remembering pleasant situations. But if a huge bear suddenly comes toward us in the woods, we can't choose whether we want to be afraid. We're afraid before we can reflect. The heart begins to race, our breath becomes shallower—the body is preparing to run. In the seconds that it would take for a person to make a conscious decision, an aggressive animal could tear his victim apart. So the body answers the threat before we begin to feel the fear.

So, too, we feel pleasure as soon as we notice something that could be useful to us. These are the small moments of happiness: if we're hungry and the bakery's smells waft our way, our mouth waters. If a friend walks toward us, a smile of welcome crosses our face, and in the same moment we experience joy. We experience feelings when we perceive the involuntary reactions of our bodies.

SCIENTISTS DISCOVER INTUITION

Do the reactions of the body move ahead of the feelings, like the waves in front of a ship's bow? A landmark experiment directed toward this question comes from the lab of the Portuguese-American neurologist Antonio Damasio at the University of Iowa, one of the most important centers in the field of emotion research. Among the resources Damasio and his wife, Hanna, have assembled is the largest archive of images of damaged brains in the world. Thanks to CAT-scan technology that creates spatial images of living brains, the Damasios have examined more than 2,500 heads. They bring these inner views of ailing brains together with the case studies of their patients, who suffer from every imaginable disorder of thought, feeling, and behavior, giving the Danasios insight into the workings of the human mind. Because their archive is so unique, experiments from the Damasios' lab will be cited often in this book.

Using relatively simple means, the Iowa scientists have shown how the first manifestations of joy, aversion, fear, and anger are, indeed, somatic. They presented experimental subjects with a game of chance and hooked them up to a lie detector.[6] This game—it has come to be known as the Iowa Card Test—consists of repeatedly pulling cards from two closed decks. The good pile yielded moderate wins and smaller losses, the bad pile a fairly large win, but more often huge losses.

After about the tenth draw, the subjects began to avoid the bad pile, and the lie detector showed the beginnings of a cold sweat and a pounding heart as soon as their hands approached the risky cards.[7] The subjects, however, didn't know why they were behaving in this way, nor were they aware of their physical reactions. Only after about fifty draws did they report a conscious aversion to the bad pile. And it took even longer—until about the eightieth draw—before they could explain this response and the principle of the game.

Intuition—this strange sense that we sometimes get when first meeting a person who later turns out to be hostile—does exist, though we can't explain premonitions of this kind, because they derive from unconscious emotions. For example, when we first meet someone who turns out to be an enemy, a threatening facial expression may quickly pass over his face, sparking an imperceptible moment of fear.

Intuition works for us even when we can't tell what is going on. A few less intelligent people never did manage to grasp the system behind the card test, but they chose correctly nonetheless. On this point, popular belief has proved to be more savvy than science, which for centuries has denied the possibility of any knowledge other than that available through reason.

But—contrary to what is often thought—emotional insight is not based on supersensible phenomena. Rather, intuition is anchored solidly in our bodies. We attain it by experience. When first pulling the cards, the participants in the experiment did not yet have a feeling for the better pile. First the brain had to learn to predict the result. A premonition happens when this calculation—one pile is good, the other is bad—is transmitted to the body before it reaches consciousness.

In the example of the aggressive bear (described by the American psychologist William James), we've already seen the usefulness of intuitive behavior that bypasses conscious thought. It makes life easier for the individual and saves valuable time in the face of danger. Sometimes, then, the body knows better than reason, or, in the words of the French philosopher Blaise Pascal, "The heart has its reasons of which reason knows nothing."[8]

IMAGES FROM OUR INNER WORLD

Like our anxious subjects with the bad pile of cards, we are often not aware of the depth of our emotions in daily life. We might know that we're blushing only when someone points it out to us. And our eyes may be sparkling with enthusiasm when we ourselves don't know how happy we are.

In such moments it becomes clear that emotions and feelings are not one and the same, although in conversation we usually employ the words interchangeably. But there is a difference: an emotion is an automatic response of the body to a specific situation—the flash of our eyes in pleasure, or the reddening of the face when we're caught in a white lie. We experience a feeling when we perceive these emotions consciously—as pleasure or as shame.[9]

Emotions, then, are unconscious; feelings are conscious. We perceive most emotions also as feelings, which is why the layman makes no distinction between them. Nonetheless, some emotions can remain hidden from us, as, for example, when we blush and no one brings it to our attention.

How does an emotion produce a feeling? With their equipment, the scientists working with Antonio Donasio were able to observe the brain in decisive moments. They asked healthy subjects to think back to very happy or very sad moments in their lives: reuniting with a loved person, or the death of a parent. For a few test runs, the researchers checked the reactions of the subjects with a lie detector and selected those who showed especially strong reactions. Then they slid them into a Positron Emission Tomography (PET) scanner, a machine that takes up an entire room. The subject lies enclosed in a narrow metal tube, strapped in so that the images don't blur—not exactly an atmosphere likely to stimulate thoughts of Fantasy Island. A solution with weakly radioactive modified glucose (serving as a contrast medium) flows through a drip into the blood. Even so, the subjects were transported so deeply into their memories that they forgot all the technology surrounding them. Some even began to cry. Meanwhile, Damasio and his colleagues watched the screen and observed the parts of the brain that the patient's strong feelings were activating.[10]

The images that the scientists presented in 2000 drew attention for two reasons. First, they showed in detail never seen before what happens inside the brain when we feel happiness and sadness, annoyance and anger. With the PET scanner, one can actually see what feeling is going on within a person at any given moment. Second, these images give stronger evidence than anything available to date that feelings actually do follow

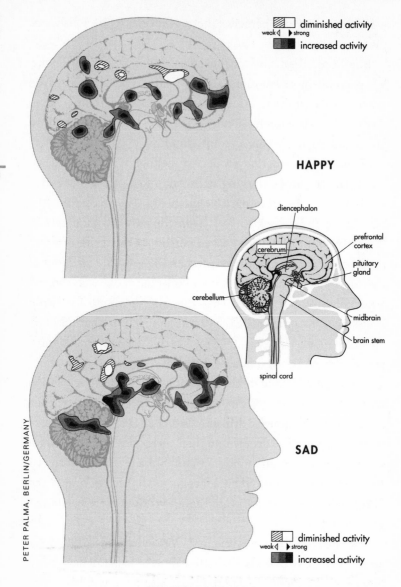

diminished activity
weak ◁ ▷ strong

increased activity

HAPPY

diencephalon

prefrontal cortex

cerebrum

pituitary gland

cerebellum

midbrain

brain stem

spinal cord

SAD

diminished activity
weak ◁ ▷ strong

increased activity

PETER PALMA, BERLIN/GERMANY

FEELINGS IN THE BRAIN

Right: The brain is constructed like a building with several stories. The foundation is the brain stem, which receives signals from the body. It grows out of the spinal cord and into the midbrain. Above the midbrain is the diencephalon, which is responsible for arousal. It controls the organism in that it releases hormones through the pituitary gland. At the very top, underneath the top of the skull, arches the dome of the cerebrum, which supervises all the rest of the brain. Its functions are sensual perceptions, thinking, planning, and all the activities of consciousness.

Left: The tomographic image shows how happiness and sadness are created in the brain. For every feeling has its corresponding pattern of brain activity. Nonetheless, some parts of the brain are active in both feelings: the data goes from the body through the brain stem. The midbrain is especially active here, as can be seen from the darker coloration. The cerebellum, which hangs like a backpack on the brain stem, processes the impulses from the brain stem and gives orders to the muscles—for example, if something pleases us, the command to laugh. Above it lies the diencephalon, which is activated to release emotional excitement. In the cerebrum the gyri (folds of the brain) behind the eyes, the so-called prefrontal cortex, are especially active. It converts the emotions to plans and actions. (Damasio, 2000)

the reactions of the body. Precisely those areas are illuminated on the monitor that are necessary to create an image of the body in the brain: underneath, the brain stem, which controls the entire organism; in the middle, parts of the cerebellum and the interbrain that process these data; and at the top, finally, the cerebrum, which brings all this information together into a coherent image and connects it to our conscious perceptions, thoughts, and fantasies.[11] We become conscious of an emotion only when it has been processed by the cerebrum.

Every feeling—and thus also happiness—depends on the brain receiving and then processing signals from the body. Even in moments of supreme bliss, when it's as if we're in another world, it's in perceiving our own body that our feelings of euphoria arise. As Damasio reminds us, our mind is, in the true sense of the word, embodied, not "embrained." A disembodied being would feel neither happiness nor sadness. And, should you tire of physical stimuli, your body, according to Damasio, can be stimulated by the brain, even unconsciously. Much as a fantasy image can be seen by the inner eye, so the brain stem can feign impulses that it doesn't really receive. Damasio believes that this enables the organism to save itself the trouble of speeding up its pulse and going through the entire program of positive emotions in less important situations—when, for example, it experiences a minor pleasure—allowing, nonetheless, a feeling of pleasant arousal, in energy-saving mode, as it were. In all likelihood this mechanism helps people left paraplegic by an accident keep their capacity for emotion alive.[12]

DOES SMILING MAKE YOU HAPPY?

It has become conventional wisdom that a sourpuss has only to smile in order to lift his spirits. Robert Baden-Powell, the founder of the Boy Scouts, even advised his young people to force a smile when they were afraid or experienced something unpleasant—the world, he claimed, would then seem friendlier.[13]

Can we really make ourselves happy with the aid of our facial muscles? Paul Ekman pursued this question scientifically, and corroborated the insight that smiling will indeed make you happy. If feelings originate in the body, then it is logical to conclude that the body can also alter feelings. Alas, this path to happiness turns out not to be as smooth as we'd like to think, for by no means does every smile attain its end. The polite expression that we strive for when we ask our boss for a raise might mask our insecurity, but it won't make us euphoric, because we've only feigned the good mood. We feel really good only when we make a genuine Duchenne smile, raising the corners of our mouth while also crinkling the corners of the eyes into crow's feet.

Since most people aren't able to control these movements, Ekman taught the participants in his experiments to train their orbicularis oculi muscle, but without telling them why. Then he was able to show that the signals of happiness didn't go in only one direction. The better the participants in the experiment learned to control their orbicularis oculi muscle, the more frequently they reported a good mood that they themselves were not able to explain. But this wasn't enough for Ekman. He also recorded the brain waves of his students when they consciously forced their face into a "genuine" smile.[14] And indeed, the resulting electric signals really were indistinguishable from those sent in the course of an amused response to a well-told joke. Smiling makes us happy, but only the right kind of smile. Tricking the brain takes skill.

2

POSITIVE FEELINGS AS A COMPASS

WHY DO WE actually have feelings? Emotions control the organism, but they could do that just as well if, like reflexes, they stayed quietly in the background. When the doctor taps you on the knee with the little hammer, your leg jerks up without any particular emotion on your part. And machines can direct their internal processes in extremely complicated ways, but no automatic welder ever has leaped for joy or, choked up by tears, gasped for compressed air.

In fact, there are even people who feel nothing at all. One of them was a patient of Damasio's who became known as Elliot.[1] Elliot was a successful lawyer and a good husband and father until a tumor the size of a tangerine destroyed the prefrontal cortex above the nasal cavity. The tumor, a so-called meningioma, was removed, but Elliot was no longer the same person.

He would have to be dragged out of bed in the morning like

a lazy kid on a school day. Incapable of organizing his time at work, he frittered the day away. And unable to work quickly through a pile of papers on his desk, he fretted for hours trying to find a method to put them in order. He lost the ability to distinguish what was important from what wasn't and could no longer make decisions.

Elliot began to lose his footing in society. He was fired from his job. Hooking up with shady characters, he constantly became mired in new business interests and financial misadventures. Although an experienced businessman, he lost everything and went bankrupt. His marriage fell apart, and a second relationship quickly broke up. Before turning forty, Elliot was under the care of his siblings and living off disability.

And yet, as Damasio had learned, Elliot's high intelligence had survived the brain damage undiminished. His reflexes, too, functioned normally. When frightened, he showed the usual physical reactions. The doctors could find no other signs of damage. Elliot was charming, attentive, sometimes even witty—and always on the cool side. He was unflappable, incapable of being provoked. He would tell the tragedy of his own life in a manner so detached that one might have thought he'd read about it. With the aid of numerous psychological tests, Damasio discovered that his patient was a man without feelings. Although his unconscious emotions were sometimes stirred, Elliot no longer had access to them.

When Damasio's colleagues showed Elliot pictures of people as they were fleeing from burning houses or being threatened by rising waters in a flood, he explained coolly that he knew perfectly well that he was supposed to find such scenes terrible, but that he, alas, felt nothing. The same thing happened when he was shown photos of his siblings or heard what had been his favorite music prior to his illness: his response was without affect, like a computer.

Computers are good for repetitive tasks, but they can't adapt to new situations. The same was true of Elliot. Although intellectually capable of assembling all the necessary information to put a series of files in sequence, he could no longer decide just how to do it, because he was unable to assess the information. Logic can think up alternative possibilities and reject those that don't make sense. But if reason alone has to choose between two equally good options, it's lost. Its only course of action is to think through all possible consequences of a decision to their ultimate conclusion—a process that often takes an inappropriately long time (and thus cost Elliot his job) and is essentially useless, since there are always things in life that can't be foreseen. Which is why reason needs help.

FEELINGS MAKE US FLEXIBLE

That help comes from feelings. While the head forms long lists of pros and cons, the gut has decided long ago that we like something, or we don't like it. No reasons given. Judgments that arise from emotion don't follow from logic but from two sources whose origins are in the distant past. On the one hand, genetic programming determines our intuition. Dishes that are overly bitter don't taste good: this is how our body protects us from poison. We react negatively—automatically—to risks that endanger us.

On the other hand, our feelings are based on our experiences, which are stored more densely and vividly in the emotional systems of the brain than would be possible in our consciousness. Just as a picture can say more than a thousand words, one emotion can often convey more than a thousand thoughts. If you see a burning cigarette lighter heading toward your hand, you don't first have to ponder the possible consequences of touching it. Once burned, twice shy.

It's smart to listen to your feelings. But it isn't always advisable to obey them blindly. An overly emotional answer to a boss's scolding has put an end to more than one promising career, and not everyone who knows how to sweettalk us into a good mood deserves our trust. Emotions developed in the course of evolution so that living things could solve relatively simple questions quickly. They are the correct means for deciding whether to run from a snake or to answer attack with counterattack. As we have seen, in such situations emotions offer people, mice, and other animals answers that are often life saving.

25

Most of our everyday problems, however, are more complicated. A quick response from the gut too often makes interpersonal difficulties even worse. An uncontrolled explosion of anger may get an adversary off your back, but it can also ruin a relationship. Animals have to follow the commands of their emotions, but we don't. We can decide against our feelings, allowing us more options to react appropriately.

Only when we're conscious of our emotions are we free to follow them, or not: perceiving our feelings gives us flexibility. Only when we become aware of our rage can we suppress the trembling in our throats and decide to speak quietly—which is often much more effective than exploding. Not wanting our quaking knees to deprive us of a new experience, we can thwart our feelings of timidity and fear. Dogs wouldn't go bungee jumping even if they could; they would be prevented by the unconsciousness of their fear—to which they are slaves.

LIFE WITHOUT UNHAPPINESS ISN'T HAPPINESS EITHER

In real life, Mr. Spock, *Star Trek*'s unfeeling Vulcan, would be a charity case. Even when we decide to resist the call of our emotions, the ability to feel is essential if we are to act with foresight, for feelings are necessary even in those rare situations in which reason alone should suffice.

This astonishing fact was demonstrated by Elliot, when the brain researchers gave him a test of chance.[2] He was supposed to decide whether he would rather take cards from a pack that regularly earned him $50 and rarely lost him $100, or whether he preferred the other pile, in which he won $100 but also lost up to $1,000.

After only a few rounds, healthy subjects choose only from the first stack. Someone without feelings, however, resolutely tries his luck with the dangerous pile. After a few rounds Elliot went broke, and he asked the person conducting the experiment for a loan.

Elliot, a highly intelligent man, quickly saw through the game and could articulate its rules, but, astonishingly, he was apparently unable to use his knowledge. And yet the choice in this game of chance was completely straightforward, in contrast, for example, to the sorting of documents, where there were many valid possibilities. Once you understand the game, it takes only a straightforward statistical calculation to predict the results. Even a computer that is programmed to maximize earnings would soon decide for the $50 pile, but Elliot lost everything.

The experiment shows why he did no better in real life. As he explained, Elliot absolutely wanted to win, and it was precisely this wish that was his downfall. He pursued every possibility. But the brain makes its assessments emotionally, not rationally. This takes place in areas of the prefrontal cortex—destroyed by Elliot's tumor—in which various possibilities are played through, and where the brain imagines how we would feel in this or that case and comes to its decision.

This process was damaged in Elliot, who was unable to develop an aversion to the risky cards even when, after pulling from the "bad" pile, he once again lost a lot of money. It was clear to him that this pack could lead to high losses, but fear and annoyance were foreign to him, and so he felt no reason to follow his insight. His failure shows how inadequate reason alone is in guiding our behavior.

A PREFERENCE FOR TRAGEDY

We are taught by nature's instructors, happiness and unhappiness. We perceive their directions most immediately in life's most basic aspects, the goals that we pursue to maintain our existence and that bring us happiness: eating, drinking, sex, friendships.

The greater our prior experience of deprivation, the stronger is our subsequent pleasure. The first splash of water on a dry throat tastes the most delicious. With pleasure as its tool, nature seduces us into doing what benefits us most.

For biological reasons, the directions given by pleasure and displeasure must aim above all to keep the organism in optimal condition. This is why pain almost always overrides all other feelings. We are not *supposed* to ignore the signal that something isn't in order. It will torment us until we do whatever we can for our body—and often, unfortunately, still longer.

Generally, we experience negative feelings more intensely and more readily than positive ones. A melodrama will move us much more easily than a comedy will make us laugh. We owe this unpleasant quirk to biology. If you show subjects in neuropsychological experiments happy and sad pictures, they will spontaneously respond more strongly to the latter, as can be read in the strong deflection of the EEG.[3] People prefer tragedy.

The value of this predilection has been shown in the course of evolution. Our ancestors, hearing the softest rustling in the bushes, were moved by fear, sadness, and anger to forget their prey, however fat and juicy, and to get themselves to safety.

To this day, we are more likely to avert risk than to seek out happiness. In every newspaper, bad news yields larger headlines than good news. Losses inflict hurt more than equivalent gains bring joy. If the mechanism responsible for this skewing of our responses is damaged, a fate like Elliot's looms.

Our systems are skewed more to the experience of unhappiness than to the enjoyment of pleasure, and we perceive annoyance and discouragement more quickly and strongly than we do joy. This inheritance of evolution, as vital as it may be in critical situations, explains many tragedies, large and small. Othello's jealous madness so overwhelmed his love for his wife that he murdered her, but a little aggravation when you're on vacation takes its toll as well. The sun shines, a light breeze cools your skin, the sea is beautifully warm, and the food tastes good. You and your companion are getting along wonderfully. But in the midst of this idyll, a crane whirrs away in front of your hotel room. All day, from morning to evening. A minor flaw in the face of all the joys of vacation, but you're incapable of looking past the annoyance. Your anger threatens to ruin the entire trip.

WHY HAPPINESS IS NOT FREE

Unhappiness comes on its own, but we have to work for happiness. While fear, anger, and sadness are responses to dangers from the external world, our feelings of pleasure have been developed by nature to lure us into desirable situations. Not only humans are programmed in this way. Male laboratory rats, for example, return repeatedly to those areas of their cages where they had once enjoyed sex, as if doing everything possible to experience that pleasure yet again.

What differentiates people from rats is the ability to see ahead. Unlike animals, we don't necessarily have to experience a situation in order to draw the right conclusions for the future.

It's enough to think an experience through. It takes only the fear of misery to deter a businessman from undertaking speculations that are all too risky. And in love, the fantasy of a night with the unreachable beloved is enough to make one's heart beat faster.

Experience and the expectation of happiness serve to guide our actions. With this insight, modern brain research corroborates a way of thinking that is central to ancient Greek philosophy but somewhat foreign to us. While many people today conceive of happiness as a matter of luck, as something that comes to us (or not) from outside, the Greek philosophers related happiness to right action. "Happiness is the consequence of a deed," wrote Aristotle. Happiness isn't a coincidental or divine gift but is given to him who makes optimal use of the available possibilities.[4] "As a good general finds the best uses for his troops and as a good shoemaker makes the best shoes from his skins," so a wise person always makes the best of his talents and the opportunities available to him. In this kind of active life lies the secret to happiness and fulfillment.

The classical philosophers drew two conclusions from these insights. First, if happiness consists of the fulfillment of human possibilities, then—since people are similar—there must be broadly applicable rules for attaining it. Then, second, we can learn happiness by following these rules. We are at the mercy of neither our moods nor our environment.

In this day and age, we see happiness as nothing more than a pleasant condition, so it isn't easy for us to follow this line of thought. Rather, we're inclined to look with envy upon "Sunday's child," someone who gets more supposedly undeserved, treasured moments of euphoria than the rest of us. We intentionally overlook the fact that, in spite of the many differences between people, humans have much more in common with one another than not, both biologically and in the disposition of our minds. We tend to view happiness as a pleasure without a history and without costs, not as a process. And this is unrealistic.

Knowing as much as we do today about the functioning of the mind, we also know that positive emotions don't come without a price. Where ancient thinkers spoke of "virtue" and "optimal satisfaction of human possibilities," modern science would stress our attaining the "optimal condition of the organism." But the central thought of classical philosophy about happiness is, in light of today's neurobiology, still valid: positive feelings are not a matter of destiny—we can and must strive for them.

3

THE HAPPINESS SYSTEM

HOW OFTEN DO we find ourselves hoping that a sense of well-being will come to us of its own accord? That our travails will finally come to an end? If only the project that has us spending evening after evening at the office were finished and done with! If only, at long last, the right person would come along and cure our loneliness! Then everything else would take care of itself.

Behind these sentiments is the idea that a life without suffering has to be a happy life. Happy is the man or woman who is not plagued by unhappiness. It seems only logical that happiness and unhappiness should be mutually exclusive, like children on a seesaw: only one can be up at a time.

But it isn't like that. As we now know, positive and negative feelings are generated by different systems in the brain. To be free of suffering is absolutely no guarantee of well-being. This is an important insight, because from it follows a series of recommendations for conducting our lives. First, I'll ask you to undertake a small experiment.

HAPPINESS IS NOT THE OPPOSITE OF UNHAPPINESS

Imagine that you're a mountain climber and are lost high in the Alps. After wandering around for a few hours, you find the path again, but it has gotten late. You know that you cannot reach the valley floor before dark. It's windy, clouds are gathering, soon the first drops of rain are falling. There's no shelter in sight. The wind is blowing the rain directly into your face, and your pants cling to your legs. You're freezing, you feel miserable, and you're annoyed about having been careless and losing so much time. Now you've no choice but to trudge on, in spite of the cold, the rain, and the growing darkness.

Suddenly you see an overhang. You crawl under it. Here there's no wind blowing and the ground is dry. You unpack your thermos, sip your hot tea, and feel the warmth suffusing your body. You feel relieved, relaxed, and even comfortable. Then you remember that you still have to get back. And your clothes are still wet, and still clinging. But haven't you just felt something like happiness? Or perhaps even happiness and unhappiness together?

Indeed, in such moments a kaleidoscope of feelings spins around in your head, some of them pleasant, others unpleasant, and all of them coexisting. Bad feelings do not exclude positive ones.

We often experience ambivalence, but frequently we aren't aware of its nuances. If you expect a raise of $500 a month as a reward for an outstanding job performance but get only $250, you're annoyed because you feel that your efforts haven't been recognized. But at the same time, you're happy about the additional income. The positive feeling of happiness melds with anger, a negative feeling. We all know the pleasure that fear sometimes gives people, as in the pleasantly terrified reactions to a horror film. Love-hate—as every young parent has experienced, if only for brief moments—isn't just a turn of phrase.

It may seem that we're dealing with a paradox here, but only at first glance. It seems obvious that someone who describes himself as unhappy cannot be happy. But then, what is meant by "happiness" and "unhappiness"? Such feelings can almost always be designated much more precisely, and what seems a confusing contradiction begins to make sense when we recognize the positive feeling as pleasure and the negative one as anger, for the two can coexist very well.

In order to better understand this kind of ambivalence, it helps to think of sensory perceptions. We all know how certain seemingly contradictory tastes and smells can be reconciled. In fact, the appeal of a food often turns out to be precisely the apparent clash of flavors: bittersweet chocolate and sweet and sour Chinese pork are examples. The nuances of taste are infinite, said Brillat-Savarin, the king of French cuisine. How poor our kitchens would be if they were limited to the five basic elements of taste—sweetness, sourness, bitterness, saltiness and savory (*umami*)—in their pure form! And so, too, the art of living with life's more complicated feelings lies in our ability to see the intertwining of happiness and unhappiness.

CIRCUITS FOR PLEASURE AND PAIN

Pleasure and pain do not exclude one another. Our bodies don't have a generator for unpleasant feelings that sometimes works harder, sometimes less so, and switches off entirely during moments of greatest pleasure. Rather, the brain has different systems for pleasant and unpleasant feelings that are capable of working together, separately and in opposition.

Even the "language" of neurochemistry uses different signals for the expression of pleasurable and unpleasant feelings. The transmitters dopamine, oxytocine, and beta-endorphone play important roles in desire, contentment, and sexual attraction. Fear, tension, and sadness, on the other hand, are controlled by substances such as acetylcholine and cortisol, a stress hormone.

The fact that desire and revulsion arise differently in the brain is something that can actually be seen. The images that Danasio took of the brains of happy and sad people show that there are different circuits for pleasant and less pleasant feelings. And certain centers in the brain are always active, although at different levels. That isn't particularly surprising, since the brain has to regulate bodily conditions whether we're feeling happiness, sadness, fear, or anger.

But, depending on the particular feeling, these regions can step into action very differently. If happiness and unhappiness were opposites, then the areas of the brain that light up strongly in happy moments would be correspondingly dim when our spirits are low, and vice versa. But that's not what happens. In no way do the images of happy and unhappy brains show opposing patterns. In the image on page 18, the more lightly shaded areas correspond to low activity, the darker areas to high levels. Only the left half of the cerebellum, for example, is at work in happy moments, but when a person is sad, angry, or fearful, both sides are working hard. And the arch-shaped structure of the cingulate gyrus on the underside of the cerebrum lights up brightly in the front right at happy moments and appears dark in the rear left, while sadness shows up bright on both front sides and dark on both sides in the back.

When we experience a feeling, then, it is always the case that various parts of the brain are active—this, too, we can see from the brain scans. There isn't one center for pleasure and another for sadness. The brain does not work that simply. The creation of emotions in the brain can be compared to the positional play in soccer. Every member of the team is necessary, and none can decide the play alone, just as a single brain center cannot release an emotion on its own. And much as the circuitry among the regions of the brain is different for every emotion, so a team on the field moves differently depending on the specific situation in the game. The team positions itself differently for a corner kick than for a free kick. In an offensive play the forward is more important than the defender, although the buildup still depends on the defense and midfield. In the end, the individual player isn't as important as the interplay of the entire team.

UNHAPPINESS ON THE RIGHT, HAPPINESS ON THE LEFT

Often the two halves of the cerebral cortex seem to divide responsibilities between them, although not in the way that has been popularized by the media. It isn't as if one half of the brain feels and the other half thinks and analyzes hard facts. Rather, both halves of the brains process emotions, though the right side tends to be more active when feelings are negative, the left side when they are positive. This difference is most clearly visible on the brain's lateral side when we compare, for example, images taken during happy moments with those taken when the subject is afraid. It seems that we have half a brain for happiness and half for unhappiness.[1]

Further corroboration: our emotional life gets mixed up if one half of the brain is damaged. Stroke patients, for example, sometimes behave very strangely indeed. People whose left prefrontal cortex has been affected often sink into serious depression; apparently the systems regulating positive feelings are damaged. A blood clot in the right prefrontal cortex, on the other hand, can have the opposite effect, leaving the patients in a state of perpetual cheerfulness. This wouldn't necessarily be a bad thing if they didn't also lose their sense of reality, rendering them incapable of seeing anything that might undermine their conviction that this is the best of all possible worlds.

They even deny their own illness. The Indian-American neurologist Ramachandran describes a patient, Mrs. Dodds, who experienced a total paralysis of the left side of her body after suffering a stroke in the right half of the brain.[2] (The connections between the halves of the body and the brain cross on the diagonal.) It wasn't only as if she didn't want to hear of any kind of disability—she really knew nothing about it. When Ramachandran asked her if she could clap her hands, she replied, "Of course!" Then she motioned with her right hand in the air and claimed in all seriousness that she was applauding. Apparently, a counterweight was missing in her brain that could have muted the overwhelmingly positive view of the left brain half and brought her back to the world of actual facts.

A finding from Damasio's laboratory shows us how precisely certain parts of the brain respond only to happiness or to unhappiness. Certain special neurons in the right half of the human prefrontal cortex react only to looming disaster. These brain cells for unhappiness react much more quickly than is possible by conscious will and decide within a few hundredths of a second whether a situation promises good or evil.[3]

When someone who is afraid of public speaking is paralyzed by stage fright as he is waiting to make his appearance, the right prefrontal cortex is practically doing somersaults.[4] Even infants react to the biting acidity of lemon juice with stronger brain waves on the right side. When they're given sweet drinks, the left side springs into action.[5] Thus, it seems highly probable that we're born with a left brain that is more responsible for the creation of positive feelings, whereas negative feelings innately owe more to the right half of the brain.[6]

That pleasant and unpleasant feelings are divided so unequally between the two brain hemispheres has to do with the way in which the prefrontal cortex computes data. This part of the brain serves as command central for behavior, and as we have seen, when it comes to behavior, emotions play an important part: positive feelings tell us what we should do, negative feelings tell us what not to do. The brain is guided both by inborn tendencies—for example, the dislike of food that is too sour—and by its store of experiences.

This is why both halves of the prefrontal cortex, where the working memory resides, are constantly sorting through everything that happens according to its usefulness for the organism.[7] In this way something like a database is created that stores our preferences and dislikes. Organizing so much information and summoning it from memory is a huge job that the prefrontal cortex makes easier by dividing it. The right half is responsible for life's nastier aspects, while the left is concerned with its more agreeable side.

The gray cells of the left brain half handle the vacation that we're about to take, while the speeding ticket we just got is dealt with by the neurons of the right side. The genuine smile, as Paul Ekman discovered, also coincides with a noticeable intensification of activity in the prefrontal cortex's left half.[8]

THE ODD COUPLE

Happiness and unhappiness have their own brain circuits and their own chemistry. But this doesn't mean that pleasant and unpleasant emotions are independent of one another. Though we can be both sad and cheerful, normally we're one or the other. The brain systems for negative and positive feelings are entwined in such a way that a good feeling can prevent bad ones and vice versa. Irritation in the evening about something the kids did can outweigh the satisfaction gained from a successful day at work. And a little bit of joy can chase away the blues—as we can see on city faces when the sun finally shines after a long stretch of rainy days.

In the brain, contradictory emotions are constantly facing off against each other, a principle that is realized within every single neuron. You've got 100 billion of these tiny synapses in your head, more than there are stars in the entire Milky Way. Every neuron is in contact with other nerve cells, some of which provide signals that stimulate activity in the neuron. From others come inhibiting impulses, and the result is a contest of strength between the stimuli. Like a small computer, the neuron draws its conclusion from the contradictory signals and communicates it in turn to other cells.

This "odd couple" interaction doesn't only take place at the microscopic level. Most of the processes in the brain are determined by the interplay of two opposing players, and the emotional circuits function the same way. Positive feelings can extinguish negative ones, and vice versa.

CROISSANTS VS. STRESS

The principle of opposing players gives us a double lever to influence our moods. Montaigne, the philosophizing French nobleman, was quite right to begin his essays on living wisely with the epigraph "*Par divers moyens on arrive à pareille fin*," that is, "By diverse means we arrive at the same end." And those who know how to combine several means will have the greatest success of all. Understanding the mind's feedback systems gives us this ability.

Being stuck in traffic on your way to work every morning is a pain: claustrophobia in the car, the noisy engines around us, anxiety about missing an appointment, and worst of all, the experience of being wedged in, bumper to bumper—these all provide a biological response to flee or to fight, and the body's automatic reaction is one of stress. Then come anger, impatience, aimless agitation, and, when we finally reach our goal, exhaustion.

Of course, the easiest antidote to this misery would be to avoid the daily traffic chaos entirely. But often this isn't possible. Our understanding of emotions, however, opens up other options for using simple means to raise our spirits—in spite of the stress.

First of all we can try to take the edge off the negative feelings directly, by using the time in the car to listen to audiotapes or a language course, thereby mitigating the feeling of powerlessness in the face of an unpleasant environment. Or we can try to awaken positive feelings. For example we could get into the habit of drinking a cappuccino and eating a buttery croissant when we first get to work, instead of plunging headlong into the day's tasks. The anticipation of this treat will lift our spirits in the car, for in expectation of something we look forward to, the brain releases transmitters that allow us to experience pleasure. And because the feedback systems of pleasure and stress are connected, the expectation of pleasure can work in direct opposition to the things that are upsetting us.[9]

We will learn other ways of using the brain's neurophysiological functions to give us a sense of greater well-being. Many of them derive, like the simple example of the driver stuck in traffic, from two things we've learned. First, we often have more freedom than we realize to improve our perception of a situation—even when we cannot directly influence the situation itself. Second, we can learn to suppress negative feelings with positive experiences.

Since the time of the ancient Greeks, philosophers have asked whether the road to happiness lies in maximizing joy or in minimizing suffering.[10] We now know that these are false alternatives. We can do both.

AN OFF SWITCH FOR ANNOYANCE AND ANGER

Pleasure and pain are eternal rivals. The two halves of the prefrontal cortex are in ceaseless competition for our mind. The left hemisphere can encourage positive feelings, presumably by moderating areas of the brain that are more deeply embedded in the skull—probably via a nerve that goes from the prefrontal cortex to the amygdala. These almond-shaped centers on the underside of the cerebral cortex can give rise to fear, anger, and disgust. We don't yet know exactly how the left prefrontal cortex opposes these emotions, but most neuropsychologists think that it sends inhibiting impulses to the amygdala. Nature might have created such signals as a kind of return call informing us that the negative emotion, the warning call, has arrived in the prefrontal cortex and thus is no longer needed. Body and mind can relax again.

So we seem to have a natural off switch for negative feelings. And with some training we can activate this off switch consciously.[11]

The neuropsychologist Richard Davidson of the University of Wisconsin-Madison has worked for years to shed light on these issues. He and his colleagues showed experimental subjects a series of slides that release emotions—naked, attractive men and women, but also patients undergoing open-heart surgery and people standing on roofs surrounded by flooding water, or the victims of a car accident. The scientist then had his subjects consciously intensify or diminish the strength of their feelings.

In order to find out how successful they were, he would sound a loud and sudden noise immediately afterward. Those subjects who were still upset by the pictures reacted even more strongly than before, and their eyes twitched involuntarily—a sure sign of fear.

Meanwhile, 128 electrodes that were placed against each subject's head gauged the activity of their prefrontal cortex.

The more active the left half of the brain was, the less likely the subjects were to be upset. They were startled by the sound that immediately followed the upsetting slides, but as quickly as a second later they apparently understood that the horrible scenes were only pictures and that there was no need to get agitated. The emotion faded away. And when Davidson repeated the signal, they hardly reacted.

But subjects whose prefrontal cortex was especially active on the right side responded differently. After seeing a grim picture, they were upset by the harsh sound for another several seconds. Their eyelids blinked intensely. Apparently they were not able to mitigate their distress. Some continued to feel upset by the photos and began to cry.[12]

The controlling of emotions is very often a matter of tenths of a second. If, in this short time, the subject isn't able to recognize the inappropriateness of fear or sadness, the negative feelings can develop a life of their own—unstoppable, like an incipient avalanche. Overcome by the power of his feelings, such a person has a much harder time calming himself down and returning to a clearer view of reality.

LETTING OFF STEAM DOESN'T HELP

Simply releasing emotions is a mechanism that can cause us a lot of trouble in any number of everyday situations. If, for example, we end a phone call by banging down the receiver in a fit of frustration, or if we slam the door behind us after our partner makes a thoughtless remark, we not only hurt ourselves by leaving what might just be a misunderstanding unresolved, we also keep the negative emotions alive longer than necessary, and now we *really* get angry.

But Davidson's experiment shows that it is clearly possible to control negative emotions the moment that they come into being. This can only happen if we become conscious of our feelings for an instant, then push them aside and get on with our lives. For some people this may seem like a superhuman challenge, but we can learn how do it.

The idea that we should control our feelings contradicts a much more widely held psychological conviction. Many people believe that they will be free of their anger if they express it, that their tears will release their pain. This rests on an often harmful concept that has proven to be completely wrong. It derives from a nineteenth-century understanding of emotions, and it is no truer than the flat earth. It sees the brain as a steam kettle in which negative feelings build up pressure. In order to avoid a dangerous overreaction, a literal "bursting with anger"—so goes the theory—the feelings have to be released. "Go ahead and cry and let it out!" is what well-meaning friends advise one another.

Of course, it is often helpful to articulate our experiences and to share our feelings with someone we're close to. In the words of the proverb, "A trouble shared is a trouble halved." But working ourselves up into a cauldron of negative emotions helps no one. No psychologist has ever succeeded in proving the unburdening effects of the supposed safety valves of tears and anger. On the contrary. Over forty years ago, controlled studies showed that fits of rage are more likely to intensify anger and that tears can drive us still deeper into depression.[13] Our heads do not resemble steam kettles, and our brains entail a much more sophisticated system than can be accounted for by images taken from nineteenth-century technology.

SUNNY TEMPERAMENTS

The control of negative emotions is one of the secrets of happiness. The way in which we respond to unpleasantness is closely connected to our general mental well-being. When

Davidson examined the psychological state of his experimental subjects, he discovered that right or left side dominance of the prefrontal cortex is also reflected in everyday life. People whose right brain half is more active and who have less control over their negative emotions tend to be introverted, pessimistic, and often suspicious. They see catastrophe looming in the slightest misfortune, have a relatively higher incidence of depression, and in general tend to be unhappy.

People with a significantly stronger left prefrontal cortex, on the other hand, usually prove to be true Sunday's children. They are self-confident, optimistic, and often in high spirits. They find it easy to be around others and seem to have been born with the ability to see life's sunny side.

In one experiment, Davidson screened scenes from both cheerful and stressful movies—of young monkeys playing in a bath, for example, or of a difficult surgery. The response of his subjects depended on the relative dominance of right and left brain halves. People with more activity on the right side reacted to the unpleasant films with greater aversion and fear than those with a bias on the left side, while the latter laughed more at the cheerful clips and enjoyed them more.[14] It seems, then, that the brain is characterized by a prevailing mood that determines whether we react more or less strongly to different stimuli. Depending on our temperaments, we live in a world basically colored either rose or gray.

This predisposition affects not only the mind but also physical health. Davidson observed that people with a stronger dominance of the left brain half are also more resistant to illness. They have more killer cells in their blood that destroy bacteria and viruses. Scientists demonstrated the impact of our emotional predispositions on the immune system by injecting people with a small dose of flu virus. The more strongly activity was centered in the left brain half, the better was the response

43

to the immunization (determined a few weeks later by the number of antibodies in their system).[15]

We don't yet completely understand these relationships, but presumably the effective control of feelings sets a kind of chain reaction in motion. People who have more activity in the left prefrontal cortex are less prone to negative emotions, which, if present, don't last as long, so their bodies release fewer stress hormones. And we know that stress hormones like cortisol can, in the long run, weaken the immune system.

Davidson suspects that when we control negative feelings, we increase the activity of the left side of our prefrontal cortex. People who make this effort not only live more happily, they are doing something for their health.

IS THERE A HAPPINESS GENE?

Davidson estimates that the proportion of people with happy, unhappy, and neutral dispositions is more or less the same, a finding that has been confirmed by other surveys. About a third of the subjects in his research showed more activity on the left side of the prefrontal cortex, whereas about a third favored the right side. The remaining third showed no clear asymmetry. Retesting several months later yielded similar results. Whether one side of the prefrontal cortex or the other dominates doesn't depend on the situation at any given moment but is an aspect of one's personality.

This imbalance between the two halves of the brain has been demonstrated to exist even in babies. Davidson examined ten-month-olds and observed in them, too, a direct relationship between brain hemisphere dominance and temperament. Babies with more activity on the right side began to cry immediately when left by their mothers and were more easily upset. Children with left dominance cried much less, and when they were left alone they seemed happy to explore the room on their hands and knees.[16]

Where does this tendency toward positive or negative emotions come from? Since it is manifested so early in life, the template for brain activity seems at least partly inborn. Is happiness genetic? Is there a happiness gene?

No one has promoted the idea of the inheritability of happiness as much as David Lykken, emeritus psychology professor at the University of Minnesota, who once wrote, "It may be that trying to be happier is as futile as trying to be taller . . ."[17] Lykken's work is based on the largest comparative study of twins that was ever undertaken. He conducted a survey investigating the degree to which almost fifteen hundred sets of adult twins were satisfied with their lives. Seven hundred pairs among them were identical twins, meaning their genetic material was identical. Without knowing one another's answers, the identical twins responded similarly more often than fraternal twins (who came into the world with different sets of genes). For Lykken, this was evidence that happiness can be genetically influenced.

Then he went one step further. In his database of twins—all of whom came from Minnesota—there were sixty-nine pairs of identical twins who had been separated shortly after birth and grew up in different families. Would they, too, answer the happiness question similarly? If so, satisfaction could hardly be a consequence of upbringing and life circumstances.

In fact, the answers of these pairs were almost as similar as those of the identical twins who grew up together, from which Lykken concluded that well-being and happiness were "at least 50 percent inherited."[18] American and European media, already fascinated by the new possibilities of genetic research, seized upon this news with enthusiasm. Typical of the reactions was a cartoon that appeared in a 1996 issue of *The New Yorker*, shortly after the Lykken publication. It shows a middle-aged man standing in front of a Rolls-Royce and a castle surrounded by magnificent grounds, complaining, "I could cry when I think of the years I wasted accumulating money, only to learn that my cheerful disposition is genetic."

What are we to make of this? The questionable relationship of money to happiness aside, there's no doubt that our genes influence our personality and thus predispose us toward cheerfulness or sadness. It has been shown conclusively, for example, that depressions are at least partly genetic in origin. People with first-degree relatives who have suffered from depression are four times as likely to experience a depression themselves as someone without this genetic inheritance. The numbers for other mental illnesses, such as schizophrenia, are similar. With these kinds of illnesses, as Lykken has determined, there is a clear genetic impact on the capacity for happiness. And since genes influence the onset and course of disease, they can bring unhappiness.

GENES ARE NOT DESTINY

But it would be stretching things to extrapolate from such extreme cases to the entire population, for genes do not function like a computer program that always does the same thing. The effect of a specific gene on the organism depends to a large extent on its interactions with the external world. And there is no part of the body in which the stimuli of the environment influence gene functioning as much as in the brain and the nervous system, those parts of the body that in the final analysis determine happiness and unhappiness.

Michael Meaney, a neurobiologist at McGill University, proved the crucial importance of early childhood to the ability of rats, for example, to cope with difficult situations when they're grown to adulthood. Young rats that had been generously licked and fondled by their mothers would later tolerate stress much better than the animals whose mothers had not looked after them as attentively. That the essential factor is the care they received—not their genes—was further demonstrated by Meaney when he switched mothers on the baby rats. Now the attentive mothers raised the neglectful mothers' babies—who became resilient adult rats. The biological babies of the caring mothers who became wards of the neglectful mothers, on the other hand, were later shown to be vulnerable to stress.[19]

Genes, therefore, are not destiny. Furthermore, unlike rats, humans are not shaped by their childhood once and for all, something Davidson discovered when he asked those people whose brainwaves he'd measured when they were babies to return to his lab ten years later. Now they were schoolchildren, and the patterns of their brainwaves showed little relation to those of the decade before. Many of the children in whom the left half of the prefrontal cortex was dominant now showed the greatest activity on the right side. And vice versa. This is how strongly the experiences of the intervening years had influenced their temperament.[20]

The brain can change as the individual grows into adulthood. Sometimes the cause is external: new experiences often change our perceptions. But the brain is capable of doing even more astonishing things. It can even reprogram itself.

Such training of one's own mind probably explains the strongest activity of the left prefrontal cortex that Richard Davidson had measured in his two decades of research. The subject was a Tibetan monk who had been flown in from Asia and had logged over ten thousand hours of meditation.

4

THE MALLEABLE BRAIN

DO YOU LIKE eating chili peppers? If so, then probably only in tiny bites, and from the perspective of your body, you're right. In the words of the Indian author Amal Naj, chili is "the only edible fruit on earth that bites back."[1] Their pods contain capsaicin, a nitrogen compound that irritates the mucous membranes and attacks the nerve receptors that react to heat, which is why we perceive it as burning pain. The ancient Chinese fought with pepper bombs, and today's police use capsaicin-laden spray. Even just the thought of biting into a red pepper pod and letting the sting of its seeds spread over your tongue may be enough to make you shudder.

But more than a billion people relish exactly this sensation. Because Mexicans, Indians, and Thais consume ground pepper pods not by the "pinch" but by the spoonful, more chili is used worldwide today than any other spice. Chili is the soul of the cuisine of entire nations, and many people can savor their food only if their mouth is on fire, for chili changes the way we taste. Fruitiness and sweetness taste different—chili fans would say they taste better—when perceived as an overtone of spicy foods. "It tastes like paper!" was the response of an Indian acquaintance to a vegetable dish that was plenty spicy by European standards.

Do people in the hotter parts of the world have different genes? Or have their curries and chili con carne killed off their taste buds? Neither one nor the other. Capsaicin irritates the mucous membranes of those who are exposed to it regularly no less than it does anyone else's. Indians, for example, extinguish the burning with yogurt. There is another difference, however, that makes the sting tolerable. It doesn't take place in your mouth, but in the brain. People who like chilies have learned to love a kind of pain that makes others recoil.

Most people who like spiciness get used to it when they're children, typically between the ages of four and seven, though sometimes earlier. In India I watched in astonishment as a mother shoved a piece of onion into the mouth of a screaming baby who was teething, and the baby was pacified. But adults, too, can learn to adapt. Even Americans who have eaten nothing but moderately spicy food can learn to enjoy chilies, as was proven in experiments at the University of Pennsylvania. What matters is that the person conducting the experiment gradually increase the amount of chili and, especially, that she praise the dish lavishly. At first the test eaters persisted only because they didn't want to appear unsophisticated in the eyes of a culinary authority, but the more they got used to the spiciness, the more they enjoyed it.[2]

That people eat chili voluntarily is remarkable, because hardly anything is programmed so deeply into our brains as our enjoyment of certain flavors and our aversion to others.

We savor sweetness, and make a face when we taste something overly bitter. These preferences are an evolutionary legacy, and we share them with mice, cats, and monkeys. But no animal would ever touch a dish that gave it pain. In Mexico rats will starve before eating the spicy remains from garbage cans. And lab experiments that tried to disabuse animals of their aversion simply failed.[3]

Human feelings, on the other hand, are flexible. We can learn to enjoy things to which we're innately indifferent—and even those that we find disgusting.

50

EN ROUTE TO NEW FEELINGS

When we experience changes of this kind, our brains are reprogrammed—something that until recently scientists would not have thought possible. Instead, they saw in the tangle of gray cells and their dendrites under the top of the skull a very complicated structure that was set at some point before or shortly after birth and that hardly changed in the course of our lives. We have known for only a few years how wrong this picture is. No system in nature is as capable of change as the human brain.

The enjoyment of chilies is based on learning that is associated with pain, but there are gentler ways of increasing our pleasure. We can learn to distinguish more nuances in wine, to appreciate an acquaintance who then becomes a friend, and to make it a habit to marvel at the morning light for a few moments before burying our heads in the newspaper.

We've learned on each of these occasions, for we've acquired a new way of experiencing or doing something. And as different as the beginning of a new friendship is from the ever more nuanced tasting of a great Bordeaux, the basic processes in the brain are the same: something works differently than before. New links have been forged in the web of neurons.

Emotions are the organism's response to a stimulus. When there's an unexpected bang behind us, we're alarmed; if we see a familiar face, we're happy. There are two ways of changing our feelings. We can change the external stimuli to which we expose ourselves, or we can learn to perceive them differently, that is, to change the way our brain reacts to them. If you don't want to suffer from the fiery chilies in your mouth, you can avoid overly spicy food, or you can learn to enjoy the burning on your tongue.

THE WORLD IS CREATED IN YOUR HEAD

The German writer Heinrich von Kleist wrote that the art of living lies in sucking honey from every blossom.[4] But that is only part of the truth. It isn't enough to obtain the nectar: we also have to savor it.

The world as we experience it is created primarily in the mind. Even with the simplest perceptual processes, it takes the brain many steps to work through the raw data conveyed by the sensory organs. When we see a film, the brain automatically creates the illusion of movement, even though only single images are flickering on the screen. When we eat an apple, we taste its delicious flavor on the tongue, although the sense of smell is at least as responsible for the perception. In fact, were your nose and eyes pinched shut you would barely be able to distinguish an apple from a raw potato.

With practice, we have at least some ability to influence the multistep process of data processing that lies between a stimulus and our response to it. We're able, for example, to develop our senses of smell and taste so acutely that we can recognize the different chateaux of the Bordeaux merely by the wine's bouquet. But we can also learn to be less sensitive to the outbursts of an impatient colleague. These, too, are rewards of the human brain's adaptability.

We see how extraordinary humans are in this regard when we compare them to other species. The German neuroscientist Gerhard Roth has tried to measure the degree to which perception and the brain's responses to it have been sensitized in the course of evolution. The neural circuits of the flatworm (the species with one of the simplest nervous systems of all) respond to each external stimulus with an average of only one impulse. That is why the worm's behavior is determined entirely externally: it is like a marionette whose arms lift when the string is pulled. But salamanders—also closely studied by Roth—respond to each signal relayed from outside by its sensory organs with several thousand impulses from the brain itself, which, by the way, is the size of a pinhead. Even such primitive animals, then, are controlled not solely by their environment but also by a simple inner life. For this reason Roth can't always predict how his amphibians will respond to a given stimulus. Sometimes they might snap for the proffered fly, even though they've just eaten. At other times, after several days of not eating, they refuse to take food. Roth estimates that Homo sapiens, with our much more complex nervous system, responds to each external signal with several million internal impulses. The brain is an organ that is involved first and foremost with its own operations. For the most part feelings are, as it were, homemade.[5]

Psychotherapy's most proven techniques rest on this knowledge. Behavioral therapy, especially, teaches us to respond with different emotions from the ones we're used to—allowing, say, a pathologically shy person to overcome her fear of parties. It even happens that after behavioral therapy someone who was afraid of spiders will let a hairy tarantula crawl over his hand. The goal of psychotherapy is, generally, to get patients to control negative emotions that they experience as serious limitations. It aims to help people out of the depths of their suffering. But similar methods can also be employed to strengthen positive feelings and help us on our path to the summit.

Was it your new appreciation for the early light that lifted your spirits this morning, or was it the other way around—that you experienced the colors of the sky more intensely because you felt better? The answer is: both. In the brain, and thus in the way we experience, cause and effect are rarely separable, and whether the chicken or the egg came first is often a question not worth asking. As we have already seen, most of the brain's circuits are so closely connected that almost every experience can work back on itself—a principle that in technology is called feedback. When we use these mechanisms properly, we set an upward spiral in motion that has an ever-growing effect on the brain: we are learning positive feelings.

THE PHILOSOPHER'S TRAINING

Like most good ideas, the thought that we can contain unhappiness and learn happiness comes from a long tradition. The philosophers of ancient Greece called their attempts to become masters of their feelings through self-control *askesis*. Today we tend to associate asceticism with a deadening of the self and think of people fasting and flagellating themselves with birch rods. But these were later developments from medieval times. In ancient Greek *askesis* simply meant "practice." "Everything is practice," Periandros, one of the earliest thinkers in the history of philosophy, is supposed to have said.

Later philosophers ran what were essentially happiness schools to train the minds of their students. The separation that exists today between science and the art of living was foreign to them. While in our own time philosophy is usually conceived of as providing a theoretical basis for knowledge, the philosophers of Greece and Rome thought that insight helped only when people were trained to apply it. "Philosophy consists of two parts," explained Ariston of Chios, a Stoic philosopher. "He who has correctly understood what to do and what to avoid is not yet wise, and won't be until . . . his mind has melded completely with that which it has recognized as right and wrong."[6]

Their goal was to form the student's character so that he would live a happier and more balanced life. The key was the purposeful repetition of certain experiences. The teachers had an entire arsenal of exercises for habituating their students to their rules for happiness. They called these procedures—by which reason was to conquer feelings like greed, jealousy and fear of death—*therapeutic.* The students were to remind themselves repeatedly that negative feelings are destructive and thus would gradually be able to free their minds of them.

In addition, "sensitizing" exercises were supposed to open consciousness to positive feelings. Asserting that no one is master of the next day, Epicurus warned his followers not to postpone pleasurable experiences. Here, too, the teachers stressed the power of habit rather than their own words. Every evening before going to bed the students were to ask themselves if in the course of the day they had lived according to the motto *carpe diem.*[7]

Finally, the students were supposed to practice exercises in which they would imagine a perspective outside themselves in order to see how insignificant their worries and needs looked from a distance. In the Garden of Epicure—this is what this philosopher's community called itself—it was common to imagine the Master's calm response to certain situations. Today's neuroscientists confirm the value of this kind of mental training, for the imagination can form the brain almost to the same degree as actual experience.[8]

In his *Metamorphoses*, the poet Ovid even took a journey into the universe in order to practice happiness: "I delight in journeying among the distant stars: I delight in leaving earth and its dull spaces, to ride the clouds; to stand on the shoulders of mighty Atlas, looking down from far off on men, wandering here and there, devoid of knowledge, anxious, fearing death."[9]

REWIRING THE BRAIN

More than two thousand years after Ovid, the physiologist Ivan Pavlov undertook a series of experiments at the university hospital in St. Petersburg. He had noticed that his dogs only had to see him in his lab coat at noon to begin salivating. A less curious person would have been content with the suspicion that the animals were looking forward to their meal. But Pavlov, a passionate researcher, wanted to know more: *How* did the dogs learn this happy response?

First, he set off a metronome. Then he spread meat powder in front of the dogs' noses. He collected their saliva and digestive fluids, which he funneled through a tube to a revolving paper cylinder. In this way he was able to determine exactly when the dogs became hungry. After a while, the saliva began to flow as soon as the dogs heard the metronome's ticking—even in the absence of meat. Step by step, Pavlov had changed the appetite's natural reactions. He discovered the foundations of learning.

For his experiments Pavlov won the Nobel Prize in 1904, and his dogs became the most famous lab animals in history. He became one of the first scientists to base his psychological discoveries on reproducible evidence. But at that time no one had the understanding of the workings of the dogs' brains that would explain their behavior.

It took many decades until scientists began to unravel the mysteries of the learning process. First, they had to gain access to the brain's smallest units, the neurons. In order to change our behavior or our emotions, the brain has to change, and these changes originate in the neurons.

Each of these gray cells is a tiny computer, and every neuron is connected to other neurons, whose signals it integrates and sends on to as many as a thousand other cells. But the neurons can change the way they process the incoming signals on their own. Compared to nerve cells, desk computers are intractable machines indeed. If PCs, with all their power, had a similar ability, they would be as adaptable—and as stubborn—as household pets, sensing and orienting themselves to the preferences and dislikes of their owners.

But how are these tiny cells, invisible to the naked eye, capable of achieving such a feat? They behave according to the saying "Like attracts like." Every neuron adapts to its surroundings—or more precisely, to the signals that it receives from its neighbors. Gray cells don't send their signals in an even stream. They fire in salvos. When two neurons fire repeatedly at the same time, the connection between them—the synapse—is strengthened. "Cells that fire together wire together," as neurologists say.

And that is what happened in the brains of Pavlov's dogs. Because the scientist set off the metronome when he fed the animals, the two sets of neurons in the dogs' brains that responded to "meat" and to "ticking of metronome" fired at the same time. The more often this happened, the stronger became the connection between them. After a while it was so strong that the neurons that fired in response to the ticking set off the circuits for appetite at the same time—much as one domino topples the next.

The principle that things belonging together join up makes good biological sense, and it applies to the brain as well. It explains why it's been many years since you've burned yourself on a stove. Thanks to a few painful childhood experiences, the mind retains such a strong connection between "stove" and "hot" that we automatically approach such objects very cautiously.

This forging of connections is called Hebbian Learning, after the Canadian psychologist Donald Hebb, who, as early as 1949, had correctly conjectured that single neurons are responsible for learning. All learning functions according to this principle, whether we're memorizing vocabulary, practicing steps to a new dance, or beginning to enjoy the taste of a new exotic fruit—in each case, we're changing hundreds of connections between the synapses in our brains.

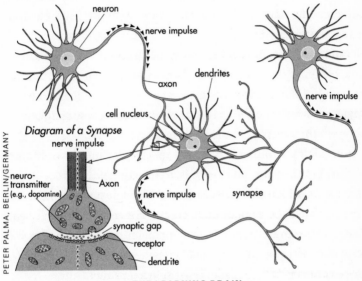

THE LEARNING BRAIN

The brain consists of 100 billion neurons, and each one is a small computer. Via a web of branches, the dendrites, it receives nerve impulses from other gray cells. It computes these impulses and passes the result through its exit, the axon, on to other neurons. The contact between two neurons is the synapse (left, enlarged). When a nerve impulse arrives, neurotransmitters (like the pleasure molecule dopamine) are released. On the other side of the gap are receptors for these substances. They pick up the chemical signal and release a new nerve impulse. When we learn something, the structure of these neurons changes. The computational processes inside the cell and even the form of the neurons change. In some places, the dendrites disappear, and new ones grow elsewhere. Thus, the neurons are changing constantly, like plants in a garden.

WATCHING THE NERVES GROW

When you've finished this book, your brain will look different than before. Changes in the nerve cells' electrical signals have been measured experimentally, but they can also be seen directly in the brain itself. This little miracle was accomplished by the German neurobiologist Tobias Bonhoeffer in 1999. With a new kind of microscope, he observed and took videos of living neurons as they grew.[10] Using tissue from rats, he placed live cells from a part of the brain that plays an important part in long-term memory into a nutrient solution, marked individual neurons with a fluorescent stain, and connected them with ultrathin electric wires. By repeatedly subjecting two neurons simultaneously to electric impulses, he stimulated two perceptions, corresponding, say, to signals like "stove" and "hot." After half an hour, bumps grew out of the dendrites of the nerve cells—so-called dendritic spines, by which the neurons establish contact. A new connection between the synapses in the brain had been forged.[11]

Bonhoeffer's films are not only spectacular images of brains in flux, but they also take us right to the core of the process.

First, repetition plays a decisive role. The more often the neurons are stimulated, the more securely a lasting connection is established. The more often we punch in a telephone number, the better we remember it. Learning emotional responses works the same way. Once connections are made, repetition keeps them alive.

Second, learning happens automatically. The neurons that Bonhoeffer worked with didn't receive a command that there was something to be learned right then. They had, after all, been removed from the brain. Nonetheless new connections were created—simply because the stimuli arrived at the same time. Everything that we perceive, feel, or think changes the brain—whether we want it to or not.

THE PARKING SPACE PROBLEM

Much as laugh lines become engraved into faces of people who are often happy, feelings, too, leave their marks on the brain.

The effect of repeated emotions like joy or sadness is like the drops of water that fall from an overhang. Each one disappears quickly, but over time many, many drops scoop out a gulley, a riverbed, a valley. Cheerfulness can become a habit, as can discontent. That is the neurological justification for the good advice to cultivate positive feelings and to keep a tight rein on our negative emotions.

Emotional reactions also establish themselves in the brain using the Hebbian Learning Rule, the process filmed by Bonhoeffer. A simple example: It might be briefly satisfactory to explode in rage at someone who was scooting into a parking space that you were about to back into, but the parking spot is now gone and, even worse, your rage has laid a path for the future. The next time someone behaves recklessly in traffic, you will probably react still more strongly, because the connection between "rude driver" and "anger" has been reinforced.[12] Fighting anger with anger is like pouring oil onto a fire. Instead of gaining control over unpleasant feelings, we become more vulnerable to them.

As we saw in the previous chapter, the prefrontal cortex is apparently constructed to control negative emotions. Even if we're feeling huge anger or fear, it's to our advantage to bring our emotions under control. When we practice self-control, there's a two-fold effect on the brain. For one, we're less likely to react negatively to start with, because the connection between the stimulus and the emotional response to it is weakened. Second, we strengthen the ability (of the prefrontal cortex, especially) to restrain such emotions, should they be released after all. For like most accomplishments, conscious control of the emotions has to be practiced. And practice, in turn, changes the structure of the brain—with the result that over time we learn to deal more easily with our own feelings.

NOTHING STANDS STILL

Although the changes in the brain begin in its smallest unit, the neuron, they don't end there. How much and how quickly habits can change entire regions of the brain was shown by the Latin American neurologist Alvaro Pascual-Leone in his work with blind people. An example: When a blind person compensates for her lack of sight by developing her sense of touch, the borders of areas of the brain shift. This is most evident in the parts of the cerebral cortex that are responsible for the index finger.[13] Because blind people read braille with this finger, they have much more room in their brains for it than seeing people have. Surprisingly, it takes only a few seconds for this region to grow at the expense of others. Pascual-Leone noticed that the areas of the brain responsible for the reading finger are enlarged as early as the evening after a blind editor's first day at work. And after a weekend's rest, they shrink somewhat.[14]

That entire regions of the brain are altered so quickly isn't a consequence of blindness but simply the result of an everyday process, as various other experiments show.[15]

Nonetheless, not all systems in the brain are as flexible as the somatosensory cerebral cortex, which is responsible for the sense of touch. Some don't change within days but take weeks or even years to be restructured. And other areas of the brain develop only at certain times of life, like in early childhood.

When things change only slowly, they often seem not to change at all. It's like watching grass grow. Many people, for example, despair because they have no sense of direction and are always getting lost. But they, too, can learn to find their way easily. They have to train parts of the brain like the hippocampus that are necessary for spatial memory. These neural circuits, however, lie deep inside the brain and are not nearly as easily changed as the cerebral cortex, for they're a much older evolutionary inheritance.

But they, too, can grow and shrink. This was shown, for example, by the London neuropsychologist Chris Frith, when he examined the brains of London taxi drivers. If you want to become a taxi driver in London, you have to pass a test that consists of no less than 467 routes. Once the aspirant finally has the license in his pocket, he steers his car, usually for many years, through one of the most tangled mazes of streets in Europe. This activity leaves its tracks in the brains of the taxi drivers, whose hippocampuses become enlarged in some parts—how much depends on the number of years these men and women have spent in the chaos of London traffic.[16]

A FOUNTAIN OF YOUTH IN YOUR HEAD

It's a long way from strengthening a neuronal connection to rebuilding an entire area of the brain, which takes several steps to accomplish. The changes begin inside the neurons. Biochemical reactions within the cell modulate cell activity, protein molecules change their form, channels in the cell wall are opened, and the amount of released transmitters increases. These processes all serve to facilitate the flow of information between two neurons, a first step in the learning process—called short-term potentiation—that is like opening the cell gates.[17]

In the next step, long-term potentiation, new informational gates are created. Now special messenger proteins affect the genetic material in the neuron and activate genes in the cell nucleus. These genes order the neurons to change their form and direct the manufacture of protein as building material for new connections. The dendritic spines grow. New synapses are created when the spines link with the corresponding dendrites of the neighboring cells. Over time more dendrites sprout from the dendritic arbor, which connects the neuron to other neurons. With these new connections numerous signals stream into the cell.

Creating long-term potentiation costs the cell some energy. For this reason the next step occurs only when it's certain that the outcome warrants it. Only when the stimuli that are to be linked in the memory have appeared together often enough do new bridges grow in the brain—the reason that remembering takes repetition and practice.

Long-term potentiation is also modified by the chemical messengers serotonin and dopamine, two neurotransmitters that play an essential role in creating positive feelings. The same substances that allow us to experience pleasure, enjoyment, and sympathy also play a key role in the restructuring of the brain. This is no coincidence, for, as we shall see, learning and the experience of happiness are inseparably linked.

Nerve growth factors must also be in place for new connections to grow in the brain. These are substances that do just what their name says: They see to it that the neurons grow new dendrites.[18] Nerve growth factors are not only a natural fertilizer for the gray cells but an elixir of life. Without them, brain cells die.

In all likelihood there is a connection between our mood and the quantity of nerve growth factors that are available to the brain. The number of these substances the body creates is controlled primarily by the transmitter serotonin.[19] If we're depressed, our serotonin level sinks, and gray cells die. Positive emotions, on the other hand, keep the brain alive, because new connections are made more easily when serotonin and dopamine circulate copiously in the brain. Thus, happiness is a fountain of youth for the brain.

THE BRAIN IS A GARDEN

But even if we're always in the best of moods, our supply of nerve growth factors doesn't last forever. In some ways the development of the brain resembles a garden: in both, matter dies readily if it doesn't grow, and what wants to grow must compete for nourishment and space. The brain is well advised to be frugal with its resources and to employ the growth factors mainly where the need is most urgent—to care for connections that are in the process of being created, or which are frequently in use and therefore seem to be especially important.

On the other hand, connections that are less active receive fewer nerve growth factors. Gradually they deteriorate, like plants without fertilizer. Using an electron microscope, we can even see how the inactive connections in the brains of animals gradually disappear.[20] Interestingly, the dying of neuron connections is as important for the organism as their creation. Only when old connections disappear can an area of the brain assume a new function—if you want to sow a new flower bed, you first have to pull out the weeds. Only when very many neurons dissolve old connections and create new ones can a region in the brain begin to restructure itself.

What the brain can do is by no means a given from birth. We can increase its abilities but we can also destroy them. Like muscles, gray cells need constant training in order to stay in shape. Talents that we don't encourage wither away. This applies to every one of the brain's accomplishments. Just as we can learn to type, speak Spanish, or sharpen our perceptions, so, too, we can train our ability to be happy.

YOU *CAN* TEACH AN OLD DOG NEW TRICKS

According to current research, there are only a few functions that are, with training, impervious to development in adulthood. One of them is sight. If the centers for sight in the brain are not trained in early childhood, they will be incapable of subsequent development. This is why a child who is born with a clouded cornea and operated on too late remains blind for the rest of his life. The light may reach the retina normally, but the brain is unable to process the images.

But this in an extreme case. Most old dogs really *can* learn new tricks. Although it's true that we learn foreign languages most easily in childhood, we can still learn French, Arabic, and even Chinese at an advanced age.

And thus it is with learning positive feelings. Connections in our brain determine how we feel, and they are more easily formed in childhood. As we have seen, circuits release emotions underneath the cerebral cortex, but the prefrontal cortex can learn to direct them consciously and to prevent negative feelings like sadness and fear from gaining the upper hand. And just as the speech centers are especially receptive in childhood, the centers of the prefrontal cortex are also particularly pliant in these early years. A Sunday's child is someone who learned to deal with her feelings early on.

Still, we are not slaves of our upbringing. Not many of the people who learned a second and then a third language picked them up as kids. And so, too, adults are perfectly capable of learning new ways of dealing with their feelings.

This was impressively demonstrated by the California psychiatrist Lewis Baxter when he worked with patients who suffered from serious obsessive-compulsive disorders—they were unable, for example, to resist the impulse to go back home again and again to check whether all the faucets had been turned off. Those patients who decided to be treated pharmaceutically were given Prozac, which is effective not only against depression but also against obsessive-compulsive disorders. The remaining patients were treated in a three-month course of psychotherapy where they learned to turn their attention away from their compulsive feelings the instant they began to surface. Psychotherapy and medication were almost equally effective. Both therapies helped about two-thirds of the patients to control their disorder.

This positive change in feelings and behavior could be seen in the activity of the patients' brains, which were examined by a PET scanner before and after treatment. There were clear differences in the prefrontal cortex as well as in two areas under the cerebral cortex: the thalamus and caudate nucleus. Before therapy, the interactions between these structures were completely confused, like an orchestra that had lost the beat. But in the course of treatment they reached a common tempo. Apparently, a connection was established between them that enabled the prefrontal cortex to control the obsessive impulses.[21]

The brain activity of patients who are cured of depression, whether by psychotherapy or medication, changes in a similar way.[22] To the same degree that one's mood improves, activity in the left brain half (which is responsible for positive feelings) increases.[23]

These studies are not only convincing proof of the brain's plasticity with regard to feelings, they point the way toward more effective treatments for mental illness. "We face the intriguing possibility that as brain imaging techniques improve, these techniques might ultimately be useful not only for diagnosing various neurotic illnesses but also for monitoring the progress of psychotherapy," wrote the Viennese-born neuroscientist Eric Kandel, who won the Nobel Prize in 2000 for his discoveries of cellular processes in learning.[24]

THE WISDOM OF THE EAST

Our consciousness has a major influence on the way emotions form the brain. With monkeys, for example, the neurons that are responsible for perception respond to light much more easily when the animals direct their attention toward it.[25] With people, too, many forms of learning are tied to conscious perception—it is impossible for a beginner to learn to ride a bike without complete concentration. It is clear that conscious engagement with an object strengthens its anchoring in the brain.

Although we still lack strict neurophysiological proof, it seems very likely that positive feelings, too, develop more strongly the more we work with them. People who enjoy life's beautiful moments fully are also behaving reasonably: They are probably reshaping their brains for the better.

This has always been the understanding of Eastern philosophy, with which contemporary neuropsychiatry has much in common. Unconscious emotions are seen as significant in both Buddhist psychology and neuroscience, and both agree that the mind is shaped by experience. But Buddhist psychology has always recognized something long contested by Western philosophy, namely that there is unconscious mental activity that enters into the mind through a gate (called *manodvara*).[26] Today's neuropsychology understands the brain similarly: emotions are an unconscious condition of the organism, while feelings are their conscious perception. According to both Buddhist psychology and brain research, the mind is formed by experiences. At this point, research in the field of neuronal plasticity is progressing so rapidly that we'll soon be able to say much more about these questions.

The German neuropsychologist Herta Flor has made significant progress in this area, showing that when we focus on pain, the changes in the cerebral cortex make us still more sensitive to suffering. In other words, the perception of pain is at least partially learned. Examining adults with chronic back pain, Flor noticed that when people received excessive attention from their partners, their pain increased. Sick people with partners who ignored the patients' complaints seemed less sensitive. She also corroborated this experimentally with patients who dipped their hands into ice water. Those who were given more sympathy showed greater brain activity: their pain was genuine. You might say that people who are more sensitive need and receive more attention. But the exact opposite is the true. As soon as the superattentive partner leaves the room, the patient's brain reacts less strongly to the bite of the cold water. People who are intensely preoccupied with their suffering sharpen their perception of it. Flor could see in the brain scan how over time ever larger areas of the brain became involved in the processing of pain: Neurologically speaking, suffering becomes programmed.[27]

The Buddhist understanding of the way in which the mind is formed by the attention we give to our own feelings has been described by Thich Nhat Hanh, a Zen monk and writer from Vietnam who immigrated to France and wants to convey the insights of his religion to Westerners. His words read like a poetic version of the central thoughts of this chapter: "Traditional writings describe consciousness as a field, a piece of land, on which all kinds of seeds are sown—seeds for suffering, happiness, joy, sorrow, fear, annoyance and hope. And tradition describes the memory of feeling as a storehouse that is filled with all our seeds. As soon as a seed is manifested in our consciousness, it will always return to the storehouse stronger than before . . . Every single moment during which we perceive something peaceful and beautiful waters the seed for peace and beauty within us . . . And during that same time, other seeds like fear and pain remain unwatered."[28]

It isn't surprising that the religious insights that are most consistent with the discoveries of neuroscience come from the philosophical and religious schools of the East. No people on the planet has been as concerned as long and as deeply with the mind as South and East Asians. The reason lies in their religions. The difference between the Western faiths on the one hand and Hinduism and Buddhism on the other is in their understanding of the source of truth. While Judaism, Christianity, and Islam find truth revealed in a holy book, the religions of the East teach us to seek what lies deepest within us. This is the path to enlightenment that, according to Hindu understanding, lets us see the divine in our own soul, and in the Buddhist faith releases us from earthly suffering.

This millennia-long occupation with the human mind makes for fruitful conversations between Western brain researchers and Eastern cultures. It isn't a coincidence that some of the world's leading neurobiological labs written about in this book have repeatedly sponsored visits by the Dalai Lama.

THE WILL TO HAPPINESS

To live wisely requires the ability to perceive, guide, and foresee our emotions. Feelings of happiness aren't a coincidence but the consequence of right thoughts and actions—a concept with which modern neuroscience, ancient philosophy, and Buddhism (which believes in a strict principle of cause and effect) all agree.

We in the West typically emphasize the value of the correct decision: if only we were to make the right choice at this or that fork in the road, everything would improve. But according to the traditions of Buddhism and the philosophies of ancient Greece and Rome, it is more important to anchor ourselves in good habits, because these form the mind. We should want to change ourselves rather than our circumstances. The rest will come, because with a mind that is prepared for happiness, we will automatically seek out those situations that make us happy.

The importance each of us gives to conscious choice is in the end a matter of faith. But two things are certain. First, our sense of happiness depends much more on the ways in which the brain perceives than on external circumstances; and second, occasional efforts aren't sufficient to change our ways of perceiving. If the brain is to be rewired, repetition and habit are indispensable. And they, in turn, depend on a willingness to make an effort.

People are willing to go to great lengths when it concerns status, career, or their children's development. But when it concerns happiness in everyday life, they can be oddly stingy with their energy. And yet, the way to happiness is quite straightforward: "The actual secrets of the path to happiness are determination, effort and time," explains the Dalai Lama.[29]

To this, science can only assent.

which do not bring happiness.

and how are habits formed? By repetitive actions, repetitive choices.

PART TWO

THE PASSIONS

5

ORIGINS IN THE ANIMAL KINGDOM

IT IS OFTEN said that we of the twenty-first century still allow ourselves to be directed by Stone Age emotions, that we're essentially Neanderthals with a tie. More than one colleague ranting and raving in the office has reminded us of a hunter swinging his club and putting the men of his horde in their place—while leaving the women for himself.

Such impressions, however, are not entirely correct. To be sure, we have at least partly inherited our feelings and behaviors from our ancestors. But why should this legacy have begun only in the Stone Age?

Our emotions, at any rate, seem to be much older. What animal lover has not sometimes observed signs of pleasure and distaste, love and hatred in his pets? When a cat is stroked, it purrs, stretches, closes its eyes, relaxes its limbs, and waits patiently for more. A dog that's been scolded slinks to the corner. Even birds chirp to get attention, and it's no coincidence that the concept of the "love nest" comes from their world. Birds seem to suffer almost as much as people in the absence of proximity to their own kind. A gray goose whose partner has died can remain without a mate and show all the symptoms of depression for years.

Such scenes touch us because we see our own emotions mirrored in animals. But they shouldn't lead us to conclude that these creatures really do feel as we do. We are unable to read what may be feelings inside animals' heads, and they have no language to express their inner lives. Whether animals feel, and how, remains thus far an unanswered question.

It is, of course, incontestable that on the surface animals show emotions that resemble ours. It is these behaviors, and not the unknown feelings, that account for our sense of having a secret relationship with them. The stronger and more basic an emotion is, the greater the similarity seems. The symptoms of fear, as we see them in cats, dogs, mice, and even pigeons and lizards, hardly differ from those of humans. But happier episodes from the animal world are familiar as well: cats playing, rats and mice exploring the world, or elephants entwining their trunks when they're about to mate. One would say that these animals are showing signs of fun, curiosity, and perhaps even love.

Is it possible that animals fear without experiencing their fear, that they love without feeling their love? It's helpful here to review the difference between emotions and feeling. An emotion is a program that runs automatically, usually involving the body; a feeling, on the other hand, is something we experience when we become conscious of emotion. Sometimes we manifest emotions without feelings—for example, when we blush without having been fully aware of our sense of embarrassment.

Awareness, then, is not a precondition for emotions, which can therefore be said to arise more simply than feelings.

Although scientists do not know whether and what animals feel, there is no doubt that they are indeed capable of emotions. We know, too, that these emotions, which are engaged automatically whether the animal is threatened, unexpectedly rewarded, or having sex, function in animals much as they do in humans.

We can conclude, then, that the basic characteristics of emotions were present long before there were humans. They are a legacy from a very distant past that influences what we feel, and when, for emotions are a precondition for feelings. In fact, the emotion determines the feeling. We see an apple, after all, only when there is an apple to be seen (unless we're hallucinating), and it is the same with feelings like pleasure and fear.

Because emotions comprise the core of every feeling, we have good reason to be concerned with their origins, and in animals we can study the origins of our more complicated feelings. Dogs, cats, and mice do not show the wealth of emotions that people are capable of, but precisely because they follow more rudimentary patterns, what is essential is much more obvious. In the mirror of the animal world, we recognize ourselves.

THE EVOLUTION OF FEELINGS

In the course of evolution, brains and emotions developed in synchrony. The more brains developed, the bigger and more complex they grew, the richer and more differentiated emotions became.

Why did nature spend so much energy in creating ever more capable brains? To equip a jellyfish that moves through the ocean and filters microorganisms from the water with intuition and an ingenious mind would have been a waste. It needs no more than a simple nervous system that controls digestion, responds to light so that it knows up from down, and to fire off poisonous stingers when its next meal brushes against it.

But an animal that actively chases after its prey depends on many more reflexes and emotions than a mere jellyfish. It has to recognize its victim, gauge the right moment to attack, and understand when it is better to flee if the would-be breakfast defends itself too aggressively.

Every creature has its own recipe for survival, a mixture of camouflage and cunning, physical strength and speed. An alligator confronts its enemies with its armored skin and powerful jaws, a horse gallops from danger, and the tiger's strength and speed render it almost invulnerable. It is the abilities of the body, correctly engaged by the brain, that always determine the fate of a living being. But over the course of evolution the center of strength has shifted upward, as the brain has grown and come to consume an ever larger portion of the body's metabolic energy—most of all in the human, whose brain requires more than a third of the body's energy.

Thus, Homo sapiens depends almost entirely on intelligence and intuition and hardly at all on the body. Without these qualities he would be lost, since, when it comes to size and agility, he is hopelessly inferior to other animals of his size. Even our nearest biological relative, the chimp, can easily grab a human and twirl him through the air.

In evolutionary terms, however, large and significant parts of our brain are much older than the human species. And in spite of the changed demands, most of these parts of the brain still function as they did in the heads of fish and lizards. To these primitive circuits we owe some of our special qualities—the terror, for example, with which a person turns and runs when encountering a harmless snake, though the same person may race a motorcycle down highways at 100 mph.

We carry around with us, along with evolution's achievements, some of its relics, for nature seldom discards anything that was once useful. Countless details in the brain are as useless as an appendix. Nothing basic has changed under the scalp since the age of dinosaurs—evolution has, as it were, only added things on. The architecture in our heads is like that of a very old city: fascinating, charming, but full of buildings that today would have been planned completely differently—and better.

OUR THREE BRAINS

The history of a city also resembles the development of the human brain in that it didn't happen gradually but in distinct phases. Our brain's structure still articulates three stages of rapid expansion—named after the creatures in which their characteristics first developed most strongly: the reptilian brain, the limbic (or mammalian) brain, and the neocortical (or human) brain.

The reptilian brain is considered the oldest of these parts. It is identical with the brain stem, to which the cerebellum also belongs. Lying at the upper end of the spinal cord, it controls the basic functions of life: digestion, breathing, and the heartbeat. The brain stem also controls simple movements like bending and stretching the large muscles, as well as posture. But above all, its circuitry plays a key role in the creation of emotions. Hunger and fear begin in the brain stem, which explains why lizards, too, are capable of fear and can even learn to be afraid of certain stimuli.[1] But the brain stem is not only a source of negative emotions: not just panic and anger but also excitement and pleasure would be unthinkable without this ancient area of the brain.

The brain's next layer developed during the dinosaur era as small, shrew-like animals were preparing to bear live offspring. Although its rudiments were already present in reptiles and amphibians, only when the first mammals emerged from the ocean to begin their triumphant march across the earth did it grow to a size that exceeded all other parts of the brain. The hippocampus and the amygdala—responsible for storing memories of feelings and places—belong to the developing nervous centers that allowed more flexible behavior and enabled animals to learn more easily to distinguish friend from foe, to locate food, and to discover which foods tasted especially good.

It's no coincidence that the subsequent enormous expansion of the emotional repertoire occurred at the same time as the emergence of the first mammals. Care for their brood, attachment to a partner or to a group of other animals of the same species, as well as the enjoyment of play all call for more than the simple responses of fear, hunger, and pleasure available to reptiles. The long period of mammalian child rearing required more developed brains, because the necessary social emotions depended on new, more powerful and capable brain circuitry. Species with simpler brains like crocodiles show little interest in caring for their offspring. Although the mothers jealously guard their eggs and tend to their brood, it isn't long before a young croc has to hide from its parents if it doesn't want to be eaten. A baby mouse, on the other hand, is suckled, licked, and stroked by its mother for weeks. The adult animal shows emotions that, in humans, we explain as nurturing love.

The last big stage in development set in a good one hundred million years ago, when the cerebral cortex greatly expanded, primarily in apes, dolphins, whales, and most of all in humans. The neocortical brain spans the brain's older areas like a dome. Because these animals with the big, new brains could learn better and more quickly than other creatures, they could adjust to changed conditions to a degree previously unthinkable. The enlarged cerebrum enabled them to plan actions in advance and to deceive other animals, to live together in complex communities, like apes, or to use a kind of language to communicate with others in the same species, like whales.

Subtle emotions like empathy also have their roots in the cerebral cortex. One of the most important scientific surprises of past years was the discovery that altruism is not so much an achievement of human culture as an accomplishment of the neocortical brain of which other animals are also capable. Behavior researchers like the Dutch primatologist Frans de Waal have gathered extensive proof for this thesis, especially from apes. Female chimps support each other during labor, young chimps of both sexes stick together against a tyrannical alpha male, and healthy animals in the group tend those who are sick.[2]

In terms of size and capability, the human cerebral cortex exceeds that of all other animals by far. We have an enormous variety of emotions at our disposal, and, most important, we can experience them as our own: We recognize feelings; we can juggle them in our imagination; we can get upset about things or enjoy them, even if they are utterly without consequence for our survival. To these expanded spheres of our cerebrum alone we owe our capacity to suffer the pangs of unrequited love on a movie screen, or to feel the triumph of our hometown team.

The more highly developed an animal is, the more complicated are its emotions. This straightforward rule becomes apparent when we look back over five hundred million years of natural history—which is how long it took for the simple nervous system of the jellyfish to evolve to the human brain.

But as many and varied as our feelings are, they all rest on basic emotions, like desire and fear, that existed in animals long before there were humans. And it is still the oldest areas of the brain that give the beat to the music of our emotions. The cerebrum, on the other hand, elaborates luxuriantly on the melody of feelings. Where simple animals are governed only by volition, we know desire and the heady rush of power, longing and silent veneration.

THE ORCHESTRA OF HORMONES

It is by no means only our brain's structure that shapes who we are. No less significant are the fluids that flow through it. The brain, after all, is not lifeless and dry like a computer, but alive, damp, and wobbly. In addition to blood and water, more than sixty different transmitters circulate within it—molecules that have an enormous effect on our actions and feelings. "The fluid brain," is what Jean-Didier Vincent, one of neurobiology's most original writers, called this concert of substances.

Some of them will play an important role in the following chapters, and they, too, have a long past: dopamine, a transmitter that is responsible for volition, excitement, and learning, also controls desire—even in bees. Naturally occurring opiates like beta-endorphin that are released when we experience pleasure (as well as pain) are also present in insect brains. Serotonin controls the flow of information in the brain and is one of the very oldest transmitters of all, having been found even in the simplest nervous systems of mollusks and cephalopods, like squids.[3]

These neurotransmitters are ever present in the brain. It is touching to watch a cat licking her young, nursing them, and carrying them carefully in her mouth to a better hiding place. This behavior, too—the essence of motherliness—is controlled by a neurotransmitter. If oxytocin is injected into the brain of a rat that has never given birth, this virginal animal is transformed within minutes into a loving mother that looks after another rat's babies as if they were her own.[4] Very similar mechanisms are at work in humans.

The thought that a few chemicals can have such a big influence on our inner lives, that they can change our mood on a dime and can even determine our behavior may scare or even anger some people. Though we have witnessed often enough how a few glasses of wine can transform a shy guest into a sparkling entertainer, or, for that matter, into a chatterbox who won't leave your side, the effects of alcohol are more like a temporary mechanical breakdown, a temporary clouding of reason, than like a fluid brain in action.

The power of molecules calls our self-image into question. We like to see ourselves as intelligent beings who are animated by hopes, thoughts, and wishes, not by chemistry. When we fall in love, or look with pride at our children, can we really believe that this experience of life's deepest joys is nothing but the flow of a few chemicals in the brain?

Hardly. But even at the physiological level, things aren't quite that simple. The formulas dopamine equals pleasure and oxytocin equals maternal love are merely conditionally correct, if only because these transmitters do not act alone. Particular neurotransmitters play a leading role in the creation of certain emotions, but they are just one voice in the choir. Thus, the oxytocin injection changes young rats into motherly animals by setting in motion a kind of domino effect that immediately releases a whole series of other substances in the brain, which, in turn, change behavior.

Just as the interplay of molecules in the brain is incredibly complicated, so is their interaction with the body. Chemical formulas aren't sufficient to explain what we feel. Neither one single transmitter nor a whole concert of such substances is capable of creating an emotion on their own. Rather, they have to act on a complicated web of brain circuits that then release reactions in the body. Moreoever, when we experience an unconscious emotion as a feeling, our cerebral cortex—the most complicated structure in all of nature—steps into action.

Though we are not simply marionettes moving at the whim of molecules, it is easy to overlook the fact that our rich inner life cannot be created in a vacuum. Thoughts, feelings, and even dreams aren't castles in the air but are built on a very solid foundation, and that foundation is chemistry. Our inner lives and the transmitters in our brains can be compared to a work of art and the materials from which it was made: the frescoes of the Sistine Chapel are infinitely more than Michelangelo's color powder. But without these pigments he could never have painted his view of the cosmos. And in just this way we're much more than the architecture of our brains, more than the substances that flow through our heads. Without them, however, we would have no inner life.

LIVING WITH THE PASSIONS

The American evolutionary scientist Sarah Blaffer Hrdy writes in her book about the history of motherhood: "Every living organism, every organ of every organism, not to mention tissues and molecules, whether or not they are still in use, bears the accumulated imprints of multiple past lives. Never permitted the luxury of starting from scratch to produce the perfect solution, natural selection recycles workable solutions for a 'good-enough' fit, meaning simply: better than the competition."[5]

Some people may be relieved to think that evolutionary biology certifies our imperfectability and lets us off the hook. After all, we're much too hard on ourselves, too often feeling that we've got no room for error and berating ourselves for falling short once again.

What we feel and what we want is to a large extent determined by programs that are older than the human species. By no means, however, does this make us into powerless creatures, helpless in the face of nature, for we are able to control these emotions. But we can't just get rid of them—even if some religions would like us to believe otherwise. ⟨ says who?

Many ascetics have made it their goal to overcome their passions and failed. Even someone with an extraordinary degree of self-control like Mahatma Gandhi, whose profound altruism enabled him to fast and suffer physical abuse, didn't succeed. Gandhi's story shows how far a man can go in fighting his nature—and where the boundaries lie. As a young man, he indulged a strong sex drive that later caused him feelings of great guilt. In accordance with certain branches of Hinduism, he saw the sexual act as a waste of energy that he should put in the service of the spirit. So he chose a life of chastity. But he continued to struggle with his sexuality even in old age. In order to test himself and to extinguish his desire, the aged man went to bed with naked girls, forbidding himself to touch them. Gandhi achieved his goal, but afterward his desire was as strong as it had been before. He may have benefited from his experiment in further training a willpower that was already superhuman—but it did not succeed in dulling his natural instincts.

The suggestion of the philosopher Immanuel Kant that we should see human passions as illnesses of the soul comes from a similar mindset. But if we follow this advice, we're declaring war on ourselves.

There are more realistic ways of living with our emotions. Above all, we should accept the legacy left us by evolution. We can't change our predispositions—nor do we have any reason to do so. In contrast to all other animals that ever existed, we are not completely helpless in the face of our drives. We can decide which to follow and which we want to avoid, and we can shape our lives so that they are in harmony with our inclinations. Since Aristotle and Buddha, sages have recommended the golden mean—an understanding of the emotions that no one has articulated as clearly as René Descartes in his "Passions of the Soul": ". . . we see that in nature they are all good and that we only have to avoid misuse and excess."[6]

There is no point in trying to find a drug against the passions, though a user's manual would be very helpful indeed. Only by becoming familiar with something can we develop a healthy relationship with it. If we want to live with our passions, we first have to get to know them.

6
DESIRE

A VIRULENT BRAIN infection left Leonard a living mummy. Although he was forty-six, his utterly expressionless face bore no lines, and he still looked like the young man who'd been struck by illness shortly before he was to have finished his studies. His limbs, incapable of almost any movement, had become stiff. He lost his voice—an affliction that tormented him almost as much as the paralysis, for he loved language. The only pleasure left to Leonard was reading, and a caregiver turned the pages for him. Burying himself in books, Leonard could communicate only with the help of a little tablet, pointing to its letters with great effort. He felt that his body was "a prison with windows, but no door," in which he had to live like the poet Rilke's panther, to which he often compared himself:

His vision, ceaselessly passing the bars,
Is now so tired that it holds nothing.
He feels as if there are a thousand bars,
And behind the thousand bars: no world.

His doctor was the young Oliver Sacks, who would later spread the fame of Leonard's fate and that of similarly afflicted patients all over the world. Sacks was experimenting at the time with L-Dopa, a new medication similar to the natural transmitter dopamine. Leonard was the first patient on whom Sacks tested the drug. Its effect was so powerful that the young doctor was reminded of paintings depicting the waking of the dead—which is why his first book (and the film that was based on it) bore the title *Awakenings*.

Treatment began in March 1969, and within two weeks Leonard was a changed man. He could run! He walked out of the hospital building to the garden, pressed the flowers to his face, and kissed them. Overflowing with happiness and suffused with energy, he *was* intoxicated by the world. "'I feel saved,' he would say, 'resurrected, re-born. I feel a sense of health amounting to Grace . . . I feel like a man in love. I have broken through the barriers which cut me from love.'" He could even drive again, and plunged into the nightlife of his hometown, New York—which seemed to him, as Sacks writes, as beguiling as a New Jerusalem.

Instead of Dante's *Inferno*, he read *Paradise*, and with tears of joy. "L-Dopa is a *blessed* drug," he wrote in his diary, underlining the word "blessed." "It has given me back the possibility of life. It has opened me out where I was clammed tight-shut before . . . If everyone felt as good as I do, nobody would think of quarrelling or wars. Nobody would think of domination or possession. They would simply enjoy themselves and each other. They would realize that Heaven was right here down on earth."

But Leonard's ecstasy lasted only a few weeks. In May he began to experience a painful longing, and then an unquenchable craving for power and sex. He harassed the nurses on the station and he asked Sacks, in all seriousness, to arrange for them to "service" him at night. "With L-Dopa in my blood, there's nothing in the world I can't do if I want. L-Dopa is power and irresistible force. L-Dopa is wanton, egotistical power. L-Dopa has given me the power I craved."

He now spoke at breakneck speed, and in the first three weeks of June he wrote an autobiography of several hundred pages. His condition deteriorated into madness. He felt that he was beset by demons and surrounded by net traps laid out to strangle him. When Leonard tried to smother himself with a pillow, Sacks stopped the medication. After a few days, Leonard reverted to the petrified state of before. He died in this condition in 1981, after further treatments with L-Dopa and similar drugs repeatedly set off more phases of insanity.[1]

THE SUBSTANCE THAT DRIVES US ON

What happened? Leonard's brain infection had attacked a few groups of cells in his midbrain, located almost exactly at the head's midpoint, where they appear as black spots about the size of a fingernail—which is why they are called *substantia nigra*, Latin for "black substance." This is where the transmitter dopamine is produced.

Dopamine is a tiny molecule consisting of only twenty-two atoms—hydrogen, carbon, oxygen, and nitrogen. Enlarged ten million times, it would resemble a tadpole: a rather long head, consisting mainly of carbon atoms, that ends in a tail on which the other little parts sit. This is the substance that was missing from Leonard's brain and that Sacks (altering the chemistry slightly) administered to him in the form of L-Dopa.[2]

As unimpressive as the molecule dopamine may seem, once in the brain, it has seemingly miraculous powers. It helps control our alertness and attention. It stimulates curiosity, the ability to learn, imagination, creativity, and sexual drive. The brain releases this transmitter whenever we desire something or someone. Dopamine is the molecule of desire.

This astonishing substance is responsible not only for arousing our desire, but it also sets the necessary systems in motion that enable us to attain our goals. Under its influence we feel motivated, optimistic, and full of self-confidence. Dopamine ensures that the brain follows up intentions with deeds—without it, the muscles wouldn't obey our will. In short, dopamine is the substance that drives us on. And because it transports us to a state of vibrating anticipation, because it makes a goal seem tempting and within our grasp, dopamine—probably more than any other of the brain's transmitters—enables us to experience euphoria.

There is hardly a situation in which this substance doesn't play a role. There's some fresh fruit in the supermarket that at that moment happens to appeal to us—dopamine is released. We feel a surge of happiness, a joyful and excited "I want it!" Under the influence of dopamine, the brain gives orders to the muscles to stretch out the arm and reach for the apple. While the brain prepares to test whether the apples actually taste as good as we had hoped, the ability to store memories is activated, enabling us to note for the future whether the experience was a good one or a disappointment.

Dopamine is involved when we attack a new problem at work, and when we pass an attractive person on the street, and, in a big way, when we anticipate sex. If we reach for a glass of beer or a cigarette, we're also looking for a pleasurable extra ration of this transmitter, for one of the main effects of alcohol and nicotine is to release more dopamine in the brain.

A second source of dopamine is the region adjacent to the

substantia nigra, the ventral tegmental area. From these two centers, branches of nerves stretch upward in every direction, distributing dopamine into the areas of the brain that do the actual work—the circuits that enable us to respond to reward, to remember good feelings, to move.[3]

This substance is so important in our lives because it has a threefold impact on the brain. First, it makes us aware of particularly interesting situations. Dopamine wakes us up. Second, it causes the gray cells to remember good experiences—dopamine supports learning. And finally, it serves to control our muscles, to make the body obey our will. Dopamine activates.

It is not surprising, then, that a dopamine deficiency robs people of their drive—even to the point of being corpselike, like Leonard. But too much of it is also disastrous: Desire becomes obsession; determination, a lust for power; self-confidence, megalomania; and a rich imagination, madness. Positive feelings, too, have their dark side—something that no neurotransmitter in the brain demonstrates as clearly as dopamine.

Tragically for Leonard, L-Dopa was new at the time, and doctors hadn't yet learned to gauge the dosage correctly. He was given more of it than his body could take.[4] It triggered the mechanisms that normally get people through their daily lives, but in him they were grotesquely intensified. But Leonard's fate demonstrated the basic ways in which dopamine works in all of us.

STEEPLECHASE IN THE HEAD

Dopamine is one of the most important transmitters by which the brain's gray cells communicate with one another. Neurotransmitters pass along signals when they're released by a neuron and flow through a gap between two gray cells to the next neuron, which then picks them up. The individual transmitters work differently in different receiver cells. There are basically two possibilities.

One is that the neurotransmitter stimulates the receiver cell directly, so that this cell releases a transmitter in turn—the message is then passed along like a letter in the post office.

The other variant is that the transmitter does not immediately release a new message, but instead changes the way in which the receiver cell reacts to subsequent messages. For example, a neurotransmitter can transform a neuron into a state of special readiness to receive or send. The neurotransmitter in this case opens the door for other transmitters. This is also how dopamine works: it can change the frequency of the ionic channels—the cell gates—and cause them to open and close. Thus it makes the neurons easier to stimulate.[5]

But scientists have not yet discovered down to the last detail how dopamine works. The functioning of neurotransmitters is being eagerly studied, and new discoveries are made almost every day. Dopamine does not appear to be the only neurotransmitter that influences arousal and desire. There are at least a handful of other transmitters that play a role in these processes, for example, noradrenaline and adrenaline, two hormones that are also important in connection with stress, sensory perception, and metabolism. Acetylcholine, dopamine's opponent, inhibits its stimulating effects. Glutamate is involved in learning. Dopamine, however, seems clearly to be at the center of all of these processes. It is something like the chemical master switch of desire.

IN PRAISE OF ANTICIPATION

A new love, a journey to a place we've never been, or even the very first images at the movie: we're restless, our fingers itch, there's a light tension in our legs, and our pulse quickens. A promise seems to hover in the air. We're hoping for something that we can't yet identify—an unexpected turn in life, a mesmerizing experience. At the same time we fear that this new thing that awaits us could prove to be not so wonderful. So we check out anything that could give us even the slightest foretaste of what's lying in store. Getting off the plane, a traveler scans the airport. A person in love jumps up as soon as the phone rings. What *are* these butterflies in our stomach? Where do they come from? And what do they mean?

It was by pure coincidence that the brain researcher Wolfram Schultz got to the bottom of this mystery—and to the heart of the puzzle behind dopamine's enormous evolutionary significance. Actually, Schultz, who was then working in Fribourg, Switzerland, was interested only in studying dopamine's impact on the movements of monkeys, a problem that he hoped would offer an understanding of Parkinson's disease (which throws dopamine levels out of kilter and thus leaves its victims with diminished control over their muscles.) When the monkeys engaged in particular movements, Schultz expected certain dopamine neurons in the *substantia nigra* to become active. But little happened. Apparently the neurons that he was studying had nothing to do with movement.

Whatever the results, the animals had to be rewarded for their efforts, and one of Schultz's colleagues placed a few apple slices in the cage: ". . . the neurons started going like crazy," said Schultz. "We couldn't believe it."[6]

What the researchers found was a synapse in the brain that is responsible for surprises. And it is this same system that is responsible for anticipation—not only in monkeys but also, as was later discovered, in humans.

Schultz and his colleagues began to study these neurons more closely. They determined that the cells were activated only when a reward was in sight. Whenever the monkeys saw an apple, the neurons were set off. If, on the other hand, the scientists proffered only a bit of wire without the skewered fruit, the nerve cells remained still.[7]

In the next series of experiments, a small lamp was lit before the animals got their apples. At first, little happened. But after a few rounds the neurons sprang into action as soon as the little lamps blinked. But then, when the scientists approached with the fruit a few minutes later, the neurons were still. So it wasn't the food itself but the expectation, the anticipation, that stimulated these neurons into activity.[8]

In the scientific literature, this brain mechanism is often designated with the imprecise term *reward system*. In fact, it isn't the reward that stimulates the neurons, but rather the expectation. Thus I will speak of the *expectation system*.

Popular opinion is quite right in praising anticipation: it is there that the greatest pleasure lies. The reward itself we accept without special excitement. An employee to whom the boss has promised a raise is happy, but much less obviously so when the additional money goes into his monthly paycheck. And thus it is with the monkeys.

PLEASURE MAKES US CLEVER

In nature, it is advantageous to economize with our attention— which is what happens when we no longer focus on something once it is expected. To return to the example of the monkeys, if it becomes clear that a certain signal will always be followed by apples, no further attention is necessary. Attention is a scarce resource, and those who don't have to keep an eye on their food are in a better position to be on the lookout for their enemies.

But what happens when expectations are exceeded? If, after giving the signal, a scientist approached the monkeys not with the customary apple but with raisins, the neurons fired off very strongly. The surprise obviously created a sense of pleasurable excitement. After a few repetitions, this reaction, too, stopped. The animals had gotten used to the better food. And so, too, when people can afford champagne every night, their enthusiasm wears off quickly.

When the researchers put the monkeys back on the apple diet, the neurons let it be known that they had gotten used to better. Now the level of arousal sank even below its normal resting level—a sign of depression. But the disappointment didn't last too long. After a while, the raisins were as good as forgotten, and the cells behaved as if there had never been anything other than apples, nor as tasty.

Wanting better is among the oldest principles of nature. Even tiny bee brains have a single neuron that functions like the *expectation system* of higher animals. Being so simple, bee brains and bee lives demonstrate the evolutionary purpose of the pleasure principle with particular clarity.

On their gathering expeditions, bees land only on blossoms that contain a lot of nectar, avoiding all the others. Somehow they must have found out where it's worth landing. The bee's brain accomplishes this with the program "apples and raisins." If a bee is exploring an unknown meadow, it dives into different blossoms and tests how much nectar they contain. And now the same mechanism is set in motion that makes lab monkeys reach for raisins. If a blossom contains an unexpectedly large amount of nectar, the neuron for octopamine is activated. (Octopamine is the name for the insect's version of dopamine. For simplicity's sake, I'll refer to it as dopamine from here on.) The bee makes a mental note: "A good landing spot." If, on the other hand, a blossom contains less nectar than the others, this neuron remains inactive, and from now on the bee won't fly to this meadow.[9]

Thus, the bee can learn, although without innate preferences and without models. Reality itself is its teacher, and the dopamine neuron tells it what is bad, good, and better. Whenever dopamine is released, it sets off the signal that the decision was a right one and that something good has happened to the organism.

As we've seen in chapter 4, the circuits between neurons change when the brain learns. Influencing the way in which genetic information is processed in the nerve cells, and thus stimulating the neurons to change their form, dopamine encourages the creation of new connections in the brain.[10] Desire and understanding are very closely linked. Desire makes us smart, and without it, learning is difficult.[11]

THE URGE FOR MORE

We see, then, that the detector for what is new and better works deeply within the brain and that without it we would be incapable of learning.

Because this mechanism is much older and more powerful than human reason, it also enables us—perversely—to act unreasonably. Unlike animals, we are concerned not only with basic needs like food. Our *expectation system* spurs on all the wishes of which humans are capable. We are programmed always to want the best there is. When we have it, we quickly get used to it, but we strive for it nonetheless, and at almost any cost.

We feel how illogical these emotions can be when we get carried away playing games, even though nothing at all may be at stake.[12] The London brain researcher Raymond Dolan has discovered some of the responsible synapses. He engaged his subjects in a kind of poker game, while he examined their brains using PET scans. If their winnings exceeded expectations, the area of the prefrontal cortex where the nerve branches end and distribute dopamine—closely related to the corresponding regions in Schultz's monkeys—showed activity. Whether the earnings were in real money or in play money didn't make the slightest bit of difference to the players' brains.

The *expectation system* is also activated by videogames, where the goal is the mere accrual of points.[13] Apparently, the mechanism doesn't ask how useful it is to get something—rather, where there's something to be had, the brain says: Go for it. This may help explain why even wealthy people rush off to sales and pour over bargain catalogs.

The goal is not to have positive emotions that endure; all that matters is to trump whatever it is we've gotten used to. A medal of honor, another increase in a salary of millions, or a bigger boss's chair may not be of much value in and of themselves, but who wouldn't do cartwheels to get them?

WHY WE STRAY

In few areas of life are we as vulnerable to the *expectation system* as in love. And nowhere else does the desire for more, for change, and for new experience cause more trouble, confusion and pain. "What does he or she have that I don't have?" is the standard question of the jilted partner—a question to which scientists have some surprising answers.

There's a story about Calvin and Grace Coolidge—he was the president of the United States from 1923 to 1929—that summarizes the problem well. As they were being taken separately around a government farm, Mrs. Coolidge entered the chicken coop when a very lusty rooster happened to be mounting a hen. The first lady seemed impressed and asked whether the rooster copulated more than once a day. "Dozens of times," was the answer. "Please tell that to the President," she replied.

Sometime later Mr. Coolidge passed by the coop. When he was told about the heroic activities of the cock, he asked, "Every time with the same hen?" "Oh no, Mr. President, every time with another." The President nodded. "Tell that to Mrs. Coolidge."

What the President correctly recognized is that the need for novelty in sexual relations is hardly rare. The *Coolidge Effect*, as behavioral scientists call the waning of sexual desire in long-standing partnerships, can be observed in many creatures and suggests that the tendency to stray is a part of our evolutionary inheritance.

The Coolidge Effect has been studied particularly closely in rats. When one of each sex is put together in a cage, they develop a lively interest in each other, and the male mounts the female. After a brief respite, they do it again—with the same energy and determination as before. After the fourth or fifth time, it's over—suddenly the male's desire is extinguished. Had he overtaxed himself? No. He was bored. If a new partner is brought to the cage, he goes right for her, and the game starts from the beginning.

As the Canadian brain researcher Anthony Phillips showed, the desire of animals for their partners is even measurable. His numbers: the mere sight of a new female behind a pane of glass increases the dopamine level of the male rat by 44 percent. Immediately before sex it continues to increase up to twice the normal level before dropping off drastically after climax. The next time with the same partner the increase is weaker, and after a few times the dopamine level is hardly more than normal: the sire's desire has flagged. But if a new female appears behind the glass pane, the level climbs immediately by 34 percent.[14]

No one would claim that this new lady rat is in any way better than the old one, or that she has a special allure. It's the charm of novelty that counts. That's why the sight of her suffices for the brain of the male rat to release the dopamine. Giving the male drugs to raise the dopamine level works just as well—his sexual lethargy disappears, and he mounts his tried and true partner with renewed enthusiasm.[15]

If love is not involved, the lure of the unfamiliar is often much more important in sex than the quality of the interaction, at least for males. The prickling in the pit of your stomach, the knocking of your heart, and the excitement of seduction can be more exciting than a good orgasm.

There are indications that in humans, the inborn amount of dopamine receptors has an influence on a person's sexual promiscuity. These, at least, were the findings of Dean Hamer, a researcher at the National Cancer Institute in Washington, who determined that there is a direct relation between a certain variant of the gene for the D4 receptor—a receptor for dopamine—and the urge for erotic adventures. Thirty percent of all men are supposed to have such a "gene for promiscuity," and over time they have 20 percent more sex partners than the average man.[16] The statistical correlation determined by Hamer is too vague to explain the (mis)behavior of all the Don Juans of this world, but his finding does indicate that the extent of this urge for novelty must be at least partly inborn.

Scientists are avidly researching these connections in males, though hardly at all in women. Male science. But simple logic tell us that women's desire is unlikely to be weaker than men's. With whom, after all, do men partner when they stray? Why do female chimps make every possible effort to hide their coupling with low-ranking males from the alpha males? And how else can we explain the fact (proven by genetic testing) that 15 percent of all human fathers are kidding themselves about the paternity of the children carrying their name?[17]

CASANOVA'S SECRET

No one embodies the idea of inconstant love as well as Giacomo Casanova, the famous eighteenth century bon vivant and seducer. Charming and witty, he conquered the most beautiful and cultured women of the day, as well as housewives and maids. He celebrated his triumphs in Europe's salons, and conversed as easily as the rest of us breathe. He was a virtuoso of the erotic mise en

scène and of the refinement of sensual pleasure. For an assigna-
tion with the beautiful Marina Maria Morosini, for example, he
rented Venice's most expensive and sumptuous garden palace.
Outfitted only for love, pleasure, and feasting, it was furnished
with a huge mirror that reflected the light of hundreds of candles,
elegant sofas, and a fireplace on whose Chinese tiles naked couples
cavorted.[18]

The staff served wild game, sturgeon, truffles, oysters, the
finest burgundies and champagne, fruits and—a delicacy in
1753—ice cream. "Gifted with the sublime capacity of thought,
man recognizes pleasure," this bon vivant explained. "He seeks
it, combines it with other pleasures, perfects it and elaborates it
through thought and memory."

Evidently his visitor also enjoyed the evening. At least Casanova
reported that he learned much from her, experiencing "sighs,
raptures, ecstasies, and feelings such as they are developed only
in a sensitive soul in the sweetest moments." After this night of
abandon, the gondola disappeared with the beloved, returning
her in the morning mist to her convent. (She was a nun.)

It wasn't Casanova's way to be inhibited by convention. That
his love was forbidden made it that much more interesting. He
wanted to try everything, see everything, experience everything.
He was drawn to new women and to much else, wanting to take
from life whatever he could get. It was one of the recurring
motifs of his life that without risk and constant stimulation he
was left unsatisfied and unhappy.

In spite of so much sensual pleasure, Casanova never attained
happiness. As he admitted, he was addicted to gambling: "I
didn't have the strength to stop when I fell out of fortune's
favor, nor was I able to desist from chasing after money." He got
himself involved in senseless intrigues, risked his life in duels,
and managed, for the most trivial of reasons, to so arouse the ire
of the authorities that he spent some of his best years in flight.

Even during comparatively calm times in his life he was driven by a real addiction to new sensations. When, as a young man, he lived on the island of Corfu for three months, he managed to work as a banker, start a theater company, form a small peasant army, flee a corsair, and unmask a false prince.[19]

ADDICTED TO NOVELTY

Casanova was an extreme case of a person driven by curiosity. But we all desire novelty. Where there's no change, there's boredom, one of the experiences that we tolerate least well of all. "Boredom is watered-down pain," wrote the German writer Ernst Jünger, and we desperately try to avoid it. Gossip, television, fashion: once again, what matters is not so much their specific purpose as that we experience something new. The digestion of newness is one of the brain's most important activities. The gray cells require nourishment.

It's in the nature of animals, wrote Aristotle, to desire change, and it's no different with humans.[20] Nature had to enable its creatures to deal with a world that is constantly changing, and that's just what curiosity does well—enabling us not just to accept new things but also to want them. When we explore the world, we're a step ahead of it.[21]

Psychological tests have shown that curiosity is one of the personality's most stable indicators, with an enormous effect on people's lives. People whose curiosity is easily aroused for a certain subject or a particular person readily become curious about almost anything else.[22]

People's needs for novelty vary. One person will stay loyal to the same company until she gets her gold watch, while someone else tries her luck elsewhere every few years. Some people live in the house in which they were born for their entire lives, while others move from city to city. Sometimes we can discern these qualities from the kinds of vacations people take. Those who travel happily to the same resort where English is spoken will be less driven by curiosity than someone for whom there can be no place that is too far away. People may be surprised by those who are so different from themselves, but there is little point in trying to reeducate someone who is restless, or immobile, for the degree to which a person needs new stimulation is probably inborn.

A hypothesis currently attracting interest postulates the existence of another dopamine receptor that influences how much stimulation a person needs. It asserts that people whose neurons are provided with relatively few so-called D2 receptors are especially curious. This applies to about 25 percent of the population—among their genes is a variant that results in diminished production of this receptor. Their neurons are less responsive to dopamine, and thus they need more than other people to attain a balance. These adventurous personalities have to do more than the rest of us to create dopamine. They seek new stimulation, they like to have their nerves tickled, and they are more willing to get themselves into risky situations. Drugs offer another way of releasing dopamine, as we shall explain in more detail in chapter 8. Indeed, people with a lesser density of D2 receptors are more likely than average to be drug and nicotine dependent.[23]

Science has not yet had the last word on the D2 theory. But there is no question about the major role dopamine plays in curiosity and dependency, and there seems to be a clear connection between the ability of the brain to process dopamine and the capacity for both curiosity and addiction. What we don't yet know is the extent of the influence of the D2 receptors in comparison with other factors.

It wouldn't be difficult, should the theory be proven, to iden-tify a few prominent candidates for a genetically determined adventure syndrome. Casanova would be a classic case. In old age, he managed not only to fill twelve volumes with memoirs,[24] he wrote science fiction in which he foresaw cars, television, and airplanes. Curiosity can result, after all, not only in searching for novelty but also in creating it.

SMALL GIFTS MAINTAIN INTELLIGENCE

The guests of Cornell University psychologist Alice Isen weren't really offered much: a bag of candies, a few coins, and a kind word ("You look great!"). But who expects such friendly gestures at the start of a psychological experiment? The small attentions had a decisive effect. The participants reported that their mood improved immediately. In and of itself that's already odd enough. Are a few pitiful candies that anyone could buy for himself really all it takes to chase away our cares, however briefly? After all, the people whom Isen had recruited for her experiment were hard-boiled hospital doctors—hardly the kind of people to be carried away by sentimentality.

But things got even stranger. In the next round of experiments, the psychologist posed a task that was very familiar to her subjects: An assistant described a few clearly defined ailments that were plaguing him, and the doctors were to establish the diagnosis. Whenever the assistant described a new symptom, Isen asked the doctors for a diagnosis on the basis of what they'd heard so far. If they had been given a small present before the experiment, they thought creatively and reached the correct diagnosis in half as many steps as when no gifts were offered. In spite of their euphoria, they remained serious and pursued the experiment conscientiously to the end, although without coming to new results.[25]

Does this mean that we should bring a little present to our doctor's appointment? There's no reason not to, but presumably this method wouldn't work if employed too often. The value of a gift of this kind is that it's a surprise. If the recipient counts on it, the *expectation system* would no longer kick in.

But why did a few pieces of candy make the doctor-volunteers into more able and inspired diagnosticians? The unexpected gift slightly lifted their dopamine levels.[26] And dopamine stimulates the gray cells to process information—the mechanism that is also the foundation of curiosity. As Schultz's monkey experiments showed, dopamine releases an unusual level of activity in the working memory, which is housed in the prefrontal cortex. And these are exactly the systems required to juggle the different data in our head. At the same time, dopamine affects deeper-lying centers that control attentiveness and provide greater focus.[27] In these ways, a pleasant surprise makes thinking more supple.

WITH HAPPINESS AND UNDERSTANDING

Under the influence of dopamine the brain learns to make connections, for this transmitter prepares the neurons for novelty. Whether it concerns the linking of a light signal to the anticipation of raisins, or fashioning a poem from sentence fragments in a writer's head, dopamine enables animals to recognize the rules in the environment, as in the first example, and to look for meaning in the world, as in the second.

The brain systems for desire intensify insight and make us inventive. That they do both proved a happy evolutionary development, resulting in a most effective synergy. The chimpanzee in the zoo piles banana boxes in order to get to the higher-hanging fruit. And we humans, too, have ideas so that we may live better and satisfy our desires. The union of curiosity and desire that dopamine creates in the brain is also the root of creativity.

Without unusual quantities of this neurotransmitter—

whether natural, pathological, or drug-induced—many works of art would never have been created. Casanova, after all, was driven not only to adventure but to brilliant writing. Oliver Sacks's patient Leonard began typing his autobiography at lightning speed when the medication L-Dopa suddenly released far too much dopamine in his brain. And Jean-Paul Sartre wrote his last books in an artificially induced surge of creativity. Facing encroaching blindness, the aging French philosopher took amphetamines, drugs that raise the dopamine level, in an attempt to win the race against time.

Too much dopamine can take people into the shadowy realms of fantasy. They suspect hidden meanings where there are none, they hear the grass growing and spin irrational thoughts.[28] But in a milder form, these feelings stimulate creativity. They enable us to see connections that are otherwise hidden and to combine things that have never been brought together. These abilities are at the heart of every creative accomplishment, whether it concerns the invention of a new dish, the design of furniture, or the solution to a mathematical problem.

Mood, then, influences mental ability. From the insights that the psychologist Isen got from her small presents there is a doubly optimistic lesson to be learned: how easy it is to raise people's spirits, and that happiness and reason are not mutually exclusive. On the contrary, the possibilities these insights suggest are legion. Students who can laugh and are comfortable in class learn more easily. Employees who enjoy their work will also be productive.

As the saying goes: The brain runs on fun.

7
ENJOYMENT

WANTING AND LIKING are two different matters. How often do we go to a party, although we're fairly sure that we won't feel comfortable? There'll just be a lot of boring people clutching their beer bottles, and, frankly, we're not even close to the hosts. Why bother? And yet we want to go, though we can't really explain why. It's as if we're afraid of missing something exciting. But as usual, once we're there, nothing happens, and for a few hours we stand around in a kind of small-talk hell. We swear we'll never again waste an evening in this way . . . until the next time.

Smokers, too, know the difference between wanting and liking. A cigarette can be wonderful. The smoke caresses the nose and tickles the throat like a thousand tender feathers. On its way down, its pleasant bite unfolds as it releases a flavor that is both austere and soft. But by the day's eighth or ninth cigarette . . . ? "Difficult to describe precisely . . ." wrote Jay

McInerney in his novel on smoking, ". . . a mix of ozone, blond tobacco and early-evening angst on the tongue."[1]

In such moments a chain smoker begins to hate himself for his dependency and weakness. He despises his cigarettes, and yet he wants them—so much so that he runs to the store in the pouring rain when his pack is empty.

We aren't accustomed to distinguishing between wanting and liking, for very often the two come to the same thing. You probably won't order something off a menu if you know you won't like it. But to confuse the two impulses can be a source of unhappiness, as the bored partygoer and the desperate chain smoker demonstrate. In the worst case, it can lead to serious addictions.

On the other hand, the opposite can happen as well: we can like something without wanting it. After a seven-course meal, you'd still like the dessert, but you wouldn't want to order it.

Positive feelings come about in two different ways: when we want something, or when we've gotten something that gives us pleasure. The brain creates the two sets of impulses—wanting/enjoyment, liking/anticipation—in different ways. The Harvard neuroscientist Hans Breiter was even able show that they activate different parts of the brain. Anticipation activates a center in the forebrain—the *nucleus accumbens,* "the leaning center," so called because it is angled like the Leaning Tower of Pisa. It's controlled by dopamine, the molecule of pleasure, and plays an important role in remembering positive experiences. But when we enjoy something, the areas of the cerebrum responsible for conscious perception are also activated.[2] And the transmitter here isn't dopamine, but opioids, natural substances that resemble opium.

THE TRANSMITTERS OF EUPHORIA

Every enjoyment is a kind of rush. Whether it's a hot shower on a winter morning, a massage, a good meal, or sex—the same mechanism is at work, and the same synapses in the brain are responsible. And they have the same chemistry: opioids are involved in the creation of every experience of pleasure. At their core all pleasures are the same. What distinguishes the delights of a massage, therefore, from the enjoyment of a cold beer on a hot summer day isn't the melody in the brain, but the different instruments on which it's played. In the one case, signals come from the pressure-sensitive sensors on the skin, in the other, from the tongue and gums. Once the stimuli reach the brain, however, the resulting pleasure is the same.

Maybe the French poet Charles Baudelaire suspected these connections when he exhorted his readers: "You should always be drunk. Everything depends on it. If you don't want to feel the awful burden of Time breaking your shoulders and pressing you to the ground, you must be ceaselessly drunk. But on what? On wine, poetry, virtue . . . whatever you want. But get drunk."[3]

The frenzy of enjoyment interrupts the flow of time—the idea isn't as odd as we might think, since opioids chemically alter our experience of time. During orgasm, for example, the clock seems to stop. Baudelaire recognized that all intoxicants have the same effect and, what's more, that we don't even need artificial stimulants to get intoxicated. The equation of "good" and "bad" states of intoxication seemed a monstrous thought at the time. Baudelaire's volume of poetry *Les Fleurs du Mal* (*The Flowers of Evil*) caused a scandal when it was published in 1857. And his collection of prose poems that includes "But get drunk" wasn't published until after his death.

More than a hundred years later, neuroscientists provided the biological basis for Baudelaire's bold claim. In 1973, three research groups determined independently that neurons in the human brain contain receptors—chemical docking stations— for opiates, among them morphine and heroin. To what evolutionary purpose? Certainly not for people to yield to the pleasures of the poppy!

Scientists searched feverishly for answers and discovered that the brain can create morphinelike substances that fit exactly onto the mysterious receptors: the first natural opiates—drugs that the body itself creates—had been found. They were called endorphins, a neologism forged from the Greek prefix "endo," for "inner" and "morphine." Soon more such substances were identified: the enkephalins. Finally dynorphins, which have exactly the opposite effect from the endorphins, were discovered—instead of pleasure, they stimulate repugnance. Today all these substances—endorphins, enkephalins, and dynorphins—are brought together under the term "opioids." Opioids are neuropeptides, molecules that are much bigger and have a more complicated structure than dopamine.

After scientists discovered these chemicals in the human brain, it didn't take them long to find the transmitters for pleasure in other animals as well. Opioids flow in the brains of dogs, rodents, and insects, and even in the simple nervous system of the rainworm. Does this mean that all of nature is moved to search for happiness?

EMBRACING THE WHOLE WORLD

Without endorphins and enkephalins the world would be terribly gray. Just how gray we know in cases where medications cause these transmitters to temporarily lose their effectiveness. Naloxon is such a medication. It is taken to cure heroin addiction, but it also kills the taste for food, stifles laughter, and transforms one's perception of the environment into something resembling soulless machinery, peopled by robots. Sex loses its appeal entirely, although the body still has all the normal physiological responses to orgasm. Without opioids, people seem to be perfectly capable of copulating—they just don't experience pleasure.[3]

The situation gets even worse when the field is left to the endorphins' opponents, the dynorphins. The misery caused by the resulting feelings are hard to describe. Experimental subjects who have ingested substances related to dynorphins report chills, insane thoughts, physical weakness, and a complete loss of self-control. Some of them found the experience so terrible that they wanted to jump out a window.[4]

Rats reacted similarly when researchers removed the part of the midbrain controlled by opioids. Everything disgusted them. When they were given sweets that they had especially favored before the operation, they spat them out. If they hadn't been fed intravenously, they would have starved.[5]

But what joy we feel when the endorphins and enkephalins are circulating in our heads! We suddenly notice an entire fireworks display of flavors when eating a perfectly normal dish. Our appetite grows and persists even when we're actually full—a reason why pleasure in eating can lead to overweight.[6] Everything seems bright and friendly. If we could, we'd embrace the whole world. We beam when we encounter perfect strangers, not only because we're feeling so good, but because they really seem nice. Our happiness is spilling over—would that we could share it![7]

When people are under the influence of this substance, they seem to be incapable of sadness. Even Helen of Troy knew after the Trojan War that her relatives needed an intoxicating drink to help ease their sense of loss. In the fourth book of the *Odyssey* we read:

> *Into the mixing-bowl from which they drank their wine*
> *she slipped a drug, heart's ease, dissolving anger,*
> *magic to make us all forget our pains . . .*

No one who drank it deeply, mulled in wine,
could let a tear roll down his cheeks that day,
not even if his mother should die, his father die . . .[8]

Neuropharmacologists today assume that this mixture contained opium,[9] and, indeed, into the nineteenth century treating anxiety and depression with opium was considered best medical practice. "For the relief of the psychic pains nothing equals opium," wrote the author of an American medical textbook of the time. "It is almost as specific in its action in relieving the mental suffering and depression . . ."[10]

Given its addictiveness, no one today would advise us to smoke opium to assuage our sadness. But the brain naturally creates a substance, beta-endorphin, which is much more effective than opium. As harmless as it is effective, it is produced by a gland of the midbrain, the hypophysis cerebri. Sometimes all it takes is a good meal.

TASTE, SOURCE OF PLEASURES

"The close relationship between happiness and roast turkey is a marvel, as is the heart's resilience when a bottle of Marcobrunn parries its every beat," wrote the German novelist Theodor Fontane.[11] Since Fontane wasn't one to drown his sorrows in liquor, and German white wine is not all that potent, the explanation for this phenomenon lies in something other than alcohol. Tasting roasted meat and wine releases beta-endorphins, which scatter sadness to the winds.

But good feelings don't come from opioids alone. The entire body is set up for enjoyment. Nothing demonstrates this as clearly as the pleasure we get from food. Nourishment is a necessity of life, but eating is one of life's great pleasures. And because our enjoyment of food is such an elementary happiness, it is the best and also the best-researched example of all sensual pleasures. The machinery of taste shows the extent to which human beings are built for happiness and how useful enjoyment can be.

If, as many religions believe, the body is God's temple, then the mouth is its gateway. It is equipped with about three thousand taste buds, tiny little nubs a few hundredths of a millimeter high, mainly on the tongue. Each of these little bumps contains about fifty sense cells that respond to the different tastes.

The taste sensors are the reason some people like spinach, for example, while others don't. A quarter of the population consists of so-called supertasters, who perceive bitterness and sweetness more intensely than the rest of us. Just what the combination of genes is that ruins the taste for spinach we don't yet know. Two groups of scientists, however, have recently identified hereditary factors that are responsible for the sense of sweetness.[12]

Altogether, more than a hundred thousand nerve strands, bundled into two cords, pass taste information from the tongue to the brain. In addition, there are sensors that report heat and cold, and others that identify texture—whether it's soft or crunchy, moist or dry. Cotton candy tastes different from caramel, although both are made of sugar. Finally, there are those sensors that register burning and thus respond to the spiciness of chilies. Every bite and every movement of the tongue sets off an entire firework display of electric signals.

But the signals don't translate into pleasure until they've been received in the brain. As I explained in the first chapter, nature invented positive feelings to seduce us into useful behavior. The pleasure we derive from taste serves to control our energy supply, as experimental psychobiologists have demonstrated on rats. If the rats—who'd been given nothing to eat—wanted to receive nourishment, they had to press a lever, which would release a nutrient solution that flowed through a tube directly into their stomachs, completely bypassing the taste/pleasure circuit. Although they could ingest as much as they wished, after a few weeks they lost almost a third of their weight. The pleasure that eating gives us is anything but a luxury.[13]

There is another reason "a thousand things are indifferent to touch, hearing and sight, but nothing is indifferent to taste," as Jean-Jacques Rousseau observed. As omnivores, humans are not limited to a small menu—unlike dogs, for example, who eat little except meat, or cows, which feed only on grass and herbs. So humans are constantly having to try out unknown foods, which we evaluate with our sense of taste. Pleasure and distaste indicate what is likely to be good for us, and what not. Taste, however, doesn't always lead us to the correct conclusion. Notorious counterexamples are the pleasing taste of the deadly amanita mushroom, or the Japanese blowfish, on which more than one gourmet has feasted to death.

Incidentally, humans do not recognize only four kinds of taste, but in all likelihood five, as scientists have recently discovered: sweetness, saltiness, sourness, bitterness, and savory, also known by its Japanese name, *umami*. This signal is released by certain amino acids, like glutamate, which are found in meat but also in foods like mushrooms, cheese, and tomatoes.[14]

Unsalted food tastes bland because the body needs salt to function, just as it also needs protein. But we tolerate bitter and sour tastes only moderately—a warning, for most poisons are bitter, and many sour fruits aren't ripe. Instead, we devour anything sweet, for sugar is straight energy. Thus the dieter's dilemma: evolution hadn't foreseen diets. It made its creatures to absorb as much nourishment as possible—as a precaution against bad times. The addiction to cake and ice cream is inscribed in our brains.

THE APPEAL OF MASSAGES

With the help of opioids, the brain evaluates everything that we experience, just as it does with food. When something good happens to us, it releases endorphins. But when bad things happen, it's the dynorphins that give the signal. In this way evolution gets its creatures to do what they should do, and to do it gladly. Mammals have to care for their young. Because they're under the influence of opioids, mothers pursue this task with enthusiasm. Endorphins and enkephalins sweeten responsibility: Reward and pleasure are always better motivators than force and fear of punishment. It is precisely those things that are most pleasant that are most necessary for the survival of the species. Sex is a good example: since nature wants us to pass on our genetic inheritance, opioids flow at orgasm.

People also like to be stroked. And not only humans, but monkeys, cats, and guinea pigs are calmed by touch.[15] Even birds, when touched, release opioids in their brain.[16] Interestingly, the surge of opioids brought on by physical contact seems to be less about creating desire than assuaging fear and calming individual members of a group when they feel abandoned or frightened. When young animals are touched, they immediately stop making unhappy sounds. If they're given opiates from an external source, their need for physical contact is diminished. People who are satisfied require less reassurance than those who aren't.[17] And a massage can do miracles when we feel lonely or depressed.

THE PATH TO HARMONY

Enjoyment is a signal that the organism is getting what it needs. But what do we need? That depends. When we're thirsty, water. When we're hungry, food. When we're sad, solace. When we're thirsty, the first gulps taste the best, and after a strenuous hike, an otherwise so-so campfire meal tastes superb. Desperate times, desperate measures—but these sometimes turn out to be rather appealing.

Whenever life's basic needs are missing, the body ascertains a deficit. When we're hungry, for example, there's an imbalance between the need for energy and the intake of nourishment. The body releases dynorphin, the opioid of discomfort, which is responsible for our perceiving hunger as unpleasant.

An impulse is set in motion to do something against the unpleasantness. We become restless, irritable, on our guard. We look for a signal to compensate for the deficiency.

We see a goal: a roast chicken! The brain releases beta-endorphin that gives a foretaste of the desired pleasure and signals that the food before us should benefit the organism. At the same time the brain very quickly releases dopamine, the molecule of desire. The circuits for wishing and wanting are closely connected.[18] Under the influence of dopamine we become optimistic and more alert, and we make an effort to satisfy our desires.

We smell the odor of meat, bite into the drumstick, and enjoy the flavor. Still more endorphin floods the brain and signals to the organism that its needs have been met and that it is returning to a state of equilibrium: it's full, and it's comfortable. We relax. Life is good.

In this way, enjoyment accompanies the return to physiological balance. If it's good for you, you'll like it. But the organism's hedonistic principle has another side: pleasure cannot last. As soon as everything is back in order, the sense of pleasure dissipates.

Enjoyment is a signal that we are moving from a worse to a better condition. Positive feelings depend, therefore, on circumstance and timing. Everything has its moment. When it's hot, you'll seek shade, and when you're freezing, you want nothing so much as a seat in front of a fireplace, or at least a cozy wool blanket. It's not the temperature as such that's so essential for our well-being, but its relation to the previous condition of the body. After all, the same cold shower that we find refreshing on a humid summer afternoon takes on a very different quality after a day on the ski slopes.

Every Hollywood director knows this. Most of us no more enjoy a film in which everyone is nice to everyone else than we do one where there is only murder and mayhem. A good plot takes the spectator on a roller coaster of feelings. In the first half hour, we fall in love with the hero. Just when we're sunning ourselves in the glow of his beautiful life and the warmth of his charismatic appeal, he finds himself in terrible danger. Horrible things happen—and we suffer with him. The greater is our joy when everything works out in his favor. The dramatists of ancient Greece called this moment *catharsis:* terror gives way to relief. They, too, knew that contrast is a key to enjoyment.

WHEN PAIN ABATES

This is why positive feelings come about when pain abates. People have always intuited a connection between pain and pleasure. But it was left to neuropharmacology of the past two decades to show just how closely they're connected.

We perceive pain in the brain, but, as we've learned, the brain is also able to block pain. If I cut my finger, pain sensors, responding to the injury, send electric signals through special bundles of fibers in the spinal cord to the brain. This information is processed in the thalamus, a center in the midbrain: we feel pain. But when it's necessary, the neighboring hypothalamus can order the release of opioids. Enkephalins or endorphins or even the bad dynorphins—all work to neutralize pain, for they interrupt the transmission of signals in the spinal cord. This is why morphine, which resembles natural opiates, is the strongest painkiller of all.

There is a precise and apt expression for the jogger's good spirits: *runner's high*. Releasing endorphins and enkephalins when we're about to be overcome by exhaustion helps the organism to run past the pain. Euphoria suppresses the sense of weakness and goads the runner on to exert himself even further.

It isn't difficult to guess why nature created this mechanism. When an animal is attacked and wounded, its instinct would normally be to lie down in order to save energy. But if opioids have stopped the pain, it can still run for its life. There are other kinds of stress besides the attack of a predator that stimulate the brain's production of opioids. Some of our busy colleagues might be looking for exactly this effect when they keep piling on the work: Stress, too, can be pleasurable. Seen in terms of evolution, this is an old mechanism. The German neuroscientist Randolf Menzel discovered that even bees have the ability to turn off pain under stress.[19]

Thanks to natural opiates women are able to endure the pain of childbirth. Natural opiates also account for the relaxed, almost beatific glow on the face of many mothers shortly after labor. When acupuncture eases pain, the likely explanation is that the minor pain induced by the needles release very large amounts of opioids.[20] There is even speculation (as yet unproven) that some people value the spiciness of chilies because they want to savor the rush of the opioids that follows the burning pain in the mouth.

There is nothing in which pain and pleasure are as entwined as in sexuality. One explanation for some masochistic sexual practices might be that endorphins offer a kind of reward for the endurance of pain, thus intensifying the pleasure. Among other effects, endorphins cause dopamine to be released in the brain, which might explain how the enjoyment of pain could lead to a further fanning of desire. But until now, even the most creative neuropsychologists have stayed away from a closer examination of sadomasochistic sexual practices.

THE SEESAW OF POSITIVE FEELINGS

The cat plays with the mouse before killing it. Sometimes appetite is more pleasurable than the food itself. In love, too, it can happen that the greatest appeal lies in the games, the flirting, the detours, and the delays. He who seeks to reach his goal by the fastest route is not a good lover. "Good things shouldn't come cheaply," explains Valmont, the practiced and sinister seducer in Choderlos de Laclos' epistolary novel *Dangerous Liaisons*. He is afraid of losing the pleasure of the long erotic contest if he gets to his goal too quickly.

Desire and enjoyment are closely connected, but they are also opposed to one another. They're like children on the seesaw: sometimes one is up, sometimes the other. To be in a state of desire means not enjoying the present to the fullest. And to reach and enjoy one's goal is also to experience the extinction of desire, at least for the moment. The urge to exert oneself is inherent in desire, whereas enjoyment is sufficient unto itself. Someone who enjoys eating a good meal, falling in love, or simply sitting in the sun is not leading armies. At that moment he isn't even fit for the small battles of daily life.

In extreme cases, enjoyment can lead to total paralysis. Rats that have been given opiates in high doses are so apathetic that their bodies become waxen and can be shaped like a ball of dough into almost any position. It has been shown neurochemically that when opioids are administered above a certain quantity, the dopamine level can temporarily sink again.[21] The neuropsychologist Jaak Panksepp at Bowling Green State University suspects that this explains the drop in energy and drive after we experience pleasure.

But we can't endure this pleasant laziness for too long, for the effect of opioids lasts only a short while—between a few minutes and a few hours, depending on the situation. After all, enjoyment serves as a signal. When the message has been delivered, the messenger has no more to say.

This is the shadow side of pleasure. If the efficacy of the happiness drug wanes, our "normal" mood returns, and after the prior euphoria this can be perceived as an intolerable decline. Recognition of the sadness that can follow lovemaking is as old as the expression of feeling itself. And the Old Testament describes the emptiness that King Kohelet felt after having amassed more property and enjoyed more delights than any king before him: "Then my thoughts turned to all the fortune my hands had built up, to the wealth I had acquired and won—and oh, it was all futile and pursuit of wind; there was no real value under the sun! . . . And so I loathed life."[22]

Desiring a goal and pursuing it, on the other hand, might last for hours, days, and years. Sometimes the banquet may be better than the hunt, and the rush of enjoyment can surpass the itch of anticipation. Anticipation, on the other hand, lasts much longer. Many people try to spare themselves the letdown by doing everything more or less consciously to avoid the fulfillment of their longings. "The way is the goal," might be their motto. There were entire epochs characterized by unfulfilled desire. The German Romantic poets went into raptures over the *blue flower*, which could never be found and thus eternally sought. The medieval bards worshipped married women, who remained, of necessity, forever elusive. A troubadour couldn't hope for more than a few quickly written lines and a stolen smile—enough to keep his longing alive, too little to ever fulfill it.

8

THE DARK SIDE OF DESIRE

SEEKING HAPPINESS, WE sometimes risk becoming the plaything of our positive feelings. Because the pleasure of the new summer dress is short-lived pleasure, we go out and buy a matching pair of Prada shoes. They were, after all, on sale. How could we resist, even if they were the wrong size? Many people who have reasonable incomes live on the edge of their credit. Pleasure is fleeting. Who hasn't tried to overcome the sense of excess that follows a cheeseburger with a double scoop of caramel swirl extra-rich ice cream—thereby undoing all the hard dieting of the previous days?

Desire can take on a life of its own, as the Canadian neuroscientist James Olds demonstrated with a legendary experiment in 1954. He placed a thin electrode into the hypothalamus of rats, the region of the brain that is responsible for desire. He attached the wire to a switch that the rats could activate to give themselves a small electric charge that would stimulate this part of the brain. The result was stunning: after a very short time, it was as if the rats were wedded to the switch. The poor creatures forgot everything else and kept pushing it again and again as if possessed, clocking up to six thousand self-stimulations an hour. To Olds's astonishment, they lost all interest in sex, and even in food and drink. For a bit of happiness they risked death! After a few days, the scientist turned off the stimulator and spared their lives.[1]

What was it that drove these rats onto such a self-destructive path? By pressing the handle, they were able to turn on their *expectation system* and flood their brains with dopamine. As we've seen, this transmitter signals the sighting of a reward and sets all kinds of bodily functions in motion to ensure that the organism actually attains its goal. Above all, dopamine ensures that the brain records the beneficial situation as positive. It becomes programmed for repetition. It was the nectar-suffused blossom that caused the bee to release dopamine, thus establishing it as the goal to which the bees would fly in the future. With Olds's rats, it was the lever that took on this role, rendering them incapable of attending to anything else—each time further strengthening the programming and thus the compulsion.[2]

In this experiment we can see the downside of positive feelings. If a stimulus triggers desire repeatedly, the functioning of large parts of the brain is changed. Becoming superpowerful, desire transforms people into driven creatures who know no limits and have lost their sense of reality. In New Zealand, the researcher John Reynolds proved recently that the brain's wiring changes under the influence of dopamine. Using an experimental procedure similar to Olds's, he found that as soon as ten minutes after first pressing the lever, the coupling strength of the neurons in the rats' midbrain, which controls external actions, had changed. The programming for pleasure had begun.[3]

AIMLESS DRIVE

Like many things that have multiple applications, the brain circuits for pleasure are vulnerable to misuse. It is only their variety and adaptability that enable them to seize our personalities. Though it might seem surprising, we don't have one circuit that controls our desire to eat, another for love, and a third for social recognition. Instead we are equipped with a single, all-purpose system for desire and its gratification. Therein lie both its power and its danger.

This insight, too, we humans owe to rats. Once again, scientists placed electrodes in the hypothalamus—this time to expose the direct effects of pleasure on behavior. As soon as the researchers stimulated the brain circuits for desire, the animals became lively and active. But how were they to channel their need for action? Having been stimulated artificially, they had no goal. So they looked for one. They began to do everything that a rat can do—eat, drink, sniffle, gnaw, clean itself, copulate, carry things around the cage, kill mice, carry their young back to their nest.

It didn't seem to matter what the rats did, as long as they did *something*. If the scientists took the food away from an electrically stimulated rat that was about to eat, it ran to the water bottle and drank. If that was removed, the rat sought out a partner with which it could mate. This aimlessness went so far that after their water had been poured from a bottle into a bowl the thirsty rats would eat food rather than drink.[4] The more dopamine circulated in their brains, the more interchangeable the activities seeking the release of their arousal became. Thus, the researchers observed agitation in its purest form: activity counted for everything, the goal for nothing.

The functioning of desire's mechanisms explains this phenomenon. Dopamine, the most important transmitter in this system, doesn't relay information as such. Rather, it alters the readiness of the neurons to receive messages—and thus it changes the way in which the organism reacts to its environment. This strengthens whatever emotions happen to dominate at a particular moment. A hungry rat will look for food with even greater enthusiasm. If we stimulate the dopamine system of an animal that is full, it will lunge for whatever is offered.

People are no different. Nothing beats boredom like desire. It lifts our mood; attaining something lifts it still more. Exactly *what* changes the mood isn't so important. A dream dress, a platinum credit card, running for a seat on the school board—anything can keep the pleasure machine running. What matters is the inner condition of desire, the anticipation of conquest. For this we are willing to give almost everything.

THE LAS VEGAS PRINCIPLE

If so predisposed, a gourmand can become a compulsive eater; a sports fan, an obsessive jogger; a happy winner, a pathological gambler. All these compulsive behaviors arise in similar ways.

In the case of compulsive gamblers, it's the hope of financial reward that sets the pathological anticipation in motion. The surge of dopamine is released when the coins tumble out of the slot machine, or when a gambler at the next table cleans up—a "fiery tingling over the whole body" is how the Russian novelist Fyodor Dostoyevsky, who lost all he had at the roulette table, described the physiological sensation. The ringing of a few coins is enough to transfix hordes of otherwise reasonable people in front of a metal box for hours, where, like robots, they pull on a handle two or three times a minute, hoping that they, too, may set off the magical ringing. It isn't by chance that this reminds us of those rats in the lab that pushed the lever to stimulate themselves, and the same thing is happening in the brains of both.

With every successful wager, more dopamine is released. Each time, the linking of "handle" with "positive feeling" is strengthened in the brain, and with it the compulsion to pull the one-armed bandit—exactly as with the rats. That the slot machines ultimately spit out less money than the gamblers put into them is something the brain's *expectation system* can't know.

The Harvard psychiatrist Hans Breiter has shown that gambling activates the same synapses in the brains of gamblers and addicts, and even in volunteer subjects who aren't dependent. But unlike the compulsive gambler, someone who plays occasionally still has her *expectation system* under control.[5]

WHEN PLEASURE RUNS AMOK

That the same mechanisms responsible for everyday learning and anticipation (and therefore necessary for living) also govern addiction is probably the least intuitive insight that the study of positive feelings provides. But for just this reason research into addiction also gives us a profound understanding of the minds of healthy people. Addiction is an accident that happens in the course of the human search for happiness.

Evolution hadn't planned for this kind of self-inflicted harm, because it couldn't plan for the distant future. A hundred million years ago, when many of our behavioral patterns were being formed in our genes, it couldn't be foreseen that large primates would one day brew alcoholic drinks, build gambling halls, and synthesize cocaine. And ten generations ago, when large-scale hunger was commonplace, no one could have envisioned the mechanization of agriculture that would contribute to obesity as a widespread pathology.

We need to understand dependency as desire that has gone out of control in the absence of counterforces. Even the Seven

Deadly Sins can be seen as an overshooting of our natural striving for happiness. Pride is exaggerated self-love, covetousness is frugality gone haywire. We become envious when our natural tendency to orient ourselves toward others gets the upper hand. People yield to gluttony when the organism doesn't respond to nourishment with a sense of satiety, and to lust when sex is so unsatisfying that we want ever more of it. Anger is unbridled aggressiveness, sloth a pleasant relaxation that knows no end.

Drugs work exactly like the fatal levers in the gambling hall and in the rat's cage, for they too give the brain a dopamine lift. Under the influence of alcohol, the dopamine level doubles, and with nicotine and cocaine it increases threefold, as the Italian toxicologist Gaetano Di Chiara has determined. Because dopamine enhances our alertness, a cigarette gives us a sense of pleasant arousal and makes us feel more energetic and capable than before. Similarly, we often become optimistc after drinking a glass or two of wine.[6]

The same mechanism is at the bottom of all addictions, and drugs differ only in the way they set it off. Nicotine releases dopamine directly in that it activates the responsible neurons. Alcohol, heroin, and morphine increase the dopamine level indirectly, inhibiting neurons that normally oppose the *anticipation system*. Finally, cocaine ensures that once dopamine has been released, it remains in circulation longer. (Normally it disappears quickly into the cell walls of the brain.) Like Oliver Sacks's patient Leonard under the effect of L-Dopa, people who sniff the white powder feel the rush of omnipotence.

The critical factor is how dopamine is released. At the crucial moment of release, the brain links the sight of the drug and the desire for it irradicably. An addicted brain that recognizes a cigarette immediately orders "Light it!" or, stimulated by "bottle," gives the order to drink. Merely the image of an injection can suffice to set off a heroin addict's synapses.[7] In this way, nicotine, alcohol, and cocaine slip into the brain structures responsible for positive feelings, like the soldiers in the Trojan horse: drugs seize the brain.

HOW WE ALLOW OURSELVES TO BE SEDUCED

Can you remember your first cigarette? Most people find it an awful experience. The smoke scratched your throat. You could barely hide your need to cough from the kids who were watching. Some of us experienced our first beer similarly. If we're honest, most of us will admit that we persisted in order to look cool, rather than because we really enjoyed the bitter taste.

Most adults can enjoy beer and cigarettes. We can even learn to enjoy the burning of chilies. But it wasn't a pleasure at first. And it is hardly ever pleasure that drives people to alcohol and cigarettes. Even a laboratory rat wouldn't suck on a liquor bottle of its own accord, although alcohol has the same effect on rats as it does on people. Scientists have to work hard to get rats to become addicted to alcohol. And the same is true for people: addictions are learned.[8] The original motivation is almost always to assuage some kind of difficulty. The German writer Wilhelm Busch wrote that people who have cares also have liquor. And, it has to be said, vice versa.

Alcohol calms and dissipates fear. Cocaine has the short-term effect of a turbocharger on imagination and wit, thus seeming to help all those people who feel stupid and boring with their friends. Nicotine helps people endure boredom and stress; it stimulates and calms at the same time, but even more important, cigarettes give young people some kind of status among their friends, and they help break the social ice.

Many studies show that it's not the search for pleasure that leaves people susceptible to drugs, but the wish to find an escape from life's problems. Drug consumption increases almost automatically when the going gets tough. Alcoholism is widespread among the unemployed, as was heroin addiction among the American soldiers in Vietnam.[9] Of these young men, 40 percent took heroin at least once to help them endure the horrors of war. Half of them took it so often that when they went off the drug, they experienced the symptoms of withdrawal.[10]

Even a brief unpleasantness can lead to increased drug use. American researchers asked experimental subjects who were not addicted to solve a difficult puzzle, all the while criticizing and demeaning them. Afterward, the volunteers were asked to participate in an experiment that was billed as a "drinking test"—they were told to evaluate and compare different alcoholic drinks. Those who had suffered the worst abuse drank significantly more than those who'd been treated appropriately. A third group that was given the opportunity to get back at their critics consumed normal quantities of alcohol—apparently vengeance diminished the need to drink away the anger.[11]

WHO BECOMES AN ADDICT?

Drugs help us forget. Clearly, however, not everyone who has worries takes drugs. And not everyone who takes drugs becomes an addict. There are many wine drinkers and even occasional cocaine users who never develop dependencies. The most likely to succumb to their addiction are cigarette smokers. Of all addictions, cigarettes are the most seductive—not only because they're ubiquitous, but because nicotine has a direct effect on the dopamine system.[12]

Why can most people consume potentially addictive drugs without becoming dependent on them? The answer lies in the quality of their lives, and on their genes. Stress, for example, whatever its source, increases the probability that in the quest for a bit of relaxation you'll succumb to alcohol, tobacco, or heroin addiction.

Some genetic factors that affect the risk of addiction are very straightforward. A high tolerance for the drug in question, for example, puts one at a much higher risk. By contrast, if drinking one glass too many results in a ghastly hangover, alcoholism is probably not in the cards.

Another genetic factor is the extent of one's curiosity. There is a close connection between the enjoyment of novelty and the danger of becoming substance dependent. Dopamine plays a role in both, and whoever responds strongly to novelty, adventure, and dangerous situations also lives with a certain risk of becoming dependent. Scientists specializing in addiction have long known that rats that are especially vulnerable to dependency show more curiosity than other rats.[13]

The familiar D2 receptor for dopamine seems to play an important role here. Scientists at the Brookhaven National Laboratory near New York even managed to get alcohol-dependent rats off the bottle by using gene therapy to increase the number of dopamine receptors in their brains.[14]

Is it possible that in the distant future genetic intervention will result in fewer addictions? Right now it's out of the question. The complex mechanisms that determine how genes influence drug consumption are still far from understood. Geneticists today are more interested in predicting a person's tendency to addiction, so that he can act preventatively. People who have too few D2 receptors are especially at risk, says the Brookhaven National Laboratory addiction researcher Nora Volkow. A great-granddaughter of the Russian revolutionary Leon Trotsky, she established her reputation by examining the brains of human addicts. She discovered that addictions further diminish the number of D2 receptors (already low), and for years.

Thus people who are or were drug dependent live with a high probability of succumbing to a second addiction. Experiments show how morphine-dependent rats that have been broken of the habit then become dependent on alcohol. Almost every heroin addict is also dependent on cigarettes or alcohol. Addictions seize all of the person. People who began smoking or drinking in puberty are at still higher risk, for the young brain is especially malleable. There is no better protection against addiction than keeping children from using drugs.

CAUGHT IN A VICIOUS CYCLE

Someone who is once addicted is often aware only of the blind need for his drug. What keeps an addiction going is the brain's programming, not enjoyment.

This is not to say that people can't enjoy their dependency. Of course, cigarettes, beer, and strong drugs can bring forth pleasurable feelings. This is especially obvious with substances like heroin, which bear a chemical resemblance to opioids and thus stimulate a sense of euphoria. Nicotine and alcohol also cause a similar reaction, though less directly, and there's no harm in occasional indulgence.

But people who use a drug regularly will need it in increasing doses. Its effect wears off as the brain gets dulled to it. Over time, the pleasure wanes, and then drug use is no longer about getting high but about maintaining a normal mood. A day without the drug becomes drab. Using it restores some sense of pleasure for a few hours, but it desensitizes the brain further, and the addict digs himself ever deeper into his dependency. At some point, the chain smoker and the alcoholic don't get much satisfaction from their cigarettes and vodka. They maintain their habit because they're hooked—the sense of pleasure is long gone.

Hardly anyone has described this condition as well as the songwriter Konstantin Wecker, who was addicted to cocaine: "What a feeling of horror there was when only a few more grams were left in the house. We tore down walls if we thought some might be stored there. We ripped furniture apart in the hope of finding any remains. It was pathetic, and I was disgusted with myself. My dealer was fair, and I loved him, and when I testified to that effect in court, it came from the heart."[15]

Compared to what comes later, the physical symptoms of withdrawal are easy. The shivering and the shaking, the nausea and the hallucinations can be tempered with medication, and after a few weeks they disappear. What is much harder to contain is the need for the drugs that has been seared into the brain.

Many people think that an addict takes his drug primarily to preempt the symptoms of withdrawal. But this doesn't explain why someone who was once addicted can still relapse after decades. Although the brain loses its insensitivity to the drug shortly after the often painful withdrawal, the number of ex-addicts who compulsively reach for a cigarette is legion, even after they've been clean for a long time.

To understand this phenomenon we need to realize that the brain creates volition and pleasure in different ways. Addiction distorts both. If a drug-free life seems bland, it's because the drug has impaired the ability to enjoy. Addiction, on the other hand, comes about because the drug has insinuated itself into the brain's systems for desire and reprogrammed them. And while the dulling of pleasure is reversible, the *expectation system* is permanently damaged.

The obduracy of addiction results from the powerful mechanisms of desire—the phenomenon of craving. Someone who was once addicted is often "trained" for life. To counteract it is like unlearning our mother tongue. The experience of addiction permanently transforms the functioning of the nerve cells in the brain, altering the way in which the genetic information is read and changed into proteins. The cells are now disposed to create substances that make the brain especially receptive to any stimuli connected with the drug. Connections that lie like thick cables between neurons in the brain cause these stimuli to release an immediate demand for the drug. They hardly ever revert to their prior condition. Neurobiologists can even see in individual brain cells exactly which rats they had succeeded in habituating to alcohol long before.

This doesn't mean that people are helpless in the face of their addictions. Dependencies can be overcome. But people who were once addicted have to work their whole lives to overcome their illness—much as survivors of a heart attack have to change their habits if they don't want to risk another one.

An addict can either attempt to avoid the siren song of the drug, or he can control the urge to give in to temptation. Both are difficult, for the brain doesn't only link the substance itself with the craving, but also all the stimuli that were ever associated with it: clouds of smoke in a bar, seeing old friends, the aroma of a few drops of rum in a cake.

Elton John, one of countless pop stars with a successful withdrawal behind him, memorably describes the absurd torments that can be visited on an ex-addict: "Sometimes, when I fly over the snow-covered Swiss alps, I think that all the coke that I ever sniffed is lying down there."[16]

9

LOVE

OF ALL LOVE stories, the Celtic saga of Tristan and Isolde is probably the most uncompromising. Although Isolde had wanted to exact a cruel vengeance on Tristan for having killed her betrothed, his gaze mollifies her and her hatred is transformed into attraction. When her maid inadvertently pours them a love potion, the two can no longer resist their passion. Nothing matters but that they be together. In their ecstasy, they're even willing to betray her husband (and his uncle), good King Mark. When their affair is discovered, they choose to die together.

Why did they go so far? "I am unable to tell you this," answers Tristan in Wagner's opera when he's questioned by the shaken Mark. He doesn't understand the power that has taken hold of him. But the music that Wagner composed for this scene reveals more: a longing that can't be put into words, a feeling that is both torment and ecstasy.

This is an experience familiar to everyone, even if, fortunately, the longing only rarely becomes as absolute as in the saga of Tristan and Isolde. We feel that love casts a spell over us and that we are possessed by it. But what has transformed us, and why it was *this* person who has become so all-important . . . we simply don't know. So it shouldn't surprise us that in times past, such an overpowering force—one that made people fall in love even against the dictates of their reason—could only be explained as fate, or magic.

THE ELIXIRS OF LOVE

But there are indeed love potions, and in ascribing attraction's power to them, the Celtic bards were much closer to the truth than they could have known.

There is, for example, the hormone luliberin that is normally created in the hypothalamus and that controls the release of sex hormones. When even the tiniest quantity of this substance is present in the midbrain, it sets off uncontrolled desire. When it was administered experimentally to male guinea pigs, they immediately began to engage in energetic sexual play with any females who happened to be near them. And the females under the influence of this substance were willing partners.[1] Luliberin works exactly the same way in humans, though it's not especially useful as an aphrodisiac, since the extra dose would have to be injected directly into the brain.

Such experiments may be distasteful, because they make sex seem totally mechanical. But the elixirs of love do much more than stimulate a readiness for sex—they can help two people to develop a mutual devotion that endures all their lives. This phenomenon was studied by Emory University's Tom Insel on the prairie vole, a wooly little animal native to North America that he injected with the hormone vasopressin. The result: from then on, they never left their partner's side. The females accomplished the same feat when given a closely related substance, oxytocin.

In fact, Insel had only accelerated a process that would have occurred anyway, for the prairie vole enjoys a most unusual love life. As soon as these finger-long creatures reach maturity, they lunge for the first available sex partner. They give themselves over to love for an entire day, the male mounting his companion up to two dozen times. From then on the two stay together forever. They move into a shared nest, he becomes a caring father to their offspring, and when an intruder approaches, the two partners defend one another and their home. Being separated has no effect on their bond, for even months later they still recognize and desire one another. This fidelity transcends even death: When one of the partners dies, the survivor remains single.

How does such a strong attachment come to pass? While copulating, the males produce vasopressin, the females, oxytocin, and these hormones affect the brain in such a way that the two partners develop a preference for one another. Sex prepares the way for love.

It was this process in which Insel intervened. When he injected the male and female prairie voles with the appropriate hormones, they became lifelong mates even if they hadn't first spent a night of passionate lovemaking together. A single substance sufficed to create a bond for their rest of their lives. And the experiment also worked in the opposite direction. When, after a night of lusty sex, the animals' love hormone was blocked, there was none of the monogamy otherwise characteristic of the prairie vole.

This lack of fidelity is apparently caused by the partners' forgetting one another, or even failing to leave much of an impression in the first place. In any case, when a prairie vole with a nonfunctioning vasopressin system is confronted with a female with which he's often had sex, he behaves as if he'd never met her, sniffing her each time as if it's their first encounter. Tests showed that the problem wasn't that he'd become more stupid, but rather that he'd lost his memory for other creatures. Partnership relies on social memory, for which the brain apparently has dedicated circuits that are affected by oxytocin and vasopressin. When we think longingly of our beloved, these are the chemicals whose effect we're feeling.[2]

Vasopressin and oxytocin create partnerships even among animals to whom such relationships are otherwise entirely alien. House mice, for example, are normally interested in their partners for the duration of sex, and that's it. Using genetic intervention, Insel taught them monogamy. Planting a single gene from the prairie vole into their genetic material and thus equipping their brains with receptors for vasopressin and oxytocin, he made faithful partners out of the house mice. House mice, too, produce copious quantities of these hormones during sex, but because there are no suitable receptors in their brains, they have no lasting impact. After the tiny genetic reconstruction, however, vasopressin and oxytocin make it possible for these animals to enjoy a durable partnership. It takes only one single gene to change a polygamous animal into one that is monogamous and set the stage for all the intricate behavioral patterns that a lifelong partnership requires.[3]

With humans, the mechanisms of attraction, love, and fidelity are more complicated. We, too, are predisposed toward monogamy, though we could hardly claim that every steamy night leads to a lifelong relationship. But it would be surprising indeed if "love potions" did not play a crucial role in humans. For five hundred million years oxytocin, vasopressin, and similar substances have governed the sexual lives of almost all creatures, from the simplest earthworms to our nearest relatives, the apes.[4]

What distinguishes us from these creatures isn't so much the basic mechanisms of love but rather the freedom that we have in dealing with them. People can give themselves over to their inclinations, in extreme cases even against their better judgment—as in the finale of Wagner's opera *Tristan and Isolde*, when the exhausted Tristan curses the "terrible potion" and suggests with the words "I brewed it myself" the deeper truth: It is a product of his own mind. Real people, too, can resist love, whether because of family opposition, or because they'd rather put their time and energy into their careers.

134

Our environment has a major influence on whether, when, and how we bond with other people. But the emotions on which this is all based are programmed into us.[5]

WOMEN'S BRAINS, MEN'S BRAINS

The attraction between the sexes begins in the brain, which is structured differently in men and women in order to ensure mutual appeal. The stage for sexual desire is set in the uterus.

A fascinating experiment undertaken by nature itself shows how the female and male poles of love come into being. It concerns a small group of villagers in the Dominican Republic who are called *guevedoces*, Spanish for "balls at twelve years of age." In the course of their maturation, the guevedoces seem to undergo a sex change. At birth there is no sign of scrotum or penis, and so, looking like girls, guevedoces are raised as girls. As soon as the hormonal changes of puberty set in, their true sex emerges: the scrotum descends from what were presumed to be labia and from the clitoris grows a penis. At the same time, the guevedoces begin to behave like young men. From one day to the next they throw the dolls and clothes that they grew up with into the corner, don shirts and pants, and begin to show interest in soccer—and especially in girls.

In the traditional world of their villages, where every fifth child can be a guevedoce, it ceases to matter that they were raised to be courted by men. They now respond to female charms, and quite reflexively. So powerful is love's genetic programming and so small the influence of their upbringing. These brand-new men have no difficulty settling into their role—they just do what nature demands of them.

Like the body, the brain is built according to a design, which is either male or female. This is set in the first weeks of pregnancy, when the fetus's brain and sex organs develop, according to either the male or the female model. Thus, a child comes into the world with the brain of a boy or a girl, and with the corresponding appearance.

But the guevedoces, whose puzzle was solved by American scientists over two decades ago, are different: of the two switches (one for the brain and one for the body), one is damaged. Although the fetus's brain develops normally, the formation of the sexual organs is delayed, and the guevedoces are born with a boy's brain and a girl's physical appearance. This unique phenomenon shows how strongly the prenatal structure of the brain determines later behavior in love.[6]

But why are they pseudofemales who become boys rather than the other way around? At the beginning of development every human is female. The basic architecture of body and brain from which both sexes develop is that of a woman—the opposite of the story of Eve being created from Adam's rib. Only later does the male Y-chromosome give the signal for male development. At about eight weeks after conception genes on this chromosome spur the gonads to produce testosterone, the male sex hormone. Using various signal paths, this transmitter instructs body and brain that a male is on the way.

Differences between the sexes are particularly apparent in the structure of the cerebrum. In women, the two halves are more strongly connected, which is why the individual brain centers seem to be somewhat less specialized than in men. It has often been surmised, but never proven, that for this reason women are usually more willing than men to speak about their feelings. What is certain is that the slightly different organization of female and male brains is expressed in thinking. Women are usually more fluent in speech and quicker in mental arithmetic and in their perceptions, and they are often more skilled with their hands. Men, on the other hand, are often better at mathematical-logical thought and spatial conceptualization.

In general, however, the significance of these differences is grossly exaggerated. A catchy title like *Why Men Don't Listen and Women Can't Read Maps*, for example, tries to suggest that all kinds of discrepancies between the sexes can be explained simply. But it isn't that simple. That the two sexes have different strengths is a matter of averages—from data that was gathered among very many men and very many women. And statistics have to be interpreted with care, especially when, by and large, the differences aren't that great. On average, the sun shines over New York 107 days per year, and over Baltimore only 105 days. Nonetheless, one would never claim that on a daily basis New York has better weather than Baltimore.

HOW SEX GETS INTO OUR HEADS

The differences between the brains of men and women are fairly small when it comes to thinking, but in matters of love, they're huge. The lives of the guevedoces suggest that the brains of heterosexual men and women are as good as programmed toward the opposite sex. And in recent years, brain researchers have begun to discover the roots of sexual preferences.

The source of sexual attraction is the diencephalon, which lies exactly in the center of the brain and where the conditions for arousal are created. It differs so strongly in men and women that it's possible to distinguish a female from a male brain with the naked eye: A particular nucleus, the medial preoptic area of the hypothalamus, is twice as big in men's heads as in women's, and it is also constructed differently.[7] Among other things, the preoptic area controls the release of luliberin, which is so important.

We see the consequences of size difference in love play, for in all likelihood the preoptic area in men serves to stimulate their desire for women. If this nucleus is stimulated, an almost fanatic enthusiasm develops for anything female that comes into view. If it's removed, interest in the other sex wanes. Male monkeys whose preoptic area has been surgically removed begin to behave like females, although they continue to practice and enjoy masturbation. This suggests that different processes are responsible for developing interest in the opposite sex and getting sexual satisfaction.[8]

A group working with the Japanese neurologist Yutaka Oomura has studied the preoptic area very closely. In order to let attraction and sex run their course under controlled conditions, they came up with a rather remarkable arrangement involving subjects who copulated in chairs on tracks, during which scientists measured the neuronal activity in the hypothalamus. All this would seem more appropriate in the sex bars of Bangkok than in a university laboratory, although the "subjects" weren't humans but macaque monkeys, and you will be reassured to hear that the experiment involved no pain for the animals.[9] Still, the bizarre experiment provided the clearest proof to date that the preoptic area is, above all, responsible for sexual desire and not for the sex act as such.[10] Just how it fulfills its task is not yet fully understood. Probably electric connections to the penis and the cerebrum are formed from other nuclei in the midbrain and the nervous system. Many researchers suspect that the brain's anatomy helps explain the frequent accompaniment of masculine sexuality with aggression. The preoptic area is connected by several fiber bundles to the amygdala—the center releases that aggression, along with other dark feelings.[11]

With female desire—much less well researched—another area in the midbrain occupies the key position, the so-called ventromedial nucleus of the hypothalamus. In mammals, it releases the mating reflex. Female rats become still so that the males can mount them, and female monkeys present their sex organs. With human females, who aren't bound by such ritual behaviors, the ventromedial nucleus probably stimulates only a general willingness for sex. This nucleus is under the influence of the sex hormones, which is a possible explanation for the variability in women's ability to be stimulated during the course of their monthly cycle.

A quick look at the brain shows the extent to which women, too, are programmed for sex, for in both sexes large areas under the skull are generously equipped with receptors for sex hormones like oxytocin. That an overwhelming number of neurons are busy receiving signals from the sex organs and transforming them into feelings of love has a good reason. If the size of individual organs were commensurate with the space given them in the brain, the penis and the vagina could easily outweigh the entire upper body. Next place would go to the lips, also organs designed for the enjoyment of love (as well as nourishment).

VARIETIES OF LOVE

For a woman to love a man, and a man to love a woman, isn't everyone's idea of fulfillment: at least seven million people in the United States prefer a partner of their own sex.

In no way does this fact contradict the discoveries about the sexual formation of the brain. The guevedoces, with their transformation from pseudogirls to men, are another example of the freedom that biology gives to variety in sexuality. The body's sexuality and the regions of the brain that control sexual desire can take different courses, and brains frequently develop in male bodies that allow a man to be attracted to other men.

This finding was confirmed by the California scientist Simon LeVay, when he performed autopsies on homosexual men who had died of AIDS. In some characteristics that are consistent with sexual preference, the structure of their brains was more like that of females than of typical males. As LeVay reported, the preoptic area was smaller than in the average male (and the links between the two halves of the cerebrum were correspondingly stronger). This certainly doesn't mean that gay men have women's brains, as is often claimed. The differences involve the regions for sexual desire almost exclusively. In brain volume, on the other hand, which is markedly different for men and women, there was no difference between homosexuals and heterosexuals.

Homosexual organizations were extremely critical of LeVay, himself openly gay. The activists were afraid that they would again be stigmatized as "sick" if their sexual preference could be shown to have an organic basis in the brain.[12]

This kind of mistrust by a minority that has been struggling for its rights is understandable. But their concerns miss the heart of the matter. In reality, LeVay's studies show how normal homosexuality is: when men feel passion for other men, it's in no way deviant, but simply a natural variant of orientation. Just as there are right- and left-handed people, and people who are gifted in music, and others in sports, there are also different predispositions in sexuality. The same is certainly true for women, although lesbian love, like so many other specifically female matters, has so far not gotten much attention from researchers.

Between homosexuality and heterosexuality lies a whole range of intermediary steps. Only rarely does a brain develop to the extremes of the masculine/feminine spectrum. Much more often, it is somewhere in between. No one is entirely male, no one entirely female.

The subtlety of these shadings can be observed in mice, whose adult behavior is strongly influenced by the social environment of the womb. A female mouse baby that lies with brothers in her mother's womb, and is thus exposed to their sex hormones, later behaves more aggressively and (oddly) bears more babies than females who developed only among other females. With male mice we see the opposite effect: sisters in the uterus give them a gentler nature. Clearly, the cause for gender behaviors lies by no means only in the genes—influences before or after birth can play an equally large or even larger role.[13]

With people, the gradations between the sexes can be still finer, not only because we're much less bound by a particular role than other creatures (thanks to our larger cerebrum), but also because the male and female poles in Homo sapiens lie very close together. The preoptic area is one piece of evidence for this: it's almost four times as big in male rodents as in the females, whereas the factor for humans is on average only two. Thus the human brain allows for countless varieties of love, from the shy romantic to the rock-hard dominatrix.

TO CLIMAX

Not every man is a Don Juan. On the other hand, there are few men who haven't thought of love as conquest and sex as triumph. To some extent, this is a part of our culture, which has been haunted by these motifs for centuries. But it's not only the qualities of the preoptic area that point to the deeper causes underlying the connection between male eroticism and aggression.

From first laying eyes on each other until climax, men and women experience sexual desire that is governed by different mechanisms. Men are under the influence of the hormone vasopressin. It is not only the tiny prairie vole that is transformed by this substance into a faithful spouse, for in both animals and humans it stimulates aggression. A contradiction? Only at first blush—after all, the father of a family is supposed to defend his wife, child, and home with all means at his disposal.

More than ten times the normal concentration of vasopressin has been measured in men during the different phases of foreplay.[14] This number should be viewed with care, because until now it has been found only in the blood, and the hormone levels could be different in the brain, where behavior is determined. That such differences do occur was discovered by the German neurobiologist Rainer Landgraf when he succeeded in measuring the release of oxytocin and vasopressin with a tiny probe directly into the brains of rats.[15] The argument could still be made that vasopressin works only in the body and not in the brain at all, but it isn't very probable, for experiments show that when vasopressin is absent, the male lacks all passion during sex. He's still capable of the physical act but finds his partner about as exciting as a wet rag.[16]

The further the foreplay progresses, and the greater the likelihood that it will lead to copulation, the more the vasopressin level drops. At ejaculation it is almost back at the normal level—another indication of how different seduction and sex are. As soon as orgasm is near, another hormone seems to dominate in men: the level of oxytocin, the female counterpart to vasopressin, now rises. Without oxytocin there is no orgasm—and thus at climax both sexes are under the influence of the substance that determined the woman's desire from the very beginning.

For females take a different path to arousal. If the vasopressin level in the brains of female rats is elevated, their sexual desire drops almost to zero.[17] The level of free oxytocin, on the other hand, begins to climb from the first moment of flirting, apparently putting them in the mood for an encounter. If the effect of oxytocin is blocked, they rebuff any male sexual advances. If the males insist, the females become rabid.

As a woman gets closer to climax, ever-increasing quantities of oxytocin are released. During orgasm itself, endorphins are added, which are responsible for orgasm in both sexes. The more oxytocin released during foreplay, the stronger the climax, as scientists who have studied women experiencing multiple orgasms have learned.[18]

MAKE LOVE, NOT WAR

Why is it that we experience orgasm? This question is as yet without an answer, although scientists have been studying it intensely for decades.

They have been especially intrigued by the riddle of female orgasm. Some even doubt that there is any reason for this unreliable response to exist at all. The interests of reproduction, after all, could be satisfied by hormones that stimulate the females to mate during ovulation. And even if one admits that females should be able to enjoy sex, these researchers think, orgasm would not have to be a precondition for enjoyment. Less radical voices explain that orgasm might serve women as a biological signal that they have found a suitable partner. There is, however, no proof for this rather masculine theory.

At least one myth has collapsed: women, it turns out, are not the only females to experience orgasm. Researchers have observed in female monkeys approaching climax the heightened pulse and uncontrolled movements that are very close to the reactions of a woman during orgasm. The Dutch sex researcher Koos Slob was the first to make this observation in his study of macaque monkeys.[19]

All primates are social beings, so why shouldn't mating have a social function beyond procreation? The bonobos, or dwarf chimps, for example, use sex to eliminate conflict. When tensions arise, the most bellicose group members are satisfied sexually. Should the conflict continue, intercourse reconciles the combatants. Since bonobos also engage in same-sex activities, it's obvious that for them mating has purposes other than just reproduction.

That such activity makes good sense is shown by orgasm's neurochemistry. Oxytocin, which both sexes release during climax, is a tool for peace. As many experiments confirm, it encourages attachment and militates against aggression. And the opioids, which are responsible for the sense of ecstasy in orgasm, also give a feeling of pleasant relaxation. A person who feels good has little reason to fight.

Sex enables us to get along with one another better, and it can actually diminish aggression and bellicosity. "Make love, not war!" demanded the flower children during the Vietnam era. They were right.

IS LOVE AN ADDICTION?

During love's most intense moments, one's partner seems like a very special being. When we're in love, nothing and no one else can put us is such a euphoric mood. These romantic feelings are often combined with a strange sense of excitement that seems to dissolve the boundaries of the individual. Poets have described this condition since time immemorial. Recently, the London researchers Andreas Bartels and Semir Zeki have shown that the intoxication experienced in love is also accessible to science.

Looking on the Internet for volunteers who described themselves credibly as possessed by "genuine, deep and crazy love," mainly women, Bartels and Zeki examined their subjects using functional MRI. First they showed the women photos of friends with whom they had no sexual relationship and asked them to think of them intensely. During this time the scientists recorded the activity in their brains. Then they were shown photos of their lovers. While their brains were being examined a second time, they were to think of their partner. Comparing the two experiences, the scientists could see what happens when the brain is focused on the lover, and it turns out to closely resemble the pattern of brains activity under the influence of heroin and cocaine.[20]

Seen neurobiologically, this is hardly surprising, for drugs and the love elixirs oxytocin and vasopressin affect the same circuits in the brain. Both affect systems in which dopamine, the hormone of desire, plays a critical role. The release of dopamine is necessary in the coming together of two people, for, as we've seen, it controls attentiveness and awakens desire.

The neuropsychologist Jaak Penksepp compares love with addiction: in the one case a bond is created with the drug, in the other with a person. This relationship becomes especially evident at separation—withdrawal from the drug and parting from the beloved. Both result in feelings of loneliness and emptiness, in loss of appetite, depression, sleeplessness and irritability.[21]

The addict usually becomes numb to the pleasant effect of a drug, and over time the attractive qualities of a loved person, too, can sometimes lose their appeal. Nonetheless, we often encounter couples whose eyes shine brightly when they look at one another, even after decades. There must be a mechanism that works against the dulling of love and protects people from experiencing their partner like a drug to which they're bound only by habit.

Here, too, oxytocin seems to be involved. Animal experiments show that this hormone, at the least, can weaken the habituation to positive feelings. If this proves true, then the magic formula for enduring love is sex. After all, oxytocin is released during sexual climax. Keeping the sense of passion roiling, it might offer couples a kind of fountain of youth.[22]

THE HAPPINESS OF MOTHERHOOD

Love also blossoms when a child is born. In some ways the affection of parents for their children bears a clear similarity to erotic attraction. People who are in love often feel they're melding into one another. Mothers and, less often, fathers experience something similar. They feel they're becoming one with their child and that its pains and joys are their own.

Are the same forces at work in both cases? Brain research makes this seem likely. If we examine the brains of mothers listening to tapes of their babies crying, the images are strikingly similar to those of lovers focused on their partners. This isn't proof, but it's a very strong indication that similar processes call forth the euphoria elicited by affection—that feeling of happiness that at its most intense resembles the effects of strong drugs.[23]

And much as oxytocin plays a role in the attraction between two partners, so it is also present in nurturing love for a child: oxytocin orchestrates all social behaviors. It has been shown in the female brain that before expectant mothers can feel tenderness for their young, they have to undergo a change that oxytocin sets in motion.

This happens in women and, still more dramatically, in the mothers of animals, which, shortly before delivering their young, can be transformed from predators to nurturers. Female rats, for example, normally react to the smell of newborns by eating them—until they themselves give birth. The expectant rat begins to behave more gently even as she builds her nest, and as soon as her young are born she hardly does anything other than nurse the little ones, licking and protecting them.

On the other hand, when scientists block the oxytocin, the mother rat devours its young immediately after giving birth. But oxytocin isn't enough to stimulate nurturing behavior. In order to get a virgin female to look after baby rats, she first has to be injected with the sex hormone estrogen, which is normally released during pregnancy. Apparently, the brain needs a message from the body that children really are on the way.[24]

Once the signals for the pregnancy hormones and oxytocin have arrived, the programs for maternal love begin to run in the mother's head, and certain parts of the female diencephalon are changed forever. Just how this restructuring happens has not yet been fully studied. According to the little that we have learned from animal experiments, it is the preoptic area—a region that is different in males and females from birth—that seems to undergo the greatest change. Apparently certain genes that control the functioning of the gray cells are turned on or off. Thus, the workings of the entire region of the brain can be changed permanently.[25]

Nor do we yet fully understand whether and in what way nursing permanently strengthens these changes in the young mother. If the female nipples are stimulated, oxytocin is released in the brain, which probably explains the enjoyment women derive from the stroking of their breasts in both lovemaking and nursing. Such feelings create a bond between mother and child, because we reflexively seek to be close to people who have given us a sense of well-being.

In a series of studies at the Karolinska Institut in Sweden, nursing mothers reported a greater interest in other people than before giving birth—also greater than the interest of nonnursing mothers—as well as a greater sense of inner peace. Possibly the oxytocin released during nursing brings forth the experience of social happiness—the joyful sense of being at peace within oneself and being able to give something to others.[26]

Whatever the effect of nursing, the brain's restructuring connects most mothers to their children all their lives. The baby's softest cry will awaken her from the deepest sleep, and a sensitive ear will often hear the cries of children other than her own.

Thus, the brains as well as the bodies of females are designed to have children. Nature rewards them with positive feelings. But not all women get equal pleasure from their children—as with sexual preferences, these gender-related factors differ from one person's brain to another's.

We mustn't forget that fathers, too, enjoy their children. We don't yet know why, for until now science has concentrated on maternal love. Because men's and women's brains are different, the happiness of a father's love might well be different from a mother's—but this is still uncharted territory.

DO CHILDREN MAKE PEOPLE HAPPY?

Children bring energy into the house and warm the hearts of their parents. They need us, when they're in a good mood they beam at us with large eyes, and to follow their development from day to day is one of the greatest experiences imaginable. Many parents say that it was in their children that they found happiness.

All the more surprising are the findings of social scientists on this subject. If, for example, you ask couples how satisfied they are with one another, those who are childless will regularly give themselves a higher score, as four independent studies from Europe and the United States have shown.

In fact, having children diminishes the pleasure that parents find in one another. Over the years, there's a characteristic up and down in the life satisfaction score that, surprisingly, is similar for mothers and fathers. Happiness in the marriage drops during pregnancy and reaches its first low point when the oldest child is crawling. After that it goes up again somewhat, until the oldest child shows the first signs of puberty, after which it falls quickly to an absolute low point. Apparently teenagers take an even greater toll on their parents' love for one another than do small children. Children up to school age may exhaust their parents, but it takes an adolescent to push them to their limits. Once the last child is out of the house, the parents' satisfaction returns to its prechildren level. But if in the course of their marriage, mother and father have gone through the valley of unhappiness, in most cases it isn't all that deep: on average the level of satisfaction in the children's teen years is about ten per cent below that of the best years.[27]

Do children not only fail to bring happiness into marriage but actually make it miserable? Not necessarily. The studies researching the ever-increasing divorce rate looked only at happiness in marriage and not at overall satisfaction. They are closely linked—obviously, marriage has a big influence on general well-being—but not identical. The emotional warmth, the fun, and the feeling of being needed that children give their parents can more than compensate for the burden they sometimes impose on the marriage.

In the end, it's a standoff. Children make us happy and unhappy at the same time. Happiness isn't the opposite of unhappiness, and the two aren't mutually exclusive. And the end result can be very positive. Although having children puts a whole new set of demands on parents, their expectations of life are, on average, higher than among childless adults. This difference is particularly noticeable in the ages 35 to 44. In this age group, less than half as many mothers and fathers die than do people without children—presumably because parents take fewer risks and pay better attention to their health.[28]

But the bottom line is that the joys and difficulties seem more or less at parity. A new German study comes to the conclusion that, all in all, parents are neither more nor less happy than childless couples. Its implications are especially important given the ever more elaborate techniques of reproductive medicine. Couples who try for their own child with huge effort and considerable physical unpleasantness for the woman should ask themselves whether their expectations might not be greater than is warranted.[29]

The only *measurable* impact children have on the parents' relationship is on the level of satisfaction, and this is negative—in spite of the fantasies most would-be parents have of family life. Because the burden usually isn't all that terrible, stable partnerships manage to cope easily and accept it as part of the bargain, for children give their lives meaning and color. But they are almost always a test for the relationship, which is why it rarely works when a couple tries to save their troubled marriage—as happens so often—with a baby.

149

1 0
FRIENDSHIP

ISAAC LIKED RACHEL. They had been friends since childhood. Physical attraction didn't seem to play much of a part in their relationship. In any case, during those years they had sex so infrequently—if at all—that Rachel never got pregnant by him. Not that Isaac, vital as he was, had no offspring. He had fathered any number of children, though not with Rachel. But he and Rachel loved spending time together. While the other males indulged in the usual status struggles, Isaac and Rachel stayed on the sidelines and observed it all as if from another world. They sat next to one another in the grass, eating fruit and grooming one another for hours. If you could ever call baboons "happy," then these two were.

For years Robert Sapolsky, a California neuroscientist, observed and documented the lives of a troop of baboons in Africa's Serengeti. Taking regular blood tests from the troop's males and examining the samples for levels of stress hormones like cortisol, he could support his claim of Isaac's well-being with actual data. (In order not to endanger nursing young or fetuses with the anesthesia, females were not included in the experiment.) In Isaac, the quantities of the transmitter were unusually low. He not only seemed more relaxed than the others—he really was.

Sapolsky made similar observations with many animals besides Isaac. The more friendships a baboon had, and the more lasting they were, the less he suffered from stress. The more often he sat with and looked after his comrades, the less life's troubles seemed to bother him. Tending to social bonds is healthful, because stress doesn't only diminish emotional well-being but is physically harmful.[1]

For Isaac, in any case, the friendship with Rachel paid off. While other males of his generation had long before been killed in fights, or died from sudden illness or aging bodies, he continued to live in the savanna, happy and healthy, grooming his friend.[2]

PEOPLE WITH FRIENDS LIVE LONGER

Good company is beneficial to humans, too. Hearing a familiar voice, we smile easily and feel secure. People who suffer from loneliness or don't get along with others will have a hard time experiencing positive feelings. Friendships and family warmth are like a loamy soil in which happiness thrives.

"If you take friendship out of life, you take the sun out of the world," said the Roman statesman Cicero. Modern sociological research confirms how important sociability is for well-being. Bonds with others are one of the few external factors that can increase life satisfaction under almost all conditions, as the English social psychologist Michael Argyle and other scientists have shown. Only the quality of the relationship with one's partner, frequency of sex, and exercise are of comparable or still greater importance.[3]

Having friends also helps increase our life expectancy. Several studies of some ten thousand Western Europeans and Americans come to this conclusion. Social contacts have on average at least as much impact on life expectancy as smoking, high blood pressure, obesity, and regular physical activity. Independent of age, health, and sex, a lonely person is twice as likely to die within the coming year than someone who feels secure in his relationships with others. Smoking, on the other hand, increases the risk of death by a factor of only one and a half.[4]

A Stanford University study yielded results that are even more impressive. Doctors divided breast cancer patients into two groups, with one getting standard medical treatment, while the other also participated with other patients in weekly group meetings in which they could share their experiences and find sympathy and understanding. Although the cancer had been diagnosed as terminal in all the patients, the women in the discussion group suffered less pain and were in better spirits than those who had received only the usual medication. And more remarkable yet, those women who were able to give voice to their experiences lived twice as long.[5]

Studies on leukemia and heart attack patients have come to similar conclusions. The results may seem odd, since as far as we know, the causes of cancer are strictly physical—even though many people falsely believe that tumors are a kind of malignant state of worry turned inward. There is no research yet that shows any causal relation whatsoever between psychological factors and cancer. The evidence for the role of genes in the creation of tumors, on the other hand, is overwhelming, with environmental toxins, cigarette smoke, and unhealthful foods often exacerbating the genetic risks.[6]

How can we explain the effect of human warmth on the health of cancer patients? People who know that they are being watched over by friends or fellow patients will, of course, be more inclined to take care of themselves and more likely, for example, to take their medications. But the watchful eye of others isn't the only explanation. Even when people are getting the best professional attention, affection helps them recover.[7]

Loneliness is a burden for spirit and body. Getting support is normally one of the best ways of dealing with stress. Lonely people have to manage without the human warmth that makes life's difficulties more bearable. Further, loneliness itself can be a source of suffering—a stress factor, even if one has no other cares.

In recent years, a new branch of science has provided a great deal of evidence for the power of feelings over health: psycho-neuroimmunology, a field concerned with the interactions of body and mind. Stress hormones like cortisol and other gluco-corticoids tax the immune system[8]—something that has been measured in lonely people[9] as well as in monkeys that were taken from their mothers.[10] There is also convincing evidence that stress reduces resistance not only to colds but also to heart and circulatory ailments.

So the puzzle of the breast cancer patients could have a double explanation. First, though stress doesn't cause cancer, it can, at least in animal experiments, hasten the growth of tumors that had other causes.[11] Second, it's possible that women who felt alone had to deal with a weakened immune system as well as with their cancer, making it that much easier for infections to take hold.

People who have to cope on their own are more physically vulnerable, while emotional ties have a positive impact on health. A statistical study of almost two thousand men from the Swedish city of Göteborg who were examined by researchers evaluating the impact of stress on health revealed the existence of one factor that protects people better than the best medical care: men survived even the worst turns of events unscathed when they had someone they could talk to.[12]

THE FEAR OF BEING ABANDONED

Our fear of being left alone goes very deep. People who are otherwise cool and detached respond reflexively to the crying of abandoned children and animals, and even the sadness of a tiny creature from outerspace who wants to call home pushes our buttons. Whether one is eight or eighty, we all can sympathize with the sufferings of E.T. It's no wonder that Spielberg's movie was so hugely successful.

The neuropsychologist Jaak Panksepp suspects that we seek contact with others in order to avoid the pain of being lonely: nature doesn't only draw us to others, it positively drives us to them. According to Panksepp, this drive for sociability is rooted in particular circuits in old and deep parts of the brain. If certain regions of the diencephalons, the thalamus, and the preoptic area, for example, are stimulated, animals howl in panic, emitting sounds they normally make only when they've been abandoned.[13]

From the point of view of evolution, this is a relatively old behavior that appeared, at the latest, with the first mammals and that probably serves to increase the survivability of newborns. A mouse, for example, is born blind and deaf and is unable to walk. Its tiny, hairless body doesn't produce enough warmth to stay alive. Without its mother, it would freeze to death. It's a profoundly dependent creature whose mother is its entire world, and if she's absent, the baby mouse shows pain—and rightly so. Like a human baby in a similar situation, it cries in fear.

Many young mammals and even chicks show this response to abandonment. Because the cries of baby rats (a very well-researched phenomenon) are in high-frequency ultrasound, humans can't hear them, but it is just these frequencies (about 40 kiloherz) to which the ears of female rats are most sensitive. As soon as a mother rat hears these sounds, she will do everything necessary to calm her young. She licks them, carries them in her mouth, and tries to take them to a safe place where they won't be afraid.

When rats mature, their fear of being alone disappears, for they're not particularly sociable creatures. But those animals that are social respond in panic to isolation throughout their lives. Many dogs howl, dig desperately into the floor, and scratch at the door when left by their owners. Parrots develop self-destructive habits, tearing out their feathers with their beak. The symptoms of grown humans who suffer from loneliness aren't quite so obvious, but they're hardly less drastic: restlessness, feelings of emptiness, tension, loss of sleep and appetite, and self-doubt can make their lives hellish.

The similarity of animals to people in this regard gives us a simpler model to study human loneliness. Animals, too, suffer from stress when deprived of contact. One of the substances involved in the chemistry of panic is the stress hormone CRH (corticotropin-releasing hormone).[14] CRH, in turn, releases the hormone cortisol, which is responsible for many stress-related illnesses in humans.

Like people, young rats pay for prolonged loneliness with their health. They become susceptible to disease, develop brains that are equipped with fewer neurons and are therefore less capable, and they remain fearful and easily confused their whole lives. Young rats that are often petted, on the other hand, shoot up like weeds, growing half as fast again as other rats in comparable conditions.

It's the same with the young of our own species. Physical gestures of affection stimulate growth, as University of Miami's

THE SCIENCE OF HAPPINESS

Tiffany Field showed in a straightforward experiment. Taking a number of premature children who had been lying in sterile incubators and received little human warmth, for three days Field caressed them, gently moving their little arms and legs. The results were miraculous. The babies gained weight significantly faster and were healthier than other preemies in the ward and could leave the incubator on average almost a week earlier.[15]

If, on the other hand, babies are deprived of contact for a longer period, the consequences are even more devastating than with rats. How necessary encouragement is for the development of small children was established as early as the thirteenth century, when the medieval emperor Frederick II of Sicily conducted what must have been one of the first controlled experiments in psychology. Wanting to identify humankind's "natural language," this researcher-monarch had a number of small children kept in total isolation when they were still too young to speak. Since they were deprived of all external influence, he hoped that sooner or later they would begin to speak the primal human language. Servants brought food, clean clothes, and the other necessities of life, but they weren't allowed to establish any other contact with the children. The experiment failed cruelly: the babies died. As a contemporary historian wrote, "The children couldn't survive without the clapping of hands, gestures, happy faces, and encouragement."[16]

HAPPINESS IN SECURITY

When people stop feeling lonely, they experience a warm sense of safety. Endorphins—those opium-like hormones that stimulate well-being—are probably an important part of this process. This can be easily proven in young rats. If they're given morphine (an endorphinlike substance) when they've been taken from their mothers, they immediately stop crying. Endorphins mitigate the effects of stress hormones like CRH that stimulate crying. If the natural effect of endorphins is blocked, the baby rats continue to clamor for their mothers long after they've returned and resumed their care for their young ones.[17] Researchers determined that the brains of nonhuman primates, too, release endorphins when the animals groom one another.

As was described in chapter 7, the function of endorphins is generally to signal a desirable situation to the brain, providing, for example, a sense of pleasure when a tasty meal satisfies hunger. In a similar way, they help regulate the need for closeness. If social beings like monkeys lack the contact with others that is necessary for survival, they lose their emotional balance and show signs of separation anxiety. When they're given companionship again, the endorphins report that the normal situation has been restored, which brings forth a comforting feeling of security.

Drugs can deceive the brain so that it is indifferent to loneliness, supplying it with the opiates that, in social situations, it normally releases on its own.[18] The lonely drinker who raises his endorphin level with alcohol doesn't need a friend. Eating sweets also releases this hormone, which is why the fictional diarist Bridget Jones tries to make her solitude more tolerable with a bar of chocolate for breakfast. And the French poet Jean Cocteau noted in his diary that opium "liberated" him from visitors.[19]

Endorphins are probably responsible for the reassuring sense of warmth that has us looking for the familiarity of a friendly face. But they are surely not solely responsible for the happiness that security offers. Oxytocin and vasopressin, for example, help stimulate love, but since they're necessary for social memory, they also play a role in other human interactions. And the transmitter serotonin, which is low in people who suffer from depression, is apparently important in bringing about feelings of sympathy—a relationship that was discovered by neuropharmacologists, not in animal experiments (for a change), but from a party drug—Ecstasy.

Ecstasy is a stimulant that releases large doses of serotonin and probably also dopamine in the brain,[20] thus giving those who take it the thoroughly pleasant sense of having the entire world as their friend—that is, they enjoy unrealistically exaggerated feelings of affection and sympathy. Indeed, until about 1980, when it was renamed by a shrewd Texan, this drug was known by its much more appropriate name *Empathy*. Scientists still speak of Ecstasy as a so-called entactogen, a drug that touches the innermost part of ourselves. The California chemist Alexander Shulgin, who created this drug in his lab in 1965 and was the first person to try it out, described his experience as follows: "I felt light, happy and inspired by an incredible strength—as if in a better existence. It was as if I was not just a citizen of the earth, but at home in the whole universe."

This is just how we feel, if less intensely, in the presence of a person we value: upbeat and trusting. But here science has reached its limits, at least so far, and to this day no one yet has been able to get to the bottom of Ecstasy's effectiveness.

GIVE AND TAKE

Why do we need friendship? Unlike baby rats, which are completely dependent on their mothers, social beings depend on group support. If a "modern" person can live in self-imposed isolation or enclosed in the cocoon of a twosome, someone who's alone, or another with another in, say, a nomadic society, has almost no chance of survival. Only the clan can offer protection and, in an emergency, help. But unlike newborns, adults cannot simply rely on maternal care and expect nourishment and affection without reciprocity. They must also give. And so we all depend on sharing for the general welfare. Not that we share equally with everyone: the closer people are to one another, the more they give each other. And the more they get, the closer they become.

To keep these rules in a clear perspective within a community requires a good deal of understanding. Every member of the group must observe how everyone relates to everyone else, what he or she gives them and can expect from them. The relationship of a couple is relatively simple by comparison, at least among animals. It's enough when the partners recognize one another and are unconditionally there for one another and their progeny. Only intelligent creatures like apes lead a complicated community life with friendships and changing social roles. Although mice, birds, and other animals with simple brains are capable of pairing off like couples, they can cope only in rigidly structured groups with precisely established rules.

Many apes depend on sharing responsibility for nourishment and defense. Their relationships help researchers understand how the mutual obligations of friendship develop, for relationships among apes are easier to grasp than those of humans, and, what's more, animals don't muddy the waters with a lot of talk.

If we like people, we invite them for a meal. Whether in the South Seas or Greenland, there is hardly a culture in which a table with guests isn't at the center of sociability. Families share the day's experiences over dinner, business people set the stage for their deals in restaurants, state visits culminate with a banquet. Apes, too, share their food, which shows how important shared meals are for the creation of social bonds.

The small South American capuchin monkeys, for example, go hunting together and steal from the nests of coatis, even taking their young from right under their noses—a risky venture, since the coati has a strong bite. Such behavior is possible only because every one of the participating thieves can rely on getting his part of the booty.

In controlled experiments the behavioral scientist Frans de Waal has researched the conditions under which capuchin monkeys compromise and cooperate.[22] He put two capuchin monkeys in neighboring cages, through which they could pass each other fruit. They could pull an apple-laden sled toward the cage with ropes, but the sled was so heavy that it took two monkeys to pull it. The contraption was rigged in such a way that only one of the monkeys could reach the fruit on the sled. It turned out that the other monkey would help pull only if it could count on sharing in the spoils. We know, then, that capuchin monkeys are able to rely on one another's sense of fairness.

But their trust is limited. One capuchin will help the other only when the reward is directly before its eyes. That the favor might be returned not immediately but only at some later time is something these animals can't grasp. Their alliances last only a short time and always have to start again from scratch. There is no such thing as a stable partnership.[23]

It's different with smarter primates. Chimps, for example, can establish bonds that last for years and exchange all kinds of favors. If one chimp likes to groom the fur of the other, the recipient can return the favor one day by sharing some of his food or joining forces against a common rival. The lives of these animals are a constant give and take. Chimps hunt together, the females share the care of their young, and high-ranking males support one another in alliances that resemble our strategies in politics and business.

Such a network of dependencies can be realized only when each knows the other's character and interests and understands who can expect what from whom. A chimp, too, will share only on condition of reciprocity, but unlike the capuchin monkeys, these highly intelligent animals are willing to wait for the delayed payback. Enabled by their memory to keep an exact ledger of credit and debit for long periods of time, they can keep track like accountants. De Waal has documented how a chimp named Gwinnie, who shared her food only grudgingly, was spurned by the others when it was her turn to ask something of them.[24]

SYMPATHY IN THE GUT

It's difficult, of course, to know what's going on in the head of a chimp, but presumably Gwinnie was the target of something like antipathy, a feeling of which chimps are perfectly capable.

With people, too, affection and antipathy develop on the basis of our experiences with one another. Surprisingly, these emotions can occur without our consciously remembering specific events. Assessments "from the gut" determine how we encounter other people, and they're often much stronger than our conscious appraisals. Sometimes we just like someone, without knowing why.

The formation of such attitudes has been shown by the neurologist Antonio Damasio in experiments with a patient whom he called David. Suffering from brain damage, David had to live with the most serious memory impairment that had ever been reported in the medical literature. He couldn't remember a new person's face, voice, or name. Nor would he later remember what transpired between them. During the course of a week he was repeatedly made to interact with two of Damasio's colleagues. One was very friendly and forthcoming, while the other was rude, refused David's every wish and forced him to take extremely long and boring psychological tests. (They were tests normally given to apes to gauge their mental capacity.)

After a while David was shown pictures of Damasio's two colleagues. Of course, he could remember neither. When asked which of the two was a friend whom he could turn to for help, he repeatedly and without any hesitation chose the one who had treated him kindly. The other colleague, who was a beautiful young woman, he rejected every time. Not that he knew to report any bad experiences with this person, but subliminally his experiences had consolidated as a feeling, and that feeling simply wasn't a good one.[25]

This is an extreme case. Healthy people can normally justify their feelings, at least partly. Nonetheless, David's fate is of general interest, because it shows that the brain can store experiences in two different ways, like a film that has two tracks, one for image and one for sound. On the one hand it registers conscious memories that are accessible to us like the pictures of a film, scene for scene. But the brain also picks up the music—the feelings that we experienced as the events were unfolding. The appropriate stimuli reawaken these feelings without having to evoke the corresponding events consciously: we hear the movie music without seeing the film. Memories of feeling come about in the implicit memory, while the scenic memory is stored in the explicit memory, which in David's case had been destroyed.

Affection arises in the implicit memory and derives primarily from our emotions, rather than from conscious memory. Such a positive predisposition is necessary for friendship to grow, because it supports the willingness to give and sharpens awareness of the other person's qualities. Only in this way, when the trust is established that enables ever greater acts of giving and taking, can an upward spiral begin.

11
PASSION—
A USER'S MANUAL

OUR PASSIONS HAVE a bigger impact on our lives than all our thoughts. While we can consciously change what we think, our passions are built solidly into us, and we have to take them as they are. They are the driving force behind our happiness, but they can also plunge us into deep sadness. This is why the art of living consists in knowing our passions, living with them and enjoying them.

It isn't surprising that people have been thinking about passion since time immemorial. But when we look for advice, we find instead confusion. Nearly everything that can be said about how to live well and cope with our feelings has already been said by some wise person. And then there's always someone else who claims the exact opposite. After two thousand years of philosophy, more than a century of psychology, and a deluge of how-to books, talk shows, and women's magazines, we know just about as much about how to live as we did before. What should we be looking for in love? Adventure? Or does the intimacy of having one partner for life bring us more lasting happiness? Do we have to work to be happy? Or is it leisure that makes life worth living?

In the meantime, the spiral of scientific discovery continues to turn. For the first time, neurobiology makes it possible not only to describe feelings, but, in reproducible experiments, to understand how feelings come into being and what purpose they serve. This opens a new gate to understanding our humanity—and with very practical implications, for in the long run we will be more productive and happier if we live in ways that correspond to human nature rather than frustrating our most basic drives.

Research can serve as a filter for truisms, separating good advice from bad. In this chapter I'll examine a checklist of a few proverbs, sayings, and aphorisms that have entered our shared thinking, to see whether they're consistent with the discoveries of neuroscience. In part, I'll be reaching back to some of the discoveries discussed in earlier chapters.

There are three insights at the heart of our inquiry that stand on solid ground and turn up again and again in different contexts.

First, positive feelings can drive out negative ones.

Second, although no happiness lasts forever, we can see to it that we experience more moments of happiness than before, and that the pleasure they give us lasts longer.

Third, less important than *what* we experience is *how* we experience it. This may seem no more than simple common sense, or even trivial, but there is a surprising amount of age-old "wisdom" that has crept into our collective thinking claiming the exact opposite.

I Can't Get No Satisfaction.
—THE ROLLING STONES
Indolence makes us sad.
—THOMAS AQUINAS

Surprising as it might be to find Mick Jagger and Thomas Aquinas concurring, they both came to the right conclusion: we are not made for living on Easy Street. This is why nature rewards us for activity, while too much comfort takes a toll on our well-being. Like the singer in the Rolling Stones' song, we might sometimes want to sit back and passively take whatever television and radio sends our way, but in the long run it won't give us satisfaction—something evolution was able to prevent.

It would have made no sense for people to succumb to their indolence over long stretches of time, since the only advantage Homo sapiens had over other species was our intelligence and skill. It was important to keep these advantages, and our brain still spurs us on to remain active—not just to observe the world, but to test ourselves in it. Dopamine plays a key role here.

This is the reason rich people who have no need whatsoever for more money continue to be professionally active instead of sunning themselves in Bermuda, why a Bill Gates can't keep from having yet another bright idea for running his latest rival out of town.

We work for more than food and rent. The philosophers and millionaires of antiquity who valued leisure knew very well that a life without goals and activity quickly leads to depression. And they were constantly busy—writing, discussing, and organizing political campaigns, sumptuous feasts, and celebrations.

Today, too, people feel better when they're busy in their free time—except in (rare) cases of total exhaustion. But depending on their temperament, many people find it difficult to get off their backsides and do something that doesn't absolutely have to get done. People like to pretend that lazing about is just what the doctor ordered. It's a fateful mistake: doing nothing hardly ever makes people happy—something that scientists have even been able to measure.[1]

For this reason it's a good idea to turn the clock of civilization back a bit now and then. A pizza from the freezer might taste good, of course, but the pleasure it gives hardly lasts longer than the time it takes to shove it into the oven and scarf it down. Baking the pizza yourself gives greater satisfaction. Just leafing through the cookbook gets the *expectation system* going. It's no tragedy if the recipe contains ingredients that aren't so easy to find: dopamine is released to guide you toward your goal. Opioids allow us to anticipate the taste of pleasures to come and to appreciate the added effort required in their preparation.

Activity, then, intensifies both the anticipation and the enjoyment itself. Because the *expectation system* isn't directed toward a particular goal, it doesn't really matter very much just what you do. Renovate the apartment, learn to ride a snowboard, dedicate yourself to a social project—they all work. Albert Einstein enjoyed chopping wood, the Roman emperor Diocletian grew vegetables. Even sweeping out a patio can be satisfying. "People are busy looking for happiness," wrote the French philosopher Alain, "but they are happiest being busy."

> *No sports, Just whisky and cigars.*
> —WINSTON CHURCHILL

This is how the English Prime Minister described his elixir of life. For this motto, fondly quoted by couch potatoes, he paid dearly. Churchill was plagued by deep depression. He sarcastically called his suffering the "black dog" that never left his side. The pathological forms of melancholy, as Churchill had to endure them, probably have their root causes in our genes. Nevertheless, even in a deep depression physical movement lifts spirits, as extensive studies from the last two decades have shown. Similarly, some studies have concluded that for people afflicted with relatively minor forms of depression, a run in the park can be just as effective as psychotherapy.[2]

The positive effect of physical exertion on healthy people is even stronger. Scientists in Europe and America carried out more than eighty large surveys, and almost all came to the same conclusion: people who engage regularly in sports feel better and have more self-confidence; they are less fearful and less often depressed.[3] We are made for movement.

Surprisingly, sports seem to help women especially. In several studies, up to 20 percent more women than men said they felt better after physical activity, though we don't yet know why this so.[4]

Running, swimming, dancing—all kinds of sports are effective, because the specific kind of movement is immaterial. Still less important are particular scores or other marks of success—on the contrary, there are indications that ambition is more harmful than useful. Goals that are set too high often can't be reached, lead to frustration and then to the failure of the best intentions. Half an hour of physical activity every day is sufficient, for having a washboard stomach isn't the point. As Rousseau wrote, "For the mind's sake, it's necessary to exercise the body."[5]

Exercise improves our mood in many ways. Moving muscles stimulates the production of hormones like serotonin and presumably also endorphins that can trigger feelings of slight euphoria. It's our body's sensory apparatus that is mainly responsible for the emotional lift we get from physical activity. There are sensors throughout the body that serve the nervous system as they watch over the organism. Thanks to these so-called visceral receptors we can track the condition of our heart, stomach, lungs, and intestines, as well as the tension of all large muscles. At every moment, the brain receives a whole concert of messages from the body, and we can learn to be alert to them and enjoy the body's smooth functioning.

Even when we're not conscious of these signals, the brain interprets them as emotions. Muscle tension and cold hands are taken as signs of fear: we feel slightly unwell and probably don't even know why.

But as the body begins to exert itself, the limbs warm up, the muscles relax, and the pulse increases a bit—and it is precisely these responses that reflect the body's sense of well-being. By moving, we can gently manipulate the neurons in our brain, coaxing the organism into the condition that it otherwise experiences in moments of happiness—and from the appropriate physiological signals, the brain, in turn, automatically generates positive feelings.

I want to have it all, and now, I must/
Before my last dreams turn to dust.
—GITTE HAENNING

Do we really want *everything*? I'm afraid so. That, at least, is how we're programmed. It's almost like a reflex: we try to get whatever we can, and then it's not enough. What we get only makes us hungry for more.

That's simply how the circuits in our brains work. In this way we're basically like Schultz's monkeys. Once they got used to the apples, the neurons that previously interpreted the reward as a very special treat were silent. They wanted raisins. As soon as something is within reach, the bar gets raised. Humans, too, are never satisfied.

The singer Gitte Haenning expressed her greed aggressively—and overlooked how boring wishes can become when they become reality. It's not easy to be satisfied, especially in a world of superfluity, where everything seems within reach. An evening in front of the television can make our lives appear boring beyond belief. Who among us gets to swing at sophisticated parties, wield power and influence at the office, and raise children who are always skipping about on a sunny lawn—and all this at the same time? Measured against such standards, we can only feel like failures. Advertisements seem to promise a way out, but the attractions of a new cell phone or a bargain plane fare fade as quickly as the sense of being full after a meal at a fast-food restaurant.

None of us is completely at the mercy of our greed, but a somewhat more critical understanding of the *expectation system* is required than Gitte Haenning suggests. Unlike monkeys, we've got minds capable of thought at this level. It's often useful to realize that desire does not always end in pleasure and to imagine what our lives would be like a few months after the object of our longing had been met. Wanting and liking are two different things.

No one should have to forgo his pleasure in shopping or his need to assert himself. In any case, the urge for more is anchored so deep within us that it's hard to get away from it. But a bit of ironic distance can help us cope with desire and not take it too seriously. The opera singer Maria Callas accomplished this in a most original way. At the height of her success, she was the best-paid musician of her time, earning more than she could possibly spend. So for each successive engagement she increased her fee by exactly one dollar.

> *Variatio delectat—Change gives pleasure.*
> —ROMAN PROVERB

It's true. By varying our pleasures we can escape the dulling of our senses. Someone who has just eaten chicken will find a banana more appealing than another chicken. After a banana, on the other hand, nothing tastes better than fish, as was determined by the scientists Edmund Rolls and John O'Doherty. In their experiments, they came across the area of the prefrontal cortex which, at least for taste and smell, is responsible for the loss of interest that accompanies familiarity. But the Oxford University scientists also made another discovery—after eating a banana, people found that the fish tasted even better than usual.[6]

Contrast is a source of happiness. That's good news, because it means that we have an alternative to the urge for more, for the *expectation system* quickly gets used to anything that gives pleasure. What had been an enjoyable surprise is now accepted as a matter of course and requires stronger stimulation—which doesn't often happen. "Nothing is more difficult to endure than a series of good days," wrote Goethe. But when we are open to *different* pleasures instead of *stronger* ones, the sense of delight is restored, and when the contrast is well chosen, our enjoyment is even more intense than before.

When you've just spent a fun evening at home with friends, it's usually not a good idea to invite the same group over again right away: they will feel that the bar has been set too high. Instead, do something different with a different group of people. Go to the movie, or make it just the two of you. After a while, the first pleasure can be repeated, because the memory of the *expectation system* doesn't last that long. The trick is to experience pleasure by rotation.

For the same reason, it's worth learning to appreciate the unexpected. We have an ambivalent relationship with all things new: "There's no place like home." But although something unfamiliar is perceived as stressful, a pleasant surprise is one of the strongest feelings of pleasure that we can experience. Humans are programmed to seek new experiences.

We struggle with our ambivalence, but our reluctance to try something new wins out more often than it should, for like all creatures, we react more strongly to the danger of something unpleasant than to the attractiveness of a promising experience. If hope has to stand up against fear, it's fear that usually wins. This is an evolutionary inheritance.

It's been a very long time since life-threatening dangers lurked behind every bush, but the old mental programs keep running. All too often our caution keeps us from pleasurable experiences. We'll order sushi for the hundredth time, even though we've long intended to try something else. And yet, thanks to our inborn passion for learning, we're in a very good position to enjoy the unexpected.

171

Everyday experiences give us a chance to make this attitude our own. Take the weather, for example. How often do we curse unpredictable, changeable weather, even though the constant change can bring excitement, varies the very light around us, and last but not least provides grist for the conversational mill.

Whoever has consciously experienced the appeal of the unpredictable will find it everywhere. It's stimulating to meet new people, because we aren't able to plan for their reactions. A thriller can be riveting because the plot takes unexpected turns. And isn't it one of the great everyday experiences of parenthood to watch our children develop their growing individuality?

Beauty lies in the eye of the beholder.
—GREEK PROVERB

Tourism is one of the fastest-growing global industries. Journeys provide a change of scenery, and people enjoy exploring unknown terrain. But after a week or two, even the most exotic locale begins to become familiar. So we pull up stakes and move on to new, still more exciting destinations. The other, often better path is to open our eyes wider. For usually we're aware of only a tiny slice of our environment. To the Bengali writer Rabindranath Tagore, this was a cause of surprise and wonder:

> *Through many years,*
> *At great expense,*
> *Journeying through many countries,*
> *I went to see high mountains,*
> *I went to see oceans.*
> *Only I had not seen*
> *At my very doorstep,*
> *The dew drop glistening*
> *On the ear of the corn.* [7]

And so it is: we're able to see, hear, smell, and taste everything that surrounds us with much greater intensity than we normally do. And the attentive observer will find unsuspected charms in even the most mundane aspects of everyday life.

Experiencing novelty in something familiar requires some practice. Most of us are in the habit of taking in as little as possible, which is how the brain protects us from stimuli that don't play a major role in our survival. Circuits under the influence of dopamine play a part here. They guide our perceptions and provide an enjoyable experience only when the new stimulus seems to be advantageous to the organism. But this limitation can be overcome. We may not have an inborn desire to get on a bike, but we can learn to ride it nonetheless.

One way of training our senses is to guide our attention consciously, by focusing, for example, only on our sensory perceptions and on nothing else, forgetting about meaning and purpose. Suddenly we no longer see falling leaves as a nuisance that has to be raked off the lawn. Instead we hear the strangely quiet sound of a leaf as it sails to the ground. For once, instead of checking off unfamiliar faces as "nice" or "not nice," we allow ourselves to see the pattern of lines and wrinkles that have been etched over the course of a lifetime.

Positive feelings then come of themselves, for the better we get to know the world, the more we learn to value it. This is explained by one of psychology's most astonishing effects: the more often and intensely we perceive a stimulus, the more positively we react to it. In one experiment, the California scientist Robert Zajonc presented his American students with Chinese ideograms, to them meaningless. But simply by seeing them again and again, they developed a preference for them. And what's more, the more often they saw a particular character, the more it lifted their spirits.

This applies to everything that we can perceive. Portraits of unknown people make them seem more pleasant; over time, Western ears find Asian folk music attractive; foods taste better, when we've eaten them frequently.[8] It is probably because of this preference for what is familiar that radio stations play the same hits again and again and why fashion brings back familiar styles at regular intervals.

Our natural tendency to be bored kicks in only when we neglect to rotate our pleasures. With even a minor change in our routine, we can avoid monotony, as fashion designers well know. Or we can become ever more familiar with what we already know, so that it is always showing new sides. There is no contradiction, then, in saying that we derive pleasure from both novelty and familiarity.

For most people, a fly is just a bother, but for an amateur entomologist it can contain an entire cosmos. She will tell us with enthusiasm that it isn't just an ordinary housefly, but the rare *hippobosca equina*, or horse louse fly, that its eye consists of more than seven hundred facets and can see ultraviolet light, and that its wings are a miracle of fine engineering. Recounting this, she will experience something like the joy of discovery.

Once again, the object of our enthusiasm is not what matters.

Whether theater, football, or the inner workings of motorcycles—any focused interest can enhance our lives. In contrast to the fun of shopping, which inevitably concludes with dissatisfaction, this kind of happiness never has to end, for every experience, every new knowledge opens doors to new experiences. We embark on a journey that can last a lifetime and where each pleasure leads us to the next.

The strongest person is most powerful when alone.
—FRIEDRICH VON SCHILLER

We mustn't allow ourselves to be intimidated by the cult of the lone wolf. The books, films, and drama of Western culture are filled with men who are willing to take on the whole world single-handed, one against all. The hero in westerns fights alone against dark forces and overcomes them. Admired by one and all and with the most beautiful woman west of the Mississippi at his side, he can now live in the frontier town that he saved. But that's not for him. And as the movie ends, we see John Wayne riding into the sunset—but for his horse, utterly alone.

German culture, especially, has been fatally imbued with the idea that solitude is a particularly desirable and noble condition. Caspar David Friedrich's lonely monk by the sea, Hermann Hesse's Steppenwolf, Thomas Mann's tragic artists: they all would have us believe that solitude brings people closer to their innermost selves.

The exact opposite is true, as both clinical and neurobiological experiments show: it's loneliness, more than any other factor, that causes stress. It's a burden on both mind and body. It results in restlessness, confusion in thought and feeling (caused by stress hormones), and a weakening of the immune system. In isolation, people become sad and sick.

People in other cultures usually see loneliness for what it is: a condition that is often painful and unnatural. Indians, for example, are endlessly surprised to find tourists traveling alone. The Indian Nobel Prize–winning writer V. S. Naipaul describes people in Bombay who became wealthy but then abandoned their luxury apartments for the closeness of the run-down, densely populated barracks in which they'd grown up. Women, especially, couldn't bear the empty silence and suffered from depression.[9]

175

This is the opposite of the sometimes equally extreme individualism of the West, which the psychologist Martin Seligman holds at least partly responsible for the prevalence of depression. Though a Westerner is not likely to share the need for physical contact that is the norm in Asia, studies of the devastating effects of loneliness suggest that we sometimes look for greater distance from others than is good for us.

> *It's better to be alone than in bad company.*
> —GEORGE WASHINGTON

Even if this motto seems to contradict what you've just read, it's true. Precisely because human closeness is so important for our well-being, the wrong company can cause more stress than solitude. Quite apart from the fact that constant conflict diminishes mental well-being, the body, too, pays a price. Several experiments conducted by the American psychiatrist Janice Kiecolt-Glaser with her husband, the immunologist Robert Glaser, show that a destructive relationship has a direct effect on the immune system. In one experiment, they provoked a quarrel between a husband and wife. A few hours later the quantity of killer cells and antibodies in the blood that attack viruses had diminished dramatically, as had their effectiveness—the worse the fight, the less effective they became. If such quarrels occur only occasionally, no harm is done. But couples who basically don't get along will pay for it with their health.[10]

In another study, scientists showed that the less students in a dormitory liked their roommates, the more often they got colds and went to the doctor. It's been known for a long time that stress can reduce resistance to the flu and minor infections.[11] There is also solid evidence that an unhappy relationship subtly causes the entire organism to suffer. When the warmth is irretrievably gone, it may be better to end the relationship.

How can people avoid the loneliness that might result? On the basis of his own experience, the French philosopher Montaigne offers unusual advice: to educate and refine our taste in the pleasures of the body. "With tooth and claw, we must cling to the enjoyment of life's pleasures that are left to us."[12] Does this mean that we should treat ourselves to hot baths, massages, scents, music, and good food to fight off the pain of loneliness? Yes! One of the greatest dangers of being alone is the loss of self-esteem, and by indulging in gratifications of this kind, we give ourselves a lift. The French nobleman's suggestion is also well worth thinking about from a neurobiological point of view: pleasure leads to the release of opioids that diminish tension and abate the melancholy of those hours during which we feel abandoned by all the world.

These natural mood-lifters also make us more gregarious. While large doses of opiates diminish the need for contact, in small quantities they stimulate it, as experiments with rats have shown.[13] When you feel the sun shining on you, you will want to share your joy with others. People in good spirits are more sociable, presumably because a slightly elevated mood dissolves the anxiety that so often makes us shrink from human contact.

If you sleep with the same woman twice,
you've joined the establishment.
—SLOGAN, 1968
A woman without a man is like a fish without a bicycle.
—GLORIA STEINEM

The first of these bits of wisdom has faded a bit, along with the belief in the coming revolution. Men no longer have to live with five women (like the legendary German communard Rainer Langhans) to be "progressive." But like so many ideas of the sixties, the hope that promiscuity offers an escape from the ennui of humdrum middle-class lives has left its mark. Who hasn't secretly asked himself whether he isn't a stick-in-the-mud for having had sex with the same person for years?

Gloria Steinem's adage became an article of faith for "the single generation." Why suffer the limitations of a lasting partnership when a group of good friends and the occasional affair might bring more happiness? But even if magazine articles and advice books are still published that endorse this perspective, for most people it doesn't work.

Granted, people who are constantly changing lovers lead more exciting lives. But a commitment to boredom can sometimes be more rewarding. Being committed to a partner creates good feelings, and physical love strengthens a relationship. There is evidence that shows that humans, unlike most of nature's creatures, are made for long-lasting ties to one partner. Most of us have a natural inclination toward monogamy, transmitted in our brains by complicated synapses in which the hormone oxytocin plays an important role. This may be a reason that lasting love relationships can give more warmth and a greater sense of security than friendships.

Surveys confirm this. They all conclude that people in couple-relationships are usually happier than single people. In the United States, for example, only 25 percent of unmarried people—and 40 percent of married adults—describe themselves as "very satisfied"—a finding that holds for both men and women. By no means is it impossible to be happy alone, but it's easier if you're part of a team.[14]

Single people suffer far more frequently from depression than those who are married, and the figure is still higher for people who are divorced.[15] Both European and U.S. statistics show that married people are less likely to suffer from physical ailments than people who are single or divorced.[16]

Loving care plays a big role here. Good friends can give a lot of support, but only rarely do they replace a partnership, for the willingness of partners to be there for each other is almost always stronger.[17] The mere touch of someone who is familiar and trusted can ease sadness. This, too, is caused by neurotransmitters like oxytocin and the opioids that are released in moments of tenderness.[18]

In short, a good partnership makes people happy. It is, along with the frequency of sex (to which it is related), the most important external factor determining life satisfaction. By comparison, financial well-being, work, home, and leisure activities play a much less important role. Nonetheless, we often spend much more time and energy on these things than on being there for the partner—something that is worth changing, for almost nothing ensures lasting happiness better than taking time for the other person and living the relationship intensely.

Gloria Steinem recognized this, if late. In 2000, at the age of sixty-three, she got married.

PART THREE

A STRATEGIC
CONSCIOUSNESS

12
CONQUERING OUR SHADOWS

SOME DAYS WE would just as soon stay in bed. We drag ourselves into the morning, and even simple things seem to take a huge amount of effort. Trivialities bring us to the edge of tears, and affronts seem to lurk around every corner. If we could, we'd walk away from everyone and everything. But being alone is also unbearable. Our thoughts flow more slowly than normal. We berate ourselves, feel empty and worthless, and see our misery as well-deserved punishment for . . . whatever. "I don't deserve any better."

We all know such dark moods of self-doubt and despair. As unpleasant as they might be, they're programmed into the brain and can actually be very useful. When we have lost something, when a relationship ends, or when we have failed to reach a goal, the organism responds with sadness—a signal that we should relinquish a possibly senseless goal. Depression is a natural energy-saving program. When we feel drained of energy, we pull back and reflect, and in the end we often attain a new strength and clarity.

A DANGEROUS ENERGY-SAVING PROGRAM

But too much sadness can also do damage. When it digs in, it develops a life of its own that has little to do with what caused it. Then we are no longer sad because a disappointed brain briefly needs reorientation—but because we're sad. The emotions that are supposed to serve the organism turn against it and the downward spiral of depression sets in—negative feelings breeding negative thoughts that get us truly depressed. Soon there's no telling hen from egg: since the situation seems hopeless, we feel we're powerless and become passive. And because we don't take our fate into our own hands, nothing improves. Depression creates a situation in which discouragement really does seem warranted. We become trapped in a vicious cycle that precludes the possibility of happiness.

Severe depression is an illness that requires treatment. As with a toothache, it's best to act quickly. The longer despair rages unchecked, the longer it takes to get rid of it, the more damage it can cause, and the greater the likelihood of sliding into another depressive phase. Someone who feels worthless for much of a two-week period, suffers from constant listlessness, tiredness, or sleeplessness and even dwells on thoughts of his own death should get the help of a physician.[1]

This is reason for neither shame nor despair. Every eighth person has had this experience or will have it at some time in his life—more than 40 million people in the United States alone. Depression is a common illness, hardly less widespread than high blood pressure and arthritis. But unlike these other illnesses, depression is eminently curable. The chance that a depressed person will laugh again is extremely high. Almost everyone improves after being treated, with more than 80 percent experiencing a complete remission.

The tips in this chapter address a less serious form of mood disorder, everyday sadness—something that is not merely a nuisance, but one of happiness's great spoilers. Psychologists and brain scientists have long puzzled over whether the kind of melancholy that we're all familiar with is related to serious depression. In the light of new research it seems very likely. Both result from the human brain's adaptability: we can learn to be happy, but we can also learn to be unhappy. Sadness is for the most part nothing more than learned unhappiness. And this gives us the ability to overcome it.

183

LEARNED HELPLESSNESS

In order to get a better handle on our negative feelings, we have to understand where they come from. The explanations given for depression are an encouraging example of how science can actually become simpler in the course of time. The second-century Greek anatomist Galen ascribed melancholy to an excess of bile, while for Freud the suspect was the unconscious raging of unresolved childhood conflicts. Today we assume that an enduring sadness simply stems from the experience of not being able to improve an unpleasant situation. "Learned helplessness" is the term given to the modern theory of depression: despondency is a product of resignation. When this kind of "down" coincides with an inherited tendency to sadness, the result can be depression.

The first person to make these connections was the University of Pennsylvania psychologist Martin Seligman. In 1965, he conducted a simple experiment in which he divided dogs into two cages whose floors were wired to give off harmless but unpleasant electric shocks. In the one cage the dogs could turn off the electricity by pushing their noses against a plate. The dogs in the other cage could do nothing to switch off the charge and had no choice but to suffer the shocks.

Once the dogs had gotten used to their environment, Seligman brought them all into a new cage with a low wall. To escape the unpleasant electric charge, they had only to jump over the wall. The dogs from the one cage, who had learned that they could do something against the shocks, left quickly. Those in the second group, on the other hand, were resigned to their fate, although escaping would have been so easy. They lay on the ground, whimpered, and bore one shock after the next. Their helplessness in the old cage had apparently been so deeply internalized that they carried the feeling into the new situation, where it made no sense. Losing interest in playing with one another, in food, and in sex, they showed all the symptoms of depressive listlessness.[2]

Our resolve in facing life head-on depends much more on the way in which we assess a situation than on reality, something that was shown in experiments with people who have been exposed to intolerable levels of noise. By pressing a button, one group could turn it off, while the other could do nothing. Afterward, all the participants were brought together in the same room, where they could turn the noise off with a lever.[3] Those who'd been in the room with the off button quickly discovered the lever, while the others wouldn't even try to operate it. Later, they sat quietly in a corner, and when they were asked to participate in a game, they made no attempts to win. They were also less able to solve simple word puzzles, even in the absence of any time pressure. In every way, they felt and behaved as if they were helpless.

THE ANATOMY OF UNHAPPINESS

"You can't do anything about it anyway." This is a depressed person's affirmation. Her despondency is confirmed by her appearance: she drags her feet, her eyes are lifeless, her shoulders droop—as if not only her spirits but her muscles have lost their strength, as if her entire being is fueled only by a pilot light.

The waning of vitality is also evident in her brain. Letting us see right into the skull, tomography shows us with particular vividness how activity diminishes in the left prefrontal cortex.[4] Because this area is responsible not only for motivation and desire but also for the control of negative emotions, the effect of melancholy is pervasive, and for two reasons: not only do we lack drive, but we also find it harder to get a grip on our sadness, shame, and anxiety. Depression is a consequence not only of the dark feelings that cast their shadow over everything we experience, but also of the absence of desire.[5]

This kind of depressed condition can also arise with frightening ease in healthy people. When the London brain researchers Chris Frith and Raymond Dolan asked their experimental subjects to read sentences such as "Life is not worth living" while playing Prokofiev's "Russia under the Mongol Yoke" at half speed, the volunteers soon complained of dampened spirits, listlessness, and a feeling of worthlessness. The activity in their brains resembled that of people who are treated for clinical depression.[6] Those who suffer from depression see their misery as tunnels without end, whereas the volunteers quickly found their equilibrium again once the experiment was over: the everyday sense of being "down" differs from pathological depression less in quality than in its duration.

HOW MISERY TAKES ON A LIFE OF ITS OWN

A few sentences can change our mood, but the reverse is also true: our mood can determine what we perceive. The border between perception and emotion is porous in both directions. In one experiment, depressed and healthy people were asked to identify optimistic and pessimistic prophesies in a potpourri of sentences. The depressed participants were better at interpreting statements such as "The future looks very black" than upbeat statements such as "The future looks very favorable." And they were also better able to remember the negative sentences.[7]

This, too, is connected with the structure of the prefrontal cortex—a part of the brain that has a large influence on our moods and serves as working memory, temporarily storing information that we need to have at hand. This is why our emotional state has such an impact on our response to what we've just seen, read, or heard. The prefrontal cortex is also linked via various nerve paths to our long-term memory. It may be because of these connections that we tend to recall sad memories when we're down—something that has also been demonstrated in psychological experiments.[8]

Once we've begun to see the world through dark lenses, the brain is tempted to keep the negative mood going. It seeks out stimuli that match our emotional state, giving dark thoughts, negative experiences, and bitter memories preferential access to consciousness. We see misery everywhere, and the whole organism reacts correspondingly. ". . . [Y]ou can think of depression as occurring when your cortex thinks an abstract negative thought and manages to convince the rest of the brain that this is as real as a physical stressor," writes Robert Sapolsky, a Stanford University biologist and neuroscientist who specializes in stress.[9]

We react to news of danger, whether it's real or imagined, much more strongly than to good news. Forgetting our pleasures and hopes until we're safe helps us respond appropriately to the slightest warning. But when we're depressed, we direct what is otherwise a survival mechanism against ourselves. Chronic melancholy is widespread because this program is so easily misled: our brain has a talent not only for recognizing threats but for imagining them. We worry about things that will probably never happen and color them in vivid detail, but just thinking of them is enough to pull us down. Depression is the price that we pay for our imagination and intelligence.

One rather radical remedy against depression is to surgically sever some of the connections between the region that conjures the dark thoughts of the future—the cerebral cortex—and the rest of the brain, resulting in an immediate improvement. Electroconvulsive therapy (ECT) works similarly. It's usually administered under brief sedation and involves harmless electrical currents that work similarly to the reset button on a computer. These impulses extinguish the storage in the short-term memory of the prefrontal cortex and break the endless cycle of brooding thoughts. Through strategic interventions like ECT even the most stubborn depressions disappear.

Fortunately, doctors rarely have to resort to such drastic measures. But the fact that they can help people out of the misery of even the most serious depressions is instructive for living with our daily troubles. It shows to what degree our thoughts and imagination can influence our mood. Very often it's our capacity for imagining misfortune that renders us unhappy.

Discontent is something for which our minds bear the full responsibility. To what absurd lengths we sometimes go to keep a bad mood going is nicely illustrated by this joke: What does a Jewish telegram say? "Start worrying! Letter to follow."

BAD MOODS KILL GRAY MATTER

When we feel threatened, we're more alert than we are otherwise. Nature has arranged it this way so that, in critical situations, we respond to the slightest sign of danger. This special sensitivity is further enhanced by stress hormones such as cortisol, that are released into the blood and then usually disappear as soon as there's no longer any reason to be afraid.

When someone suffers from depression, however, the stress hormones don't disappear. Depression is a state of permanent stress: we perceive any careless remark as a slight, every triviality as a small catastrophe—and as further proof of the world's evil. As a result, more stress hormones are released, which makes us still more sensitive. Thus the vicious cycle continues endlessly, until, sometimes, it gets so bad that the depressed person retreats into a darkened room and doesn't leave.[10]

Even worse: when the depression lasts too long, the brain itself comes under attack. Of all the discoveries that recent research into depression has brought to light, this may be the most disturbing. Depression not only involves an imbalance in the neurotransmitters, but also affects the hard-wiring of the neurons. To what extent the damage can be undone is still unknown.

In the process, the brain loses its adaptability—melancholy is a state of rigidity that paralyzes all initiative and ossifies the depressive condition. Our ability to feel fades, and our judgment and concentration diminish. Tests have shown that depressed people are less able to solve even simple tasks, such as the sorting of playing cards.[11] At the beginning of a depressive phase, the working memory is affected, and the stress hormones impede the brain's ability to think.

Abilities that aren't exercised deteriorate. The circuits in the brain begin to shrink as soon as we use them less. And this is what happens in a depression. As the feeling of hopelessness increases, the brain sends stress hormones, which can harm the neurons and do lasting damage to the brain.[12] If this condition is prolonged, the consequences can be devastating: gray cells shrink. Then the brain works less and less well, and the spiral continues downward.

In people who have suffered repeatedly from serious depressions, the space in the prefrontal cortex occupied by certain kinds of neurons is diminished by a third, as the psychiatrist Grazyna Raykowska of the University of Mississippi Medical Center discovered.[13] Other parts of the brain lose so much matter that they just shrivel up. This has been observed, for example, in the hippocampus, on which memory depends.[14]

Normally, the brain learns and forms memories when the neurons, like climbing plants, constantly grow new fibers, which then link them to other neurons. In depressed people, however, the brain seems to freeze, like vegetation in winter.

PILLS AGAINST UNHAPPINESS

The discovery that depression could be a result of too little neuron growth has radically changed the direction of research into unhappiness.[15] Until now, scientists have assumed that periods of sadness were simply the cause of a chemical mixup in the brain due to a low level of certain transmitters, for which the success of pharmaceutical treatment was cited as evidence. For almost five decades doctors have been prescribing medications for depressed patients that elevate the levels of the transmitters serotonin and noradrenaline, which are chemically related to dopamine. More than 60 percent of patients diagnosed with serious depression have been helped by these drugs, and an even greater number when the pills were combined with appropriate psychotherapy. Prozac, probably the most famous medication of this kind, has in the meantime been superseded by medications from the class of the so-called serotonin reuptake inhibitors that are still more successful. The conclusion seemed obvious: depression could be explained by a deficiency of serotonin and noradrenaline.

However, it was soon determined that reality was more complicated. If the amount of serotonin is lowered in the brains of healthy people, their mood remains stable. So, whatever the claims, depression can't be explained only as a serotonin deficiency. A medication like Prozac, sometimes lauded in the media as a happiness pill and described as rose lenses for the mind, has almost no effect on well-balanced people. It raises the mood only of those who are truly depressed. Prozac and similar medications are pills *against unhappiness,* not *for happiness.* They can remove the bad feelings, but they don't create positive ones.

This may be explained partly by the fact that the level of serotonin seems to be linked to the stress system. When a large amount of serotonin is circulating in the brain, fewer stress hormones are released. By making more serotonin available, antidepressants diminish susceptibility to chronic stress and the negative feelings that accompany it, as was shown by Juan Lopez and Elizabeth Young at the University of Michigan.[16] But when people are free of stress, the medications have no effect— as little effect as aspirin has on the well-being of people who have neither pain nor fever.

Why does it take so long for antidepressants to take effect in depressed patients? The quantities of transmitters in the brain change as soon as the medication gets into the blood, that is, after just a few hours. Nonetheless, it almost always takes about four weeks until patients report improved spirits. Apparently, for Prozac and similar drugs to become effective, they have to take a detour, and that takes time.

It's possible that the medications awaken the brain from something like a hibernation.[17] When they release more serotonin and noradrenalin, the gray cells begin to grow again. This has two possible explanations. For one, the presence of fewer stress hormones reactivates the growth of the gray cells. Secondly, serotonin and noradrenaline work directly on the neurons, indirectly activating certain genes in the nucleus. These genes, in turn, stimulate the growth of nerve growth factors, the brain's natural fertilizer.[18] And as soon as the gray cells sprout again, the symptoms of depression disappear. The frozen brain is brought back to life.

SHOWING MELANCHOLY THE DOOR

When the brain is inactive, we feel depressed. This is why the standard reaction to unhappiness—withdrawal—only makes things worse, for then the brain *really* begins to lose any incentive to become active again. Listlessness and paralysis, both emotional and intellectual, spread and take hold. Doing nothing is no cure for a bad mood.

In serious depressions, medication is often the only means to prod the brain out of its immobility. But the much more frequent common sadness of everyday life is best overcome with a double strategy that involves gently stimulating your brain on the one hand and, on the other, guiding your thoughts and feelings to deprive the depression of a foothold.

Sadness can be the consequence of an acute emotional strain. The loss of a close person, a bit of bad luck, stress in work or family, or even a sudden change of location like at the beginning of a vacation can result in so much stress that the organism demands a retreat. This need is expressed by a feeling of listlessness, sadness, and tiredness. It may be wise to give in to its demands for a while. For how long depends on the cause. A recovery that last weeks is hardly appropriate after the strain of a long journey, but the death of a family member is another matter entirely. As the French say: "Reculer pour mieux sauter," step back in order to jump better.

But the feeling of being "down" often takes on a life of its own. If there once was a cause, it happened a long time ago, and now the melancholy feeds on itself. Nothing seems appealing. To further fuel the vicious cycle of listlessness and inactivity by being passive makes no sense whatsoever. Whoever has had a leg that was in a cast for a long time knows how dramatically muscles can weaken in the course of an enforced rest, and how feeble the desire is to take those wobbly and difficult first steps. But there's no getting around it if one wants to walk again. Similarly, we have to reaccustom the brain to activity after an extended period of depression.

RELAUNCHING THE BRAIN

Activity—any activity—helps against sadness. You take up life's reins again. When you do something, you engage your brain and deprive it of the opportunity to go down thought's darker paths.

How much our emotions and our ability to reason influence one another has been shown by PET scans tracking people through different moods as they work through problems. Since feelings and problem solving are processed in areas of the cerebrum that overlap considerably,[19] there's apparently less space for pessimistic emotions when we direct our attention elsewhere.

Even better for our spirits are activities that bring a sense of success. It's important that we set goals when we're going through periods of sadness, though we shouldn't overdo it, since the brain isn't up to its normal level of activity.

For this reason, it's best in such times to engage in simpler tasks. Housekeeping, cleaning up, shopping and taking care of correspondence and e-mail serve as a gentle warm up. They require relatively little effort, are stress free, and give a sense of accomplishment. Because the little jobs of daily life are often neglected, a "down" phase is well spent taking care of them. And when you see the result, you make the pleasant discovery that the melancholy even yielded some good outcomes.

That the experience of success becomes especially important when people are having a hard time can be explained by the functioning of the two halves of the prefrontal cortex, according to the neuropsychologist Richard Davidson.[20] When we're sad, its left half, which both directs us towards goals *and* controls negative emotions, is insufficiently active. But if we decide to strive for even a small goal, we reactivate this part of the brain that is so important for our well-being. And when our plan is transformed into reality, these neurons in the prefrontal cortex give a signal and release a feeling of success that we have every reason to enjoy.

193

RUNNING AWAY FROM MELANCHOLY

We've already seen that physical activity and sports result in positive feelings, which makes them an ideal tool for driving away depression. Physical movement has a two-fold effect on our feelings.

First, when it's done right, it always gives a feeling of success. We can all set goals for ourselves that correspond to our abilities. People who aren't used to regular physical activity can have the same sense of triumph after jogging a mile as an athlete who has run a marathon. More important than absolute achievement is that you gauge the level appropriately, so that you don't give up. People who don't like physical activity balk at the effort, the sweat, the ordeal of it all—but therein lies its power. There is a guaranteed reward for beating your inner couch potato: just knowing that you've done something for yourself by facing down your sense of lazy comfort can chase away a good deal of sadness.

Second, physical activity has a direct effect on the brain. Movement encourages the growth and even the new formation of neurons, as the California neuroscientist Fred Gage has shown. He put rats on a simple treadmill in a cage and observed greatly improved scores in subsequent memory tests. Even mice that had not learned well were better able to do so after running. Gage found one solution to the riddle in parts of the brain that are critical for memory. The rodents that ran had more nerve growth factors and twice as many newly formed neurons as those that had just hung around.[21]

But activity doesn't only make us smarter. By stimulating neuron growth, movement works against depression's most dangerous symptom: the disappearance of gray cells. Exercise is a kind of natural Prozac. This analogy works also in that physical movement releases serotonin—the same transmitter whose levels are increased by pharmaceutical antidepressants.[22] In contrast to medication, which only diminishes sadness, movement also yields positive feelings, because physical effort releases the euphoria-inducing endorphins. This might explain why regular exercise for half an hour three times a week is as effective against melancholy with some people as the best medications currently available.[23]

THE ROBINSON CRUSOE THERAPY

To recharge the brain is one measure against melancholy; arming ourselves against negative thoughts and feelings is the other.

The English literary hero Robinson Crusoe put this second principle into operation. He, too, was plagued by depression after he was washed onto his island, helpless, without companionship, with no hope of being saved. But, Crusoe said to himself, no situation is so hopeless that one should give up. So he took a pencil that he'd saved from the stranded ship and made a list of plusses and minuses. Some examples:

EVIL	GOOD
I am cast upon a horrible, desolate island, void of all hope of recovery.	But I am alive; and not drowned, as all my ship's company were.
I am singled out and separated, as it were, from all the world, to be miserable.	But I am singled out, too, from all the ship's crew to be spared from death; and He that miraculously saved me from death can deliver me from this condition.

EVIL	GOOD
I have no clothes to cover me.	But I am in a hot climate, where, if I had clothes, I could hardly wear them.

Then he drew his conclusions: "Upon the whole, here was an undoubted testimony that there was scarce any condition in the world so miserable but there was something negative or something positive to be thankful for in it; and let this stand as a direction from the experience of the most miserable of all conditions in this world: that we may always find in it something to comfort ourselves from, and to set, in the description of good and evil, on the credit side of the account." This happiness saved his life. Had he given into his all too understandable despondency, he soon would have died in his isolation. He wouldn't have had the opportunity to meet his companion Friday, and he wouldn't have been saved by an English ship.

Did he talk himself into a fool's paradise? No, for both sides of his ledger are true. The question is only on which side you stand, and it's usually more useful to see things optimistically. Deciding for the glass that is half full instead of the one that is half empty is one of the most effective of all antidotes for depression.

All this sounds so hopelessly simple—almost too good to be true. The National Institutes of Health spent ten million dollars to test Crusoe's method in one of the great therapy experiments of all time. The psychologists proudly called it *cognitive behavior therapy*, though a better name might have been The Crusoe Therapy. The study lasted six years and involved hundreds of participants suffering from moderately severe to severe depression. Sixty percent of them were cured by the cognitive behavior therapy—the same success ratio as with patients treated pharmaceutically.[24] If medications and cognitive therapy are combined, the percentage is somewhat higher still, and the danger of relapse is reduced.[25]

Psychoanalysis, on the other hand, is not only much more expensive but also less effective. After the lengthy and expensive treatment on the couch, hardly a third of the patients improve.[26] One might as well swallow sugar pills. Indeed, numerous studies have shown that about a third of people with depression are cured by taking placebos—pills with no active ingredients at all. Sometimes good common sense is better than the most complicated intellectual constructs.

In cognitive behavior therapy, the psychologist supports patients as they change their ways of thinking. This can be very useful when negative thought patterns have been deeply engrained during a prolonged depression. For everyday purposes, it's not really necessary. The Crusoe Method is so simple and yet so effective that it can be used by anyone.

OPENING OUR OWN EYES

How do we attain this change in perspective? When we suffer from depression, entire streams of negative thoughts pass before us. We see all our intentions failing and are convinced that they *had* to fail, because in the end we're losers. Everything that happens confirms our worst fears.

We spin inner monologues. A colleague passes without looking up. She doesn't even say hi. You think: She probably wants to get back at me. But she has no reason to. She can't stand me, and her behavior proves it. And isn't she justified in her dislike? I *am* hard to take. Even my voice is hoarse. Wouldn't it be better to steer clear of the cafeteria today and not bother everybody?

Many of us are so accustomed to this kind of silent script that it goes by us very quickly and as if by reflex. Our first job, then, is to notice it. There are numerous strategies for doing this.

Crusoe's tactic is especially effective: if you write down your fears, self-accusations, and struggles, you may be shocked at first at how numerous they are. But merely writing down the ways in which we torment ourselves helps us to overcome them.

Putting our fears and feelings of worthlessness down on paper also makes them tangible—and thus easier to test than ideas that just swim around in our head. The trick from then on lies in dropping the dark thoughts at the moment we notice them. There are two ways of doing this. The better of the two is to turn your attention immediately to something else and to walk away from the negativity. This isn't always possible, however, because some fears force themselves into consciousness no matter how hard we try to keep them out. In this case it helps to imitate Robinson Crusoe and write down arguments against thoughts that are tormenting us. When we think someone is snubbing us, for example, it's likely that she's just thinking of something else.

If you're wondering whether you'll have to stand vigilant with pencil and paper until the end of your days—you won't. Writing things down is only a way to get started, like training wheels on a bike. The mastery over our dark thoughts and feelings quickly becomes a habit. As the gray cells are reprogrammed, the left front lobe is trained to master negative emotions a tenth of a second after they first appear. As this ability grows, the bitter feelings vanish.[27]

1 3
THE POWER OF PERSPECTIVE

THE BRAIN IS the central switchboard for good feelings. Unfortunately, it has a tendency to twist and turn in ways that sometimes prevent our being as happy as we could be. We accept these sleights-of-mind not because they're useful, but because we aren't aware of them.

Though we're almost incapable, for example, of imagining the effect of an unfamiliar situation on our mood, the brain vastly exaggerates the consequences of both positive and negative expectations. Ask yourself, for example, whether you would fare better if a) you won the jackpot in the lottery, or b) (may this never happen) you had an accident and were confined to a wheelchair.

Presumably, like almost everyone else, you'd prefer to be a millionaire. Some people would even say they'd rather be dead than paraplegic. But, as American scientists have shown, such conjecturing has little to do with the real feelings that people have in the years after an accident. In a study that has become a classic of social research,[1] the investigators polled people who had nothing directly at stake, but they also asked real lottery winners and accident victims about their life-satisfaction. They discovered how well people adapt—to both the good and the bad. Winning a million dollars does not ensure lasting happiness, and the life-satisfaction of paraplegics is much greater than one might expect. For a few weeks, of course, the lottery winner is on cloud nine, while the paralyzed person mourns his lost freedom of movement. But soon everything seems the same as ever. The newly rich don't feel better off, since in the meantime driving a Mercedes instead of an old Chevy has become normal. The difference is that they now dream of a Ferrari. The person in the wheelchair, on the other hand, has gotten used to the help of others. After a time of depression, most regain their emotional vitality almost completely, and their level of satisfaction is on average not much lower than that of healthy people. Whether accident victim or lottery winner—if you accepted your life beforehand, you will do so now. And a complainer remains a complainer.

This applies even more to less drastic changes in life. We make investments in the expectation that they will make us richer and thus happier. We change jobs, because we think we'll derive more satisfaction from the new one. We move in the hope that we'll feel more at home in a new neighborhood. But at the end of the day life goes on as it always has.

Not that change is unimportant. But we often overestimate its effect on our life satisfaction. Because we get accustomed to both positive and negative changes very quickly, external circumstances affect our sense of well-being much less than we would think. (There are exceptions, such as certain chronic pains like arthritis, and noise—which many people never get used to.[2] People who are sensitive to noise should never believe

199

the real estate agent who says that before long you'll hardly hear the racket coming up from the street under the window.)

When we judge our lives, we often make the mistake of confusing satisfaction with happiness. What's the difference? Happiness is what we feel at the same moment in which we have an experience. It exists only in the present. Satisfaction is that which remains in the mind. It is created in retrospect, like a newspaper review evaluating a film in a few lines.

Someone asking us whether we're happy in our new apartment will probably get an answer that addresses our satisfaction, since it's not likely that we'll first go over every minute since we moved in. In general, people who frequently experience moments of happiness are, all in all, satisfied. Nevertheless, it's quite possible to be satisfied without being happy. By the same token, there are people who feel happy but nurse a sense of dissatisfaction. This might not sound so tragic, but confusing the two concepts can lead to bad decisions and take a significant toll on our well-being.

TRAP #1: SELF-DECEPTION

We spend more time at work than with family and friends. No wonder people put so much emphasis on having a suitable occupation and working in a compatible environment.

If you were a teacher, for example, you'd probably assume that teaching in a good school would be more fun and more satisfying than teaching in a bad one, especially in the United States, where a bad school can mean metal detectors screening for weapons in backpacks, fewer books, vandalized classrooms, drug dealers on the neighboring streets, and gang attacks on teachers.

In the classrooms of good schools, on the other hand, the children of lawyers, doctors, and businesspeople are nurtured for success, much as they are at home. Parents pay high fees, and classrooms are equipped with the newest PCs and connected to the Internet. Kids with problems have ready access to tutors and psychologists. Compared to the poor areas, the work in these schools is easy, and success is more or less assured.

But the teachers see it differently. To learn about the impact of the work environment on satisfaction, the sociologist Norbert Schwarz gave teachers in Houston, Texas—200 at good schools and 200 at bad ones—questionnaires about their day that they filled out every evening. They were asked whether the work was satisfying, whether they felt happy, and how satisfying their lives were in general. The astonishing results: inner-city teachers and suburban teachers responded the same. Were they really immune to their daily failures and fears?[3]

Schwarz wanted more precise answers. He equipped the teachers with Palm organizers that would give off an hourly signal. When the teachers heard the beep, they were supposed to register their level of happiness into the PDA. (Those teachers who didn't want to be interrupted could enter the information after class.) These statistics showed a rather different picture. The teachers in the good schools were in great spirits in the morning. When they went home at lunch, their mood fell to an average level. Those who taught in the inner city showed the exact opposite: during the hours that they had to be in the classroom, the happiness levels were low, but once school was over, they improved.

That's how poorly people assess their own lives. The teachers in the run-down neighborhoods weren't aware of the degree to which they were affected by the blighted environment in which they worked. And their colleagues in the good schools underestimated how much they enjoyed their jobs. Both groups are hurt by their distorted views: it doesn't occur to the teachers in the poor schools to look for a better job or to fight for better conditions, while the others don't realize how good they've got it, and are less satisfied than they might be.

What went wrong? The teachers' memories played a trick on them. Instead of remembering their emotions as they really were, they measured them against the norm they'd gotten used to. Asked in the evening how happy they were, those in the bad schools determined that their day was like any other—by that standard, okay. They didn't realize how they *really* felt at work. The same process (but the other way around) took place in the minds of their privileged colleagues.

Both groups of teachers confused happiness and satisfaction. The one was happy, the other unhappy, although both were reasonably satisfied. Both completely deceived themselves about what gave them a sense of well-being. Sometimes we don't know our own lives.

What, you ask, is the harm? Plenty. Emotions like fear and depression cause stress, even when we don't consciously perceive them. And, as many studies have shown, stress makes people sick, weakens the immune system, and increases the risk of suffering from heart and circulatory ailments, among other illnesses.

TRAP #2: BAD TIMING

You've had a great evening, but when you're ready to leave the party and put on your coat, an old friend squeezes by without even saying hi. Now the evening is ruined. That's how lax memory is in its grasp of reality—sometimes a few seconds count more than a few hours.

The mind shades reality in its own color, and sometimes it even turns truth into its opposite. And it's no wonder. As I've described in chapter 4, every external stimulus causes more than several million signals in the brain to be set off. The brain has more than enough opportunities to manipulate reality, and it makes generous use of them.

In falsifying memories of our own feelings, we're engaged

in a mental act that resembles a perfect and unsolvable crime: we've covered our tracks. There's no measure by which we can objectively test what we really felt at any given moment. While emotions can be read from the reactions of the body, feelings are a purely private matter that exist only in the brain, and if the brain has erased its tracks, only indirect clues remain—if that.

The Nobel Prize–winning Princeton University social psychologist Daniel Kahneman found a way to catch these deceptions and uncover the rules behind them. He asked patients who had to undergo an unpleasant medical examination to note their pain on a scale of one to ten, minute by minute. The total score yielded a quantifiable indicator of their discomfort.

But the treatment varied for the two groups. One was treated according to the standard method, in which the pain increases during the course of the procedure and ends abruptly. With the other group the doctors prolonged the exam for a few moments, so that the pain diminished gradually before the exam was over. The patients in the second group had to endure discomfort for longer and their scores were correspondingly "higher."

But when asked later, it was the second group that reported less pain. That they suffered more both objectively (a longer time in treatment) and subjectively (higher score) no longer seemed to count. The patients were more satisfied with the process that caused them discomfort longer and were even willing to be subjected to a second exam (thus justifying the longer exam, although it was unnecessary for the diagnosis).

In this case, too, people were tricked by their memory, which is indifferent to the duration of a feeling—a finding that Kahneman could corroborate with other experiments. The brain stores the memory of the feeling only at its most intense and in its final moments. The moment of greatest discomfort was the same in both diagnostic procedures, but the final minutes of the longer exam were less unpleasant, which is why the patients preferred it. The last impression sticks. Our brains want a happy ending.[4]

We can put this automatic distortion mechanism to use in daily life. Leaving a party at its liveliest is smart, because it's the last experience that counts. And it's worth trying to emulate people who know how to enjoy short moments of intense happiness, because the memory always retains these high points.

TRAP #3: FALSE EXPECTATIONS

Our expectations distort our feelings and emotions even more than our memories do. Also-rans can tell a story or two about this one. Winning a silver medal at the Olympic Games brings glory, but a bronze makes people happier. While the runners-up imagine themselves on the top step and are upset, having missed their goal by a few tenths of a second, the bronze medal winners feel terrific, as the social psychologist Victoria Medcec discovered at the Barcelona games in 1992. Those in third place were happy that they won a medal at all and made it into the record books, whereas the silver winners were mainly aware of what they'd just missed.[5] "For there is nothing either good nor bad, but thinking makes it so," says Hamlet.

Could it be that pessimists are more satisfied because reality has only pleasant surprises in store for them? This claim is often made. The social psychologist Allen Parducci has even developed a whole theory of happiness based on the idea that well-being is a consequence of mid-level hopes. He also believes that sporadic moments of happiness make people unhappy because they raise expectations. He writes, "If the best can come only rarely, it is better not to include it in the range of experiences at all."[6] The secret to happiness, claims Parducci, is to have had many bad experiences: expecting the worst, we're then pleasantly surprised that life hasn't done us a bad turn after all.

Parducci is wrong. His experiments are based on manipulated games of chance that aren't applicable to everyday, complicated lives. Pessimism nourishes excessive worry and anxiety, which already diminish the capacity for happiness. Moreover, it often prevents positive experiences, for whether we hope for the best or fear the worst determines our attitude in confronting a situation. Discouragement is not a good motivator.

A student who thinks he has no chance of passing a test is just as happy not to study in the first place. Optimism is an indispensable motivator. As many studies show, people who are optimistic are not just happier but they're more successful students, athletes, and salespeople.[7] In matters that are at least partly under our control, realistic hopefulness is helpful. Only someone with an exaggeratedly rosy view of the future is likely to be disappointed. A smart student expects a good grade, not an A+.

TRAP #4: SIDEWAYS GLANCES

Who among us hasn't envied neighbors and colleagues who always seem to be doing better than we are? But envy is mutual. It turns out that those whom we envy are the very ones who look at us in disapproving admiration, casting a sideways glance at our happiness—an effect that the American social psychologist Ed Diener has shown statistically.[8] One of the two must be wrong. Or perhaps both?

There is no objective norm for satisfaction. Our hopes and fears provide the measure with which we evaluate reality. Often we have to compare ourselves to others in order to decide whether we're kings and queens or losers. "If people just wanted to be happy, it wouldn't be so hard, but they want to be happier than others—and that is almost always difficult because we imagine others to be happier than they really are," wrote the philosopher Montaigne.[9]

People who compare, lose. Casting sideways glances not only makes us dependent on others but leads to bad decisions. With what subtlety and scant awareness we trick ourselves has been shown by Norbert Schwarz. He looked at satisfaction in the lives of people who are partners—something that we would expect to have little relation to the neighbors' love lives.

But this isn't the case. Schwarz asked male students who were living with a woman about their sex lives. Among all kinds of diversionary questions, he wanted to know how often the young men masturbated. The answers were to be entered anonymously into a questionnaire, of which there were two versions. One group was given a scale that ranged from "less than once a week" to "several times a day." Most of them marked once or twice a week (i.e., in the middle of the scale), which, according to most research, is the answer one would expect. The possibilities given to the other group ranged from "never" to "several times a week," placing the average response at the upper end of the scale and thus suggesting something abnormal. The students could only draw the conclusion that they were masturbating excessively—a worrying thought, especially since the question about frequency of sex with one's partner was also gauged to manipulated scales. These students might well ask: could something be wrong with their relationship?

Schwarz determined that after taking the survey, the students in the second group were indeed plagued by such doubts and expressed more discontent than average about their current relationship. And these men also indicated that they would be much more likely to have an affair. Thus do arbitrary and often unconscious judgments affect our lives.[10]

Everyone experiences such situations almost daily, though it's not usually devious experiments that make us dissatisfied and lead us to mistaken conclusions. There are entire armies of models who would have us believe that an ideal figure and flawless complexion are completely normal. The stories we hear from other children's mothers make our own kids look like brats and failures. And those of us who read in the business pages about supersuccessful CEOs might regard our own lives as wasted. Unlike the participants in Schwarz's experiment, who were ultimately told about the deception, in daily life we have to remind ourselves how badly the habit of comparison can lead us astray.

TRAP #5: ENVY

"What makes someone with a hunchback happy?—When he sees a hunchback that's still bigger," claims a Yiddish proverb. Pleasure in the misfortune of others—schadenfreude—can be satisfying because such moments throw our happiness into positive relief. And psychological experiments have confirmed the sad truth that merely seeing someone in a wheelchair raises the spirits of most people and results in high satisfaction values on questionnaires.[11]

But it's a temporary comfort. It's easy to find people who are worse off, but we'll also always find someone whom we can envy. Even the most successful of us are vulnerable. "If you desire glory, you may envy Napoleon. But Napoleon envied Caesar, Caesar envied Alexander, and Alexander, I dare say, envied Hercules, who never existed," as Bertrand Russell wrote.[12]

Evolutionary psychologists have tried to explain the seeming tenacity of envy as a Darwinian survival of the fittest: when everyone in nature is competing with everyone else, it isn't enough to have enough—only those will survive who are better and have more than others. Which is why we're programmed for envy.

Whether this is really the case is as hard to prove as it is to disprove. Envy might have an evolutionary purpose, but that doesn't mean it's inborn. Nonetheless, it is true that people will be envious, even when it's harmful to themselves—as long as the harm to the other person is still greater. During a conflict over wages in an English aeronautical turbine plant, for example, the workers were willing to sacrifice some of their income as long as the group of competing workers earned less. Such absurdity surprised even the social psychologists who studied the case.[13] The workers knew, of course, that the position they took was directed against fellow union members, but in their mind it was a question of justice.

Envy often makes no sense, even when it's superficially understandable. Very often we're envying someone who isn't nearly as well off as we think: we see the pluses, but not the minuses. We're annoyed by the success of others and often don't recognize the price they had to pay for it. For this kind of thinking the Stoic philosopher Epictitus found a nice example and some biting words two thousand years ago: "Someone was favored over you? You weren't invited to the dinner? But you didn't have to pay the price the host demands; he'll invite you in exchange for praise, for favors. If you think it's worth it, pay the price. If you want the meal without having to pay the price, then you're as shameless as you are stupid."[14]

We don't have to judge as harshly as Epictetus. Maybe we really are born with the tendency to be envious, in which case it would be an emotion that is hard to get rid of. But with a little clear thinking, envy could be channeled into more sensible paths and help us to better recognize our own wishes.

TRAP #6: THE RAT RACE

With an ad declaring that you're spending money badly if it doesn't make you happy, Lexus marketed its luxury limos—driven by Bill Gates, among others. Money really can be wonderful. If you have enough of it, you can ride home in a taxi, while everyone else waits in the rain for the bus. With money we can be attractive and sexy, because nice clothes and a good haircut are expensive. Money gives us freedom—it pays for the babysitter when Mom and Dad want to go out in the evening. People who not only earn well but are actually wealthy are independent and can live their dreams. Instead of being jerked around by your boss and having to get by on two weeks' vacation, you're free to travel, start your own company, initiate a charitable project.

"I've been poor, and I've been rich, and I can tell you: rich is better," said the singer Sophie Tucker. Who wouldn't agree? In 2004, the American Freshman Study, a national survey by the University of California at Los Angeles, 78 percent considered it "very important" or "essential" to become "very well off financially." The bourgeois Marxist Bertolt Brecht articulated a similar point of view: "You live comfortably only if you live prosperously."

Nonetheless, there's surprisingly little to be seen of money's effect when people are asked about their satisfaction. Whether money increases happiness is a central question in all capitalist societies, and social scientists have gone to considerable lengths to answer it. Exactly 154 large surveys were undertaken after World War II, in Europe, the United States, and many other countries that address just this topic.

They all came to the same conclusion: money brings satisfaction, but the effect is minimal. Adding a few hundred or even a few thousand dollars more to your paycheck is like drinking vintage champagne instead of ordinary champagne: you'll hardly notice the difference. Even with the superrich, money's effect is hardly measurable. The psychologist Ed Diener determined in interviews that the level of life satisfaction of the fifty richest Americans (valued at more than a hundred million dollars each) was barely more than average.[15] And most multimillionaires agree with the thesis that money can make people happy *or* unhappy—a situation that the psychotherapist Jense Corssen taps into by offering seminars for the children of entrepreneurs in which they're taught how to live with their inheritance. Being wealthy doesn't have to hurt, he promises. "I teach the young people how to be happy in spite of their wealth."[16]

Factors other than the size of our bank account clearly weigh far more in determining our satisfaction. Only at the bottom end of the income scale does more money yield a clear improvement.[17] If a single mother working the night shift has to stand over greasy french fries all night, earning just enough for herself and her children to squeak by, then every dollar will improve her life noticeably. She can work a job with a better schedule and spend more time with her children, and she doesn't have to torment herself for not being able to give them the cash they need for class trips. A minimally satisfactory income is determined not only by the most elementary needs like housing and food. Poverty is also defined by the income standard of the people around us. The more expensively her children's classmates are dressed, the more an impoverished mother has to spend on her own children's clothes so that they won't be teased.

But as soon as income exceeds this poverty threshold, the relation between wealth and well-being disappears. When we get a raise, our happiness lasts only as long as the higher standard of living feels new. If you earn thirty thousand dollars, someone earning three times as much seems wealthy. But she sees it quite differently. "What would you do if you suddenly had a million marks?" the German banker Josef Abs was once asked. His answer: "I'd really have to cut way back."

Enthusiasm over access to better restaurants, a beautiful car, and a bigger apartment wanes quickly. The same adaptive mechanisms are at work as with the monkeys who soon stopped enjoying even the raisins. "The treadmill of hedonism" is what the social psychologist Donald Campbell called this fruitless struggle.[18]

And worse: chasing after fame and money diminishes life satisfaction. Several recent studies make ambition look like a real instrument of torture. As the American social psychologists Richard Ryan and Tim Kasser and their German colleague Peter Schmuck discovered in large-scale international surveys, people for whom money, success, fame, and good looks are especially important are less satisfied than those who strive for good relationships with others, develop their talents, and are active in social causes. The rat race—the chase after recognition for money and status—doesn't pay. Not even the fulfillment of their wishes can compensate the ambitious: wealth and influence bring them no happiness, because as soon as they've attained their heart's desire, they set their sights on a new one.[19]

According to these studies, big ambitions have a more than average likelihood of being accompanied by anxiety and depression. It isn't clear if chasing after success is a cause or consequence of emotional instability. Probably the two go hand in hand. If you want to rise, you often have to defer the reward. Instead of a vacation in Hawaii, you hear the lure of those overtime hours at your desk. And not even that guarantees success: whether we attain our professional ambitions depends at least as much on coincidence and the goodwill of others as on our own achievements. And this can give rise to feelings of helplessness and dependency—paving the way for fear and depression.

THE ANSWER: KNOW YOURSELF

We all have illusions about what's good for us. But it's easy to avoid these mistakes and become more aware of what makes us happy and unhappy. What's important is to have a good perspective and to choose the right moment.

Seeing our own lives from another person's point of view is usually not especially helpful. We humans experience fear and joy, and sadness and anger similarly, but our emotions are triggered differently. Although emotions are inborn, most preferences and dislikes are acquired. The culture of our environment, our upbringing, and our personal life histories help determine who likes opera and who likes rock. Further, small genetic differences can affect our interests: someone born with a poor visual/spatial sense is unlikely to have a good time playing Ping-Pong or volleyball.

212

Someone who tries to model himself too closely on others is therefore unlikely to find either happiness or satisfaction. The demand that we lead our own lives may sound trivial, but it runs counter to all we've experienced. Parents do their best to instill their values in their children from day one. In school, all children are supposed to learn by the same method, although we've long known that people differ in their strengths and talents.

It's possible to avoid a lot of unhappiness if we know how we respond to a given situation. How do we learn to listen to the brain? It doesn't help much to think about our experiences, because memory manipulates our memory. Instead, we need to be more attentive *in the moment* than we usually are.

When we notice emotions as soon as they happen, they're not yet distorted by comparisons, thoughts, and memories. In this moment feelings can be signals for our inborn preferences and dislikes. An instant suffices in which to become conscious of an emotion. More than that isn't necessary, and dwelling on negative emotions can even be harmful. When a heedless driver makes us angry, it helps to be aware that we feel we're being treated with disrespect. We're spared a tantrum, and it becomes easier to keep a cool head and turn to other matters.

Positive feelings, on the other hand, should be savored. Though—wrongly—we're willing to yield to our anger and sadness, we often take pleasant feelings—the kind we have when we're sitting across from someone we like and trust—for granted. If everything is going well, our mind quickly begins to wander, and our thoughts turn to something that's troubling us. When this happens, we lose a lot. When we're only dimly aware of our happiness, we not only forfeit the happiness, but also the knowledge about what it is that we like and what helps us.

213

HAPPINESS DIARIES

It isn't enough to be happy. We have to be aware of our happiness. This is also the credo of the Italian psychiatrist Giovanni Fava. He has developed a treatment called "Well-Being Therapy" that helps people who want to cultivate positive feelings and enjoy them more.

The idea came to him while working with depressed patients who were getting better. Fava noticed that their widespread reluctance to acknowledge their happiness deferred the healing. These people are usually very dissatisfied, but often much less so than they think. In order to counteract this, Fava invented a simple procedure: the patients were to keep happiness diaries. If you keep track of your good moments, your attention will be drawn like a searchlight to everything that you respond to positively. And because the happy moments are put down in black and white, the brain can't talk itself out of them later on.

Fava reported that his patients, many of them still very "down," often balked at his suggestion. They were afraid to appear before the doctor with empty notebooks. He encouraged them to try it nonetheless, and they almost always came back with full pages: there are good moments even in periods of greatest depression and dissatisfaction.

When Fava's patients consciously experienced a sunny moment, they were to describe it in detail, as well as their own feelings, and score their well-being on a scale of 1 to 100. And thus they discovered that their lives were much better than they'd thought. Moreover, they learned what does them good.

In a second round, Fava wanted the patients to figure just how they'd been able to be so dismissive of the happiness that they had, in fact, experienced. One patient, for example, reported a positive moment when he was warmly greeted by nephews he was visiting. But this was immediately followed by the thought: "They're only happy because I brought them a present." Being aware of the ways in which the brain ambushes us keeps us better grounded in reality. After ten weeks, the people who tried Fava's method were freed from their deep depressions. They were less fearful, and more satisfied with their lives than before.[20]

Above all, they saw that it isn't the one big change that turns lives around. Satisfaction is like a mosaic created out of many happy moments. To be aware of these moments of happiness is a sure means of leaving misery behind you.

Just what it is that makes people happy is something we each have to discover for ourselves. Life is not a hundred-yard dash in which we all take off from the same starting line and finish in the same home stretch.

14

RAPTUROUS MOMENTS

"BLISS" IS A lovely word whose sound already hints at its meaning: a feeling of intense elation. A moment in which the whole world seems to light up with happiness must have been what Rosa Luxemburg was experiencing when she wrote the following lines: "Do you know where I am, where I am writing this letter from? I've taken a small table outside and am sitting hidden between green bushes. To my right are ornamental yellow currants, which smell like clove, to the left a privet, and before me the white leaves of a large, earnest and tired silver poplar are rustling . . . How beautiful it is, how happy I am, I can almost feel the mood of approaching Midsummer—the full, lush ripeness of summer and the intoxication of life itself."

Rosa Luxemburg wrote this letter to Sophie Liebknecht from prison in 1917. It was her third year of incarceration, and she knew that as a leading pacifist, she would be kept in prison until the end of the war. But the boredom, the abuse, and the uncertainty of her future seemed hardly to touch her. Something in her was stronger. "I lie alone quietly, clad in the many black wraps of darkness, boredom, the confinement of winter—and yet my heart beats with an incomprehensible, unknown inner joy, as if I were walking in brilliant sunshine across a blossoming meadow . . . How strange it is that I am constantly in a state of blissful intoxication—and for no particular reason," she wrote in astonishment in another letter of the same year.

But she knew exactly what the source of her happiness was. Her ability to let fears bounce off her was strengthened by her conviction that she had been imprisoned for a larger cause. Her suffering, she felt, had meaning. Luxemburg owed her extraordinary gift for happiness to her intense powers of perception. She herself described the enthusiasm for the bird-song and the rustling of the leaves as the source of her positive feelings: "I believe that the secret is nothing other than life itself."[1]

Today we know how justified this supposition was. Perception and mood are closely related. A depressed person has no interest in the world. His orientation is entirely internal. Preoccupied solely with himself, he broods ceaselessly trying to get to the bottom of his misery. But someone who manages to turn his attention outward has little room left for worry and fear. Being involved with other people and things interrupts the constant circling of dark thoughts and feelings. Thus unburdened, a happy brain begins to forget itself: we become completely involved in what we're doing and in what is happening around us. And then—with no external cause—we can feel the purest and perhaps most beautiful elation of all: happiness at being alive.

WALKING ON WATER

The brain behaves as if it can't bear a vacuum. Imagine sitting in a room with nothing to do. Somewhere a radio is playing. Whether you want to or not, you're listening to the music: our attention doesn't always obey our will. The brain rushes to any stimuli that present themselves. (Which explains why we look at a lot more ads than we're really interested in.) You can ignore the interruption only if you've got something else to do. When you're engaged in a serious phone call, for example, the brain blocks out background noise. The gray cells have more important things to attend to.

Worries, too, can absorb the brain when it's running on empty. Who hasn't brooded over the next day's uncertainties when trying to fall asleep? That's why counting sheep really can work: the neurons are busy and keep worries from surfacing. Imagining colorful scenes is still more helpful, since they're more interesting.

That in idle moments we tend to be occupied with disagreeable fantasies rather than with pleasant memories has to do with the brain's evolutionary programming. If a fearful and a cheerful thought present themselves simultaneously, the former will win out every time.

In unfocused moments we can begin to brood and are often overcome by fear and self-doubt. The Gospel According to St. Matthew describes the connection between perception and feelings in the wondrous scene on the Sea of Gaililee. Peter is in his boat when he sees Jesus, who is walking on the water. Peter begins to run toward him, but then, distracted by a strong wind, he looks away and is seized by fear. And right away he begins to sink.[2]

The London neuropsychologist Nilli Lavie proved that disturbing stimuli fail to reach most of the centers of the cerebrum and thus consciousness when we concentrate on other things. In her experiment, the volunteers were told to study the words on the monitor and pay as little attention as possible to the confused patterns of dots that were streaming across the background.

They succeeded when they were so absorbed by their task that the working memory had no capacity left for the dancing dots. Because the stimulus that the experimental subjects wanted to perceive (the words) was strongly differentiated from the disturbance (the dots), Lavie could show that the volunteers were actually immune from the distraction. The cerebrum processes immobile and moving images in different parts of the brain. The brain scans in Lavie's experiments showed that only the centers that processed the words were activated. The regions that were responsible for the moving images, on the other hand, were not.[3]

PLEASURE IN PERCEPTION

If we look, listen, or feel intensely, we can forget everything else, even ourselves. Sometimes this kind of focus comes as if by itself, as when we watch—as if hypnotized—the spray of the sea, or when we're having sex.

To focus our concentration by force of will is difficult. What helps is to experience the joy of discovery, of perceiving the world quite differently than usual. Have you ever listened to the many different sounds of rain as it strikes windowpanes, roofs, and trees? Or have you watched the sunlight breaking on your fingers and bringing forth a wash of tiny points of light in all colors of the rainbow?

Such moments tend to dispel worries and fears. But this alone doesn't explain the happiness that we sometimes feel in such moments. What *is* the source of our joy when we listen and look? The pleasure in discovery plays an important role, because new stimuli activate the *expectation system*. Dopamine helps direct attention to these signals and ensures that we feel an agreeable tension. This program even runs in the brains of animals—in a cat, for example, when it is fixated on a bird.

Humans, uniquely, can also be moved by symbols. Flowers on a table make us happy, even though they have almost no practical value to the organism. It's not as if we're about to eat the roses. Rather, we owe our feelings to the same emotions that make it possible for letters on the page of a novel to make us laugh. We don't actually see more than the printer's ink on a page, but the brain adds meaning, and thus a whole stream of images, scenes, and emotions appears before our inner eye into which we can dip as if into another life. This ability to imagine comes from an inborn tendency to interpret all the signs in our environment. Romantic feelings are a byproduct of evolution.

Most people see much more in a sunset than the image of a red disk that is slowly sinking. At the end of the day we spontaneously think of sleep and dreams. We may remember our first love, or how our own children once played on the beach at dusk. Some people might think about the passage of time, or perhaps even of their own death. As Heinrich Heine wrote, teasing his contemporaries for their weakness for romantic feelings:

> *The maiden looked long at the ocean,*
> *Her sighing was touching and deep.*
> *It was clearly a heartfelt emotion,*
> *For the sun going down made her weep.*
>
> *Why, ma'am, 'tis no cause for sorrow—*
> *There's simply no need for alarm.*
> *The sun may go down, but tomorrow*
> *It sneaks right back up—that's its charm.*

What Heine didn't realize is that the brain automatically charges most scenes with emotion. What differentiated the romantics of the nineteenth century from people in less sentimental times isn't that they were moved by the drama of nature, but that they celebrated these feelings in poetry, painting, and music.

We find something similar in the letters of Rosa Luxemburg, surely not a person known for sentimentality. When she sees and smells the blossoming bushes and listens to the wind blowing through the poplars, she remembers and anticipates the approach of summer. But her associations probably reach further. She may think of the sequence of the seasons, of fruitfulness and mutability, and presumably also of her hope for a better world. She simply enjoys being alive. That's how much everyday experiences can inspire us, if we only stay with them for a moment. We easily forget how much this joy depends on the human brain's impressive powers. Even the most intelligent monkeys derive no pleasure from flowers and sunsets.[4]

WHEN TIME STANDS STILL

Devoting ourselves to an activity can give intense focus to both our attention and our perception and is thus also linked to positive feelings. It doesn't matter so much what kind of activity it is, as long as it is carried out with concentration. Skiing or reading, a conversation, any work taken seriously—the important thing is to find a task that takes full advantage of the brain.

To be absorbed by an activity can be so pleasant that we engage in it again and again for its own sake. At such times it seems that things are happening not by our own agency, but automatically, as if driven by a power that uses us as a tool. The I is forgotten, and our preoccupations fade away so that we can better concentrate on the task at hand.

Even time seems to disappear. The German bestselling novelist Heinz Konsalik, the apparently tireless author of 155 books, has described this condition as "losing myself in my characters and plots. There's no time, no food, no peace. After eight or ten hours at the typewriter, I'm completely worn out. Then I need twenty minutes to get back into our world."[5]

The psychologist Mihaly Csikszentmihalyi has made it his life's work to document such experiences, which he calls *flow*. He conducted interviews with athletes, surgeons, conductors, and others who work at occupations requiring complete concentration. But he also spoke with hundreds of office workers and others with normal jobs. He came to the conclusion that in moments of intense focus experiences resemble one another and are largely independent of the specific activity. Because Csikszentmihalyi knew that memory distorts experience, he didn't rely entirely on recall. Asking the interviewees to record their feelings regularly, he discovered that people tend to idealize their free time. As a rule, the interviewees felt better when engaged intensely in an activity than when they spent evenings and weekends doing nothing. Factory workers indicated that they were twice as happy at work as in their leisure time. With office workers and managers the difference was still greater.[6]

By no means does this mean that the factory workbench or the office desk is a better environment than the garden at home. Rather, most people are forced to be busy at work, and this raises their spirits. At home, on the other hand, they can be idle. A disagreeable sense of torpor was reported three times more frequently during off-hours than while at work.

TOO EASY IS AS BAD AS TOO DIFFICULT

Could Sisyphus have been happy? This hero of Greek mythology wasn't tormented by the strenuousness of the task that the gods had assigned him—the physical effort of rolling the same stone up the mountain over and over wasn't really the problem. Nor was it so terrible that his success was momentary, that each time after reaching the peak, the boulder rolled right back down to the bottom. There are, after all, many jobs (think of housecleaning) whose results are transitory. The worst part of Sisyphus's task must have been its monotony.

As Csikszentmihalyi learned in his interviews, *flow* is possible only when the activity requires just the right amount of exertion from the brain. In those cases, the effort doesn't have to lead to exhaustion and negativity. Rather, it releases a pleasant stimulus, even a light euphoria. But if a task is too difficult or too easy, the positive feelings don't occur.

That there's no satisfaction when the demands exceed our ability makes sense: not to experience success is to invite frustration, self-doubt, and a sense of helplessness. But the opposite condition—being underchallenged—is hardly less unpleasant. Boredom is among the feelings we tolerate least well. The brain doesn't like a vacuum. When the gray cells are insufficiently engaged, unpleasant thoughts, fears, and depression intrude. We try anything to avoid such situations, or at least to tickle the brain with stimuli. (This must be the reason so many people turn on the radio the moment they've closed the car door.)

Nilli Lavie's studies showed that tasks that are too simple do indeed have a similar effect on the brain as ones that are too difficult. As soon as the brain is understimulated, it can no longer differentiate between important and trivial stimuli. In Lavie's experiments, the subjects began to attend to the distracting patterns in the background as much as they did to the words on which they were supposed to be focusing. This is just what happens when *too much* is asked of the gray cells. When Lavie had her subjects remember rows of numbers and names of politicians at the same time that photos of pop stars were being shown on the monitor, the participants couldn't focus for long. As soon as the rows of numbers became more complicated, the scans showed how the brain became increasingly occupied with the irrelevant faces instead of with the task at hand.[7]

The reason is that too much was asked of the working memory. The neurons in the prefrontal cortex normally filter out what is unimportant so that it doesn't reach consciousness. When the working memory has to keep too much information, like names and rows of numbers, it breaks down, and our consciousness is then flooded with whatever stimuli happen to stream in. Whether the brain has too much or too little to do, it loses its ability to focus.

223

Being underchallenged, therefore, has the same devastating effects on emotional balance as being overchallenged. According to extensive psychological studies, people who are understimulated at work are more likely to suffer from depression and anxiety.[8] Very gifted children, for example, often being forced to adjust to a normal learning pace, suffer intolerable boredom that can cause real psychological suffering and even suicidal fantasies. Only when these students are genuinely challenged do they get better. The solution is to let them skip a grade or to give them more difficult work. Some parents send their highly gifted children, for example, to an afterschool course to learn Japanese.

If schoolchildren or working adults are to do their tasks well, their responsibilities have to be appropriate to their abilities. To achieve this kind of balance in a class with thirty students is a challenge for the teacher, because the line between too easy and too difficult is thin indeed. But people can only succeed to the limit of their abilities—and enjoy it—when the right balance is met.

THE SECRET OF FLOW

Where do the good feelings come from when we are intensely occupied with an activity? This is an area still in need of more research. But dopamine probably plays an important part, because this transmitter (as I've already explained) controls attentiveness and arouses pleasure.[9]

Dopamine has a direct effect on the neurons in the prefrontal cortex, which is responsible for the working memory. Some scientists even think that it is among the most important tasks of this neurotransmitter to ensure that the brain is able to sift important information from disturbances.[10] When we concentrate, it's likely that the dopamine level rises. At the same time, dopamine is a kind of mental lubricant. Under its influence the brain processes data more quickly, so we react and think faster, make mental associations more easily, and are more creative. This would explain the perhaps unintuitive finding that increased concentration both enables sustained levels of high achievement and simultaneously brings forth positive feelings.

The effect of dopamine might even explain why people like to participate in strenuous and yet "useless" activities like whitewater rafting, football, and chess. It's possible that real enthusiasts experience a kind of addiction to this natural drug that is released in moments of special attentiveness.

To this is added the expectation of success. If we have a goal before us and think that with a little more effort we could achieve it, we're excited by the challenge. When we've made some progress, we realize that the effort has paid off, and we experience a small sense of triumph. And then we're confronted by the next step—a new challenge—and desire kicks in again. In this way, the mild depression that often follows an achievement fails to materialize. If the difficulty of a given task is at the appropriate level, the hedonistic seesaw alternates constantly between desire and reward, both releasing dopamine and opioids. If the activity is too simple, there's no challenge and thus no stimulation. If it's too difficult, there'll be no reward.

In order for *flow* to set in, we first have to force ourselves to focus. When we're distracted, it helps the brain to return to the task at hand as quickly as possible, so that it can pass the threshold beyond which the powers of concentration take over. From this point on, people stay on track effortlessly, especially if the task demands a little more of us than we're used to. For this reason, forcing ourselves a bit to undertake a challenging task can often be rewarding.

It's a good idea if the goals we set for ourselves are small from the outset. There's hardly a climber who could muster what it takes to climb a cliff if she thought only of the ultimate goal, the summit, which usually can't even be seen from the base. Every alpine climber unconsciously divides her ascent in such a way that she repeatedly has the experience of success from the very beginning. She's happy when she's pulled herself up by an elusive grip after climbing twenty feet against the cliff, and again after fifty feet when she's reached an overhang, and finally after a hundred feet when she has climbed the length of the rope and found a ledge to stand on. And so it goes for several hundreds and even thousands of feet of easier and more difficult stretches, all the way to the summit.

These partial victories warrant more attention than the end result. Not only do they yield more positive feelings, but we have more control over the small triumphs than over a distant goal. A sudden storm can destroy any hopes a climber had for the summit, and more than one scientist has lost his shot at fame after many years work when it turns out that a competitor published the results a few weeks earlier. For this reason it is often said that the path should be the goal. We can't forget the striving for a reward quite so easily, because the inborn *expectation system* is very powerful. But we can choose where and in what form we seek and, in the end, find our reward.

THE STATE OF ABSORPTION

People as far back as ancient Greece—as with many of the ancient cultures of the East—understood exaltation as a gift of the gods. This is why mystics of almost all religions have experimented with techniques that aim for such experiences. The methods that they discovered rely on mechanisms similar to the joy we experience when we look at something intently or engage in concentrated activity. Meditation, for example, is controlled perception that enables us to lose ourselves and experience euphoria.

When a Zen monk counts his breathing, when a Yogi repeats his mantra, or when a Christian is lost in prayer—the person meditating always directs his perception toward a simple focus. In this way he occupies his brain, prevents it from turning to everyday cares, calms his mind, and relaxes his body.

That meditation has measurable effects was first shown by the Harvard neurologists Herbert Benson and Robert Wallace over three decades ago. It has been confirmed by many studies since. When thoughts are calm, muscles relax and the electric brain activity shifts to the steadier rhythm of the so-called alpha waves. Finally the pulse drops, as does blood pressure and the utilization of oxygen. At the same time, fewer stress hormones circulate in the blood, which is why it's thought that regular meditation might strengthen the immune system. The whole organism attains a more balanced state—one that the brain interprets as anxiety free, relaxed, and pleasant.[11]

Sitting motionless isn't for everyone, but many people who do practice the discipline of meditation experience a kind of quiet joy as soon as their thoughts have come to rest. This alone can be extremely pleasant, but experienced meditators speak of much more than only the effects of pure relaxation—they report moments of intense spirituality. As you sink down ever deeper, you lose awareness of yourself, as well as a sense of time and space, experiencing instead a melding with the entire universe. Michael Baime, a physician who conducts stress research at the University of Pennsylvania and has been practicing Buddhist meditation for thirty years, describes such a moment as follows: "There was a feeling of energy centered within me . . . going out to infinite space and returning . . . There was a relaxing of the dualistic mind, and an intense feeling of love . . . clarity, transparency and joy. I felt a deep and profound sense of connection to everything, recognizing that there never was a true separation at all."[12]

RESEARCHING MYSTICISM

Baime was among the first people to be examined by scientists wanting to find out what happens in the brain during such experiences of the infinite. Does mystical experience have a basis in the neurons? Might there even be circuitry for God in the human brain, as newsmagazines and several scientists have speculated?

Such questions have been on the agenda of serious science for only a few years. For a long time many scholars were inclined to dismiss reports such as Baime's as the fantasies of hysterics and weirdos. At most, they would entertain the possibility of a neurological defect. It's been known for a long time that epileptics have extraordinary experiences during attacks, which they sometimes interpret later as encounters with God. Such an episode might have converted Saul on the road to Damascus, when he became a disciple of Christ and renamed himself Paul. In any case, the vision that the saint describes in the Bible corresponds quite closely with the symptoms of temporal lobe epilepsy. On the road to Damascus he saw a bright light flash above him, he fell to the ground and heard a voice asking, "Saul, Saul, why are you following me?"[13] He was then blind for three days, during which he could neither eat nor drink. Later mystics such as St. Theresa of Avila reported similar breakdowns and, from the nineteenth century on, epilepsy is well documented in a number of famous people who were intensely occupied with religion. Fyodor Dostoyevksi, whose novels include no less than thirty epileptic characters, had his first attack when he was nine. As an adult he sometimes collapsed every few days. Lights flashing before his inner eye, he often felt an almost supernatural happiness before losing consciousness.[14]

But now researchers—among them the radiologist Andrew Newberg, like Baime at the University of Pennsylvania—are working to prove that clinically healthy people, too, can have mystical experiences and that such conditions are accessible to science. Newberg transformed the setting of his experiment as much as he could: candles illuminated the darkened lab, the subject was enveloped in clouds of jasmine-scented incense so that he didn't think of high-tech medicine but of a temple. A woolen blanket protected him from the cold while he sat meditating in the lotus position. His body was still, and his mind became increasingly absorbed. A tube was inserted into his veins, and a thread was wound around his finger.

The subject signaled the climax of his experience with a short tug, and Newberg released contrast fluid through the tube. The fluid flowed to the brain and gathered in the neurons, which were especially active. After a few moments, Newberg led him into an adjoining room and had him lie down on the bed of a scanner that recorded how the contrast fluid and thus the brain activity is distributed.[15]

Newberg examined eight volunteers who, like Baime, had long experience with Buddhist meditation. He also asked three Franciscan nuns to his lab to devote themselves to prayer. Said Sister Celeste, one of three nuns: "[There was] . . . a feeling of centering, quieting, nothingness, [as well as] moments of fullness of the presence of God. [God was] permeating my being."[16]

MELDING WITH THE COSMOS

According to Newberg, these states of exaltation are not imagined but absolutely real. As proof, he offers functional neuroimages demonstrating to his satisfaction that the mystical experience corresponds to a biological process in the brain. Just as meditation measurably changes the condition of the body, so also the effects on the brain are provable.

The brain scans show clearly when the meditator has succeeded in focusing his perception on his breath or on another goal. The parts of the prefrontal cortex that are responsible for the control of attention are especially active in these moments. In addition, several centers beneath the cerebral cortex that watch over processes in the body are unusually active.[17]

The changes in the activity under the top of the skull and behind the temples—the parietal and temporal lobes of the cerebral cortex—are not quite as pronounced. The parietal lobes serve among other things to create an image of the body in the brain. Without it, we would have no sense where in space our arms and legs happen to be. The brain needs these images when we learn new movements or want to find our way in an unfamiliar environment. Because the meditator remains motionless, less data reaches the parietal lobes than usual. Newberg suspects that this absolute concentration on a particular point of focus further diminishes the flow of information to the parietal lobes. When the circuits in the parietal lobes are, as it were, clamped off, they can only interpret this as the limitlessness of the body and the dissolving of the self into space, as if it had gained access to the infinite, as if it had melded with the whole world.

229

ENCOUNTER WITH GOD?

The temporal lobes, on the other hand, have centers that are involved in creating feelings and storing long-term memory. They are connected with circuits beneath the cerebral cortex, thus linking external perceptions to basic feelings like hunger, sex, and fear, as well as to the person's own life history. For this reason, brain researchers have called this area the gatekeeper to consciousness. When it is stimulated in an unaccustomed way, people often experience overwhelmingly powerful feelings, sometimes to the point of ecstasy. Afterward, the subjects report deep insights and mystical experiences. This is precisely what happens to epileptics, whose neurons fire off wildly for a few seconds during an attack, while a whole thunderstorm of electrical impulses shower down on the temporal lobes.

Scientists now know how to create such experiences artificially. The neuropsychologist Michael Persinger of Laurentian University in Ontario, Canada, uses an electromagnetic helmet that some call a "God machine." This headgear contains magnetic spools that send magnetic fields towards certain parts of the brain with great precision. The effect of the magnets influences the electrical activity of the neurons much as the magnetic fields in a television deflect the electric current. Employing "transcranial magnet simulation," researchers can stimulate targeted regions of the brain. Using himself as a subject, Persinger exposed his own temporal lobes to magnetic stimulation. Afterward, he reported having experienced God for the first time in his life. Nine of fifteen volunteers on whom he repeated the same experiment reported similar experiences.[18]

This experiment raises a fascinating question: do people who meditate learn in the course of their long training to create the same effects in the brain as a magnet stimulator? If so, they could stimulate certain parts of the brain to extraordinary activity and turn others off—thereby giving themselves access to very unusual experiences. Reprogamming itself in this way would signal a brilliant triumph of the human brain.

Persinger stimulated the left temporal lobe more strongly than the right because he surmised that the latter plays a more important role in creating a sense of self. He thought that simulating the left side while leaving the right relatively still would result in a kind of mental paradox. Perhaps the brain can interpret the contradictory data only as a separation of mind and body, or as the influence of an external power with access to the innermost part of a person—God?

Whenever it can, the brain automatically seeks to avoid confusion and to explain away contradictions. The particular interpretation that it's inclined to make is determined largely by one's life history. A person who is rooted in Christianity or in another theistic religion will see his experience as an encounter with God. A Buddhist, who believes in an immortal personal core but not in a higher being, understands such an experience as a moment of enlightenment, as insight into the truth of our own being. In this way, the same mystical experiences, accompanied by the same processes in the brain, yield different interpretations in different religions.

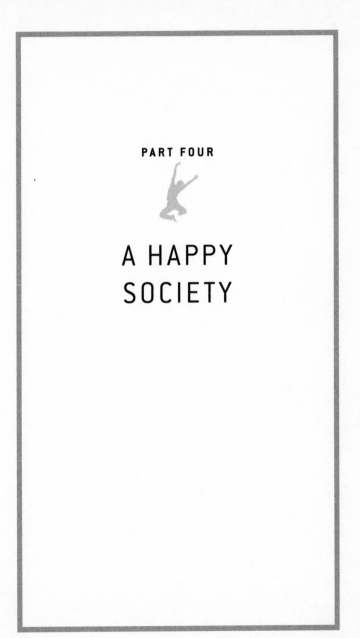

PART FOUR

A HAPPY
SOCIETY

THE MAGIC TRIANGLE

WE MAY BE looking for happiness, but we're not finding it. Although incomes have increased enormously in the last fifty years, the percentage of people describing themselves as happy is no higher today than it was half a century ago.[1] Compared to then, life now offers us much more. What were once luxuries can be afforded by almost everyone. Salmon and champagne are sold at Wal-Mart, and for the price of a suit you can fly to Tahiti. For most of us. leisure time is no longer a scarce resource, and the ways of spending it are limitless. If you want to learn to throw a pot, speak Chinese, or give erotic massages, you can enroll in an adult education class that will teach you just that. Have you long dreamt of piloting a plane? You can make it happen. In the United States (as in all developed countries) the good life has become the "average" life. But this doesn't seem to have done much for well-being. Bertolt Brecht described this dilemma in his *Threepenny Opera:*

Aye, race for happiness
But don't you race too fast.
When all start chasing happiness
Happiness comes in last.[2]

POLITICS AT A DEAD END

As far as life satisfaction goes, the Americans, whose Declaration of Independence gave them the right to strive for happiness, rank toward the top of the mid-range for industrialized countries. The Swiss, Dutch, and Scandinavians score as the happiest, while the Spanish bring up the rear.

It doesn't matter if we look at studies comparing different countries or those showing trends over time—they all point in the same direction: levels of satisfaction in the industrialized countries haven't begun to keep pace with the standard of living. There's a world of difference between well-being and being well-off. If, as the philosophers of the Enlightenment demanded, it's government's responsibility to increase the happiness of its citizens, the Western politicians of the last decades have all failed. According to Francis Hutcheson's *Examination of Good and Evil* (1726), government's goal should be "the greatest happiness of the greatest number." This idea is at the root of the Declaration of Independence, as well as the premise of European democrats.

But in real life, governments aim instead to increase economic productivity above all—and thus the standard of living of their citizens. Only if greater prosperity led to greater happiness would it serve the happiness of the largest possible part of the population. As statistics show, in industrialized countries this is apparently not the case.[3] If the purpose of human and mechanized labor is to produce happiness, our economic system with its huge creation of wealth is grotesquely inefficient.

It's another situation in developing countries, where every

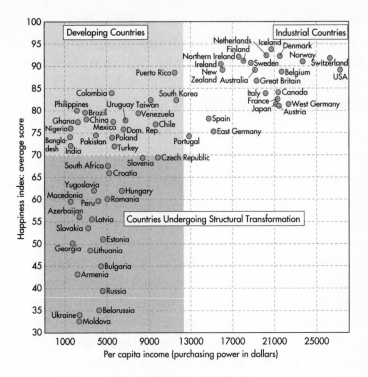

THE HAPPINESS OF NATIONS

Measuring people's satisfaction with a "happiness index," we see three different clusters. Citizens of countries that have recently undergone a profound change or a major crisis are the least satisfied, because they often live in uncertainty and insecurity. Well-being is much higher in stable, developing countries. In this cluster, the happiness index climbs with income—from impoverished Bangladesh to Puerto Rico (almost ten times as wealthy), which is on the threshold of the industrialized countries. Finally, in the most developed countries, the material needs of most people are generally satisfied. Here, greater prosperity no longer brings additional well-being. Although the West Germans are almost a third richer than the Irish, they're less happy. These data are from the late 1990s, and the recent events in the German Democratic Republic are reflected in the figure for East Germany. (Ingelhart and Klingemann, 2000)

added dollar can make a real difference, and the curve of satisfaction climbs steeply from poor countries like the Republic of Moldova to the top earners among the threshold countries like South Korea.[4]

The reasons are obvious: where essentials are lacking, happiness is rare. A peasant in Nepal whose land yields just enough rice for his family is under constant stress. Will next year's harvest be enough? Will the roof of his hut keep the rain out for another season? Is his coughing child seriously ill? Even a modest increase improves the life of this family significantly, making a doctor's visit and perhaps an education for the children affordable.[5]

THE PROMISED LAND, WHERE PEPPER GROWS

Even in the poorest regions of the world, economic power is only one of several factors that determine happiness. In relation to their meager wealth, some countries have managed to achieve a very high level of well-being for their citizens.

Among them is Kerala, a state in India's torrid south where thirty-three million people live in a small space densely planted with coconut palms, bananas, and spice plants. In spite of bountiful harvests, the Keralites—almost all subsistence farmers or fishermen—earn on average less than forty euros a month.

And yet Kerala is in many ways highly developed. While half the men and even more of the women in other Indian states are illiterate, in Kerala almost everyone can read and write. Most have even attended secondary school. Kerala has a thousand-year tradition of martial arts, ayurvedic medicine, and dance theater. There are excellent films in the Malayalam language. And while the population in many areas of the third world has to labor for starvation wages in the fields of wealthy landowners, almost every peasant family in Kerala owns land from which it lives.

People born in Kerala today have a good chance of reaching old age. The average life expectancy is seventy-four—a sensational figure for such a poor region. The Brazilians, for example, who are about six times wealthier, live on average to age sixty-six. Even African Americans—relatively speaking, an almost immeasurably wealthier population—have a life expectancy that is lower than Kerala's.[6]

BODIES, SENSORS OF HAPPINESS

What does life expectancy say about happiness? Health contributes to positive feelings, and, conversely, the absence of anger and stress is good for one's health.

The people of Kerala owe their longevity to the excellent medical care and hygiene that's available to them. Unlike many developing countries, Kerala invests in schools and hospitals rather than in steel plants and airports. But its inhabitants also owe their physical well-being to having easier lives than other Indians. With their own land, a secure income, and a functioning village community, people look with more confidence to the future and suffer less stress than the inhabitants of teeming slums.

The interaction between body and mind is even more important as a population becomes better educated and is served by more doctors. Infections can be fatal in less developed areas, but as soon as medical care and hygiene improve, deaths from diseases like tuberculosis, dysentery, and cholera decrease markedly, and people live to old age. But the higher the life expectancy, the more people die of stress-related illnesses—heart attacks and strokes, for example, which are the main causes of death in industrialized countries.[7]

That there's a direct correlation between a sense of emotional well-being—and thus the absence of stress—and life expectancy has been shown by many studies. It's lifestyle, more than genetics, environment, and medical care, that determines how long a person is likely to live. In fact, its influence is stronger than all these other factors together![8] The body is a sensor of happiness.

THE PARADOX OF MONEY AND HAPPINESS

Life satisfaction and life expectancy go hand in hand with social justice. In both regards, Kerala, poor as it is, is a leader among

239

developing regions. Where the split between haves and have-nots is greater, as in Brazil, people die younger—even though a poor Brazilian earns significantly more money than someone in Kerala's middle class.

That longevity is related not to absolute wealth but to its equal distribution can also be observed in industrialized countries. Where people enjoy the smallest income spread, as in Sweden and Japan, they live the longest, although both countries have completely different social and health systems. On the other hand, greater social inequality is statistically correlated with lower life expectancy.

Surely it's no coincidence that in international comparisons those citizens are most satisfied who enjoy the most equitable income distribution. In Scandinavia, in the Netherlands, and even in Switzerland the discrepancy between rich and poor is much less than in Germany or, for example, in Italy.[9]

The comparison among different states in the United States is particularly striking. Although the United States has excellent hospitals in general, average life expectancy in individual states varies by as much as four years. People can expect to reach seventy-seven in North Dakota, but only seventy-three in Louisiana. Neither income, nor the origin of the population, nor cigarette consumption can explain these differences. Futhere, there's almost no difference in the number of deaths caused by cancer and other diseases with a genetic component.[10] Rather, the explanation lies in the income differentials between rich and poor, which is almost 50 percent greater in Louisiana than in North Dakota.[11] Citizens of states with large gaps in income levels die at a younger age, primarily because of the stress caused by stark social contrasts.[12]

We see, then, that the relationship between money and happiness is complex. Above a certain income level, the increase in satisfaction brought by wealth is minimal, but the distribution of wealth in a society is of enormous significance.

In many parts of the world, income differentials have grown

over the past three decades,[13] most dramatically in Eastern Europe. The statistics from Russia and Lithuania are the worst of all. There the mortality rate (the number of deaths per 1,000 people) has increased by a third since 1989, and life expectancy for men is now less than sixty. In Hungary, which made the transition to capitalism early on, the mortality rate climbed 20 percent from 1970 to 1990, although income increased threefold during these same years! But the prosperity benefited only a few, while most Hungarians own no more today than they did in 1970.[14]

According to the figures of the U.S. Census Bureau, the gap in incomes in the U.S. has grown hugely in the past two decades. In 1979 the 5 percent top-earning American households were on average eleven times wealthier than the poorest 20 percent. By 2000 the difference had increased to a factor of nineteen—almost doubling the gap.

According to conservatives, it hurts no one when the rich become richer, as long as those who are less wealthy don't become poorer. If the size of one's bank account is all that matters, this is true. But if you look at the consequences for well-being and health, it's false. When social discrepancies grow, everyone loses, rich as well as poor.

APULIA IN AMERICA

The trend toward an increasing disparity in income was anticipated in the first half of the twentieth century by the citizens of Roseto, a small town in eastern Pennsylvania. In the first half of the twentieth century, they seemed blessed with virtual immunity against diseases of the heart and circulatory system, the most common cause of death in developed countries. No one died of such illnesses before reaching old age, and men older than sixty-five had a mortality rate exactly half that of the American average. Although Roseto's inhabitants were all of Italian descent, they could hardly attribute their health to the much-vaunted Mediterranean diet. In fact, the Roseto "lifestyle" was actually very unhealthy. Its citizens smoked and worked hard, and, since olive oil wasn't available in the United States in those days, in Roseto the traditionally fatty southern Italian cuisine was cooked in lard. Nor were there any genetic peculiarities to explain the robust constitution of Roseto's citizens.

What did differentiate these people from average Americans was their social cohesion. The town consisted of the descendants of a small number of clans, who had all emigrated from Apulia at the same time and remained inseparable in the New World, where they preserved all the rituals of a small Italian town. People met for their evening walks, gathered for games in one of the many clubs, and celebrated in processions and church festivals. Since envy is divisive, the display of wealth was frowned upon. Although many families had attained some measure of prosperity, it was impossible to distinguish rich from poor—whether by clothing, cars, or housing. Old people lived with their children, three generations under one roof. Crime didn't exist.

But as Roseto became like the rest of America, everything changed. People grew more prosperous, and the community fell apart. After 1970, many young people left the town to study, returning with ideas different from those of their parents. Some drove up in Cadillacs. They built big houses, dug swimming pools, and fenced in their gardens. People retreated into their four walls and savored their wealth. The more Roseto came to resemble a normal American small town, the more closely rates of illness and mortality approached the national average. As the close communal ties withered, so did their protective power.[15]

THE PROTECTIVE SHIELD OF SOLIDARITY

As long as their community was intact, the people of Roseto seem to have lived with less stress than other Americans. The cause was twofold. First, they felt no compulsion to outshine their neighbors. Second, those who were poorer and less successful didn't have to fear for their social status. After all, what makes people unhappy isn't having little but having less than others. It's the sense of having *less* that can make people feel worthless. The people in Roseto were spared the experience of watching helplessly as others pulled ahead and left them forever in the dust.

Furthermore, everyone could rely unconditionally on family and neighbors. The support of the community was so strong that old age and bad luck lost their terror. Roseto's citizens knew that they would never be helpless in the face of life's inevitable ups and downs.

This sense of inner balance was reflected in the sensationally low rate of stress-related diseases of the heart and circulation. Cancer, on the other hand, which does not have psychological causes, occurred with the same frequency as elsewhere in the United States.[16]

It has been known for a long time that social solidarity makes difficult conditions more bearable. The union movement of the nineteenth century was based on this principle. What is new is the recognition that a well-functioning communal structure benefits even physical health. We have already discussed this in chapter 10 in connection with the value of friendship. People live better and longer when they are socially rooted. This connection between well-being, life expectancy, and social cohesion has been convincingly corroborated by many studies since the pioneering work of social scientists in Roseto.[17]

Members of a society can enter into workable relationships only when their lifestyles and interests are similar. If the social distinctions become too large, the communal net dissolves in a tug-of-war. Rich and poor live in different worlds, and neither strays into the territory of the other.

A positive example on a larger scale is provided by the

Netherlands, whose inhabitants have had to deal for centuries with the constant threat of North Sea floods. They developed an egalitarian society in which even the queen rides a bicycle and is photographed in rubber boots on a dyke during a storm surge.[18] To this day, the income gap in the Netherlands is relatively small and the level of life satisfaction correspondingly high.

ENGAGEMENT OUT OF SELF-INTEREST

The flood of research on the beneficial effects of solidarity is incompatible with the currently fashionable ideology of the entrepreneurial self. We're supposed to lead our lives as if we were companies in the marketplace. Advice books urge their readers to imitate the techniques and rhetoric of business consultants. One of these books recommends that we all brand, "reengineer," and benchmark ourselves against the best and the brightest. In the words of the New York entrepreneur and billionaire Ron Perelman, "Happiness is a positive cash flow."[19] Nothing could be further from the spirit of Roseto. All "management by vision" notwithstanding, the future of such strategies is not promising, for they load an almost inhumane burden on anyone who tries to live by them.

For most people, the retreat into private life means a self-inflicted rejection of happiness—and not only because they enjoy less a supportive and less congenial environment in their homes and neighborhoods. The greatest loss is the satisfaction that comes from the very activity of community involvement, as the English social psychologist Michael Argyle demonstrated in his study on free time. Most of the people he surveyed indicated that nothing could outweigh the pleasure that they derived from their work as volunteers. On a scale of enjoyment gauging the value of their free-time activity, only dancing was higher. What they especially enjoyed was getting to know like-minded people, seeing the results of their work, and gaining life experience.[20]

Whether among amateur actors, or in an environmental action group, getting involved is recommended not only for moral reasons but also out of simple self-interest.

A CIVIC SENSE RELIES ON TRUST

An unspectacular activity like singing in a chorus, for example, can accomplish much more than merely improving the singer's mood. When the Harvard political scientist Robert Putman looked into differences in quality of government, he asked why some Italian provincial governments function wonderfully (like the northern region of Emilia-Romagna), while others are plagued by corruption, mismanagement, and chaos. He found one explanation in the contrasting social structures of the villages and towns. Where people liked to work together toward common goals, they were usually blessed with good government, no matter that the context—football clubs, PTAs, choral societies, and the like—was usually apolitical.

Putnam argued that when people engage together freely, their interests converge. In a community with an active public life, it's difficult to act in secret, and politicians, knowing that their misuse of power won't be tolerated, are more honest from the get-go.

By contrast, weaker social ties make it easier for corruption to thrive. An individual feels helpless in the face of clans and old-boy networks. In order not to fall behind, everyone cheats as best they can—and those in power pocket more and more.[21]

In the long run, mismanagement and misrule can thrive only where there's no opposition. A civic sense assumes trust, but the reverse is also true: the more people are willing to act on each other's behalf, the easier it is to prevent the abuse of trust. Honest leaders and effective laws and institutions are important, but without a well-developed public life, their effectiveness is stymied. A civic sense is the foundation on which democracy rests.

Where there is a strong civic sense, the discrepancy in incomes is relatively small, and where social cohesion is weaker, the gap in wealth grows correspondingly. Putnam found that in the United States, states with a more equitable distribution of resources also enjoyed a stronger network of associations, civic and social action organizations, and clubs. Not only do more people vote, but they have more trust in one another—and a greater likelihood of reaching old age.[22] Justice, civic sense, and life expectancy are all connected: where the social structure is intact, people live happier lives.

A LIFE IN SLOW MOTION

Mass unemployment, too, shatters social cohesion. Surveying life satisfaction in different regions, the Swiss scholar Bruno Frey came to the conclusion that unemployment has a negative effect on the well-being of *all* members of a society, including those who have jobs.[23] At fault are the widespread fear of job loss and the absence of solidarity. Even those who are better positioned feel the effects of social rejection.

The suffering that the enforced lack of activity causes the unemployed is shown by a famous example from Austria. Marienthal was a thriving little town south of Vienna, until its largest employer, a textile factory, began to founder in 1929. After a struggle of several months, the factory shut down. It was a time of great economic hardship, when no one who had lost a job had any hope of finding another.

Thanks to unemployment insurance, no one was destitute. Nonetheless, the inactivity among the previously proud workers had a devastating effect, as was documented in detail by the Austrian social scientists Marie Jahoda and Paul Lazarsfeld.

Marienthal suffered an agonizing decline. Without any hope of turning things around by their own efforts, its citizens resigned themselves to their fate and showed all the symptoms of learned helplessness. After a year, the rich social life of the town was almost completely extinguished. The park that the workers had laid out went to seed, although the townspeople had more than enough time to care for it. But the unemployed could summon only enough energy to run their own small households. "I have no interest in going out any more," complained one of them. Depressed, they didn't even manage to use the extra time to read. The number of books checked out of the free public library declined by half. The number of newspaper subscriptions dropped even further. A previously active Socialist Party functionary said, "I used to read the worker's paper until I knew it by heart. But now, though I've got more time, I just look at it a little, and then I throw it away."

The unemployed of Marienthal lost their sense of time. In diaries that they kept at the request of the researchers, they recorded entries like the following: "4–5 pm: Fetched milk. 5–6 pm: Walked home from the park." A stretch of a few hundred yards that would previously have taken five minutes, now took an hour! In order to better understand what was going on, Jahoda and Lazarsfeld positioned themselves at a window overlooking the main street and measured people's pace as they walked by. It was less than three kilometers per hour. The unemployed were crawling by at a speed less than half that of a purposeful pedestrian. And the longer they were without a job, the more passive and flaccid they became.

ILLNESS AND INACTIVITY

Nineteen thirty isn't 2006, and Marienthal isn't Europe. The unemployed receive much better financial support now than they did then, and the economy isn't even close to the kind of crisis that people went through in the 1930s. But the devastating consequences of inactivity are much as they were.

Many of those who suffer long-term unemployment have no realistic hope of ever finding work again, no matter how hard they try—especially if they're over fifty. And, as some half dozen studies show, they are less satisfied with their lives than are people with jobs. Some analyses even come to the conclusion that the loss of employment has a stronger impact on well-being than the death of a spouse.[24] People without work are more likely to suffer from psychological trouble and from stress-related illnesses like heart disease. They also have a diminished life expectancy.[25]

248

Sayings such as "There's no right to laziness" may be punchy soundbites, but the freedom of the unemployed person to sleep late is worthless, because he hasn't chosen the circumstances himself. To feel unneeded is humiliating. Like the people of Marienthal, the unemployed can easily succumb to depression and self-neglect. Unemployment is one of the most devastating examples of the damage that can result from learned helplessness.

Social welfare staff tend to manage lives rather than to help people onto their feet, though the United Kingdom and the Netherlands have shown how it is possible for people to find work again and to overcome their feeling of helplessness, if they are actively supported in their search for job.[26]

THE BLESSING OF SELF-DETERMINATION

The key to happiness in society is to be in control of our own lives. "Losing one's autonomy can be a devastating experience," says the New York stress researcher Bruce McEwen.[27] It doesn't particularly matter whether people have to submit to the will of others or to circumstance (like the unemployed of Marienthal)— the experience of having no control always results in stress that is damaging both psychologically and physically.

We experience this helplessness-induced stress even in

relatively trivial situations—at the airport, for example, when the ground crew announces again and again that for mechanical reasons, takeoff has, unfortunately, been delayed. We know in principle that whether we arrive at our destination a little earlier or a little later hardly matters in the long run, and that it's senseless to get upset—after all, what say do we have over the timing of takeoff? But it is exactly this powerlessness that is the problem.

The stress response to loss of control is an ancient legacy of evolution. The stress researcher Robert Sapolsky, observing baboons in the Serengeti, noted how much the low-ranking males suffer when they have to obey the will of the alpha animal. Although the underdogs in no way suffer from want—there's plenty in the Serengeti for everyone—the leaders of the horde are notably healthier. The lower baboons are in the hierarchy, the more stress hormones circulate in their blood, the more often they're sick, and the younger they die.[28]

In humans, very subtle—and completely ordinary—forms of subordination can influence long-term well-being and health. This has been demonstrated by any number of examples:

◆ The citizens of East Germany enjoyed much less choice in their lives than West Germans. State power was widely feared. Feelings of helplessness were expressed even in body language, as the psychologist Gabriele Oettingen showed when she compared the gestures of customers in workers' bars in West and East Berlin in 1986. While in the West about three-quarters of the faces expressed at least an occasional smile, in East Berlin it was less than a fourth. Still more noticeable was the difference in posture, which, according to Oettingen, expresses either self-confidence or depression. In the bars of West Berlin one out of every two customers

249

sat upright, while in the East it wasn't even one in twenty![29]

♦ As a rule, the lower employees are in the hierarchy, the less control they have in shaping their jobs—with negative consequences for their health, as a study of more than ten thousand government officials in the United Kingdom showed. The results are similar to Sapolsky's. Clear differences could even be seen between the heads of offices and their main department heads. Those in the lowest levels of the hierarchy called in sick three times as often as their bosses. Their risk of death was also an almost unbelievable factor of three. And yet the differences in income among Her Majesty's servants were relatively small, and they all received medical care from the such as nutrition, physical activity, and smoking, explain these huge differences. The cause is a hierarchical structure that accords different degrees of authority in their jobs. The lower their rank, the more often the bureaucrats expressed their sense of powerless in sentences such as "Other people make decisions about my work," or "I can't even decide for myself when to take a break."[30]

♦ Even a relatively small increase in autonomy can make people much happier—and lengthen their lives. This was evident when doctors in old age homes in the United States encouraged residents to decide the details of their daily lives themselves.[31] They were no longer simply presented with their meals, but could chose from a menu. Instead of being transported by bus for coffee and cake, they could choose from among several excursions. And while previously the caretakers watered the plants, the old people took over this responsibility for themselves. These almost ludicrously small changes worked miracles: the old people assumed greater responsibility for the other aspects of their lives, got together more often, became ill less frequently, and in interviews expressed greater happiness. Most striking of all, the annual death rate was reduced by half.

The more the old people were encouraged by the staff to take their lives into their own hands, the better they did. And the reverse was also true—their condition deteriorated as responsibility was taken from them. Even subtleties counted. When students came to visit the old people, the health of all the residents improved. But those who could determine the timing of the visits did best of all.[32]

DEMOCRACY MAKES PEOPLE HAPPY

The happiest Europeans live in Switzerland. The explanation lies surely not in the beautiful landscape, nor in their ethnicity, because whether they speak German, French, or Italian, they're still more satisfied than their neighbors in Germany, France, and Italy. Switzerland's prosperity and its propensity for cleanliness are also negligible factors.

More important for people's well-being is the unique way in which their communal life is governed, as the Swiss economists Alois Stutzer and Bruno Frey discovered.[33] In Switzerland, several political systems exist concurrently, because important decisions are not made in the capital, Berne, but in the twenty-six cantons. The cantons apply the instruments of direct democracy: referendums enable citizens to amend the constitution, enact new laws, abolish existing ones, and control the budget.

But the degree of participation that the individual cantons allow their citizens varies enormously. In some cantons, such as Basel-Land, the government has to consult with the electorate on expenses above a certain level, and if voters want to get an issue onto the political agenda, it only takes a few signatures. Because the chances for success are good, the citizens of these cantons have a strong incentive to participate in politics. But in other cantons, Geneva, for example, the hurdles are higher. There the political system is more like a parliamentary democracy, such as in Germany.

Stutzer and Frey asked 6,100 Swiss about their life satisfaction and compared the figures with opportunities for influence. The result: the more people could participate in public decision making, the more satisfied they were with their lives. This effect is so strong that moving from Geneva to Basel-Land, seen statistically, does more for well-being than a rise from the lowest income level (about $1,000) to the highest income level ($3,600). Political influence has a much greater impact on satisfaction than the size of one's bank account. Democracy makes people happy.

Are people in Swiss cantons where ordinary citizens play a larger role in public decision making happier because schools, hospitals, and swimming pools function better there? Or is there a direct satisfaction that comes from the ability to take the fate of their community and region into their own hands? To this question, also, Stutzer and Frey have an answer: the second explanation seems to apply. Among foreigners, who also benefit from the fruits of a better administration, but have no vote, life satisfaction in a direct democracy rises noticeably less than among citizens. A happy country is one in which politics is more than a spectator sport.[34]

THE MAGIC TRIANGLE OF WELL-BEING

A civic sense, social equality, and control over our own lives constitute the magic triangle of well-being in society. The better these three criteria are met, the more satisfied people are with their lives. But one can't view these factors in isolation. They need and reinforce one another.

We've seen this in our examples. In Marienthal, civic sense was forfeited when people lost control over their own lives. The garden laid out by the workers went to seed when people were excluded from the economic life of their society and made to feel helpless.

In Roseto, on the other hand, solidarity was such a strong feature of the social fabric that people lived with a sense of great security. The foundation of this solidarity was social balance. Where discrepancies in income existed, their external signs were blurred. When this changed, the sense of community was lost.

Finally, in Switzerland, citizen control over cantonal life creates the conditions for people to join together and work on behalf of their region. And this is why the Swiss are more satisfied than other Europeans.

Civic sense, social equality, and control over our own lives increase well-being, because they diminish the stress that people are otherwise vulnerable to when they live together. At the same time, they increase our freedom to shape our lives according to our talents and opportunities.

A happy society gives its citizens the ability to decide life's many small and large questions for themselves. It helps individuals realize their plans and hopes. According to the Indian economist and Nobel Prize–winner Amartya Sen, who studied the state of Kerala, the aim of every social development should be to increase the choices of the individual. Other goals, such as increasing prosperity, are a second priority.[35]

But enjoying freedom means taking responsibility. Widespread prejudice notwithstanding, this obligation is a pleasure rather than a burden, as the comparison of the Swiss cantons shows. Individuals profit from the advantages of a happy society when *they* make it work. After all, government can't carry its citizens on their quest for happiness.

Different points of the magic triangle require different levels of effort. The individual has little direct influence on economic justice. A society reaches this goal slowly, usually by raising the quality of education for a large number of people and gradually changing their culture.[36] But when they exercise control over their own lives, citizens set changes in motion. Sometimes this requires governmental or workplace reform that can take years, or even decades to implement. But a measure of freedom can often be won in small steps—for example, when childcare facilities establish flexible opening hours and schools take advantage of flexible schedules, thus enabling parents to be less constrained in their jobs.

A sense of civic responsibility means that everyone can initiate changes of this kind. Civic responsibility means engagement. Even acting only on our own behalf gives us a sense of self-determination, whether it be participating in the PTA to reshape the curriculum, taking on a leadership role at the office, or voting to replace the president of the soccer club after the season's losses. Practicing civic responsibility increases our well-being twice over: through the results of our actions, and by the pleasure the activity itself accords.

Inactivity and the feeling of helplessness are the greatest enemies of happiness—a thought you have encountered throughout this book. Activity, on the other hand, is the key to positive feelings. This applies to the private happiness of the individual, and even more to the happiness of society as a whole. A happy life isn't a gift of fate. To make it happen, we have to act.

EPILOGUE
SIX BILLION PATHS TO HAPPINESS

OUR LUST FOR life is inborn. The itch of anticipation, the ecstasy of enjoyment, and the warm flow of sympathy are part of the basic equipment of our brains. They are gifts that are necessary for survival.

People can be happy in almost any situation. External conditions determine well-being much less than we usually think. Extensive studies have shown that the enjoyment of life is neither a question of age nor of gender. It doesn't depend on your IQ, or on how many children you have, or on the size of your bank account. A craftsman in Bangladesh has different but not fewer opportunities for enjoyment than an office worker in Boston. Both—all of us—have to use the opportunities at hand.

Many people look for happiness "like a drunk for his house," in the words of the French philosopher Voltaire. "They can't find it, but they know it exists." But since our capacity for positive feelings is hardwired into the brain and influenced only minimally by external conditions (according to many studies, less than 10 percent), there is only one explanation for Voltaire's conundrum: hunting for happiness, we trip over our own feet.

In this book, I've tried to introduce a few strategies for achieving well-being and to show how and why they work. Unlike many such efforts, these suggestions don't rest primarily on experience and transmitted wisdom. Rather, they are based on recent discoveries in neuroscience, especially on the insight that the brain is malleable and that it can change in adulthood—which is what enables us to train our relationship with our feelings. And neuroscience has shown something else: happiness is more than simply the absence of unhappiness. We have dedicated circuits in our heads for positive feelings, enabling pleasure and enjoyment to thwart negative emotions such as sadness and fear, much as wind drives away fog.

Our ability to make our lives happier rests on these two basic principles: we can strengthen the circuits for the positive feelings with conscious practice, and we can seek out situations that give us pleasure and enjoyment. A few examples will refresh your memory.

- ◆ The well-being of body and the well-being of mind are inseparably linked. Emotions have their origins in the body. Exercise and sex have proven the surest means of raising our spirits.
- ◆ Activity makes us happier than doing nothing. The often-heard advice to take a vacation when you're "down" is wrong. Our controls over thoughts, intentions, and feelings are closely connected in the brain, so we worry easily when the brain lacks anything else to keep busy.

256

On the other hand, the brain's *expectation system* releases a sense of anticipation as soon as we set a goal, and we experience triumph when we reach it. Thus, activity almost always leads to positive feelings.

◆ An alert mind increases a sense of well-being even when it's only observing. Concentrated perception is often accompanied by feelings of elation. This sense of mild ecstasy resembles anticipation. It, too, we owe to the *expectation system*. This capacity for enjoyment through attentiveness is something we can learn.

◆ By giving in to negative emotions like anger and sadness, not only do we fail to appease them, but we actually reinforce them. Letting off steam can only hurt us. The conviction that it is otherwise rests on a psychology that has been disproved. On the contrary, it is possible—and much better for our emotional balance—to control such feelings consciously.

◆ Variety gives pleasure. The *expectation system* is quickly dulled to pleasurable stimuli, which set in motion a vicious cycle of desire and reward. When we change our pleasures more frequently, we avoid taking something for granted. And in learning to value the unexpected and to see from new perspectives, we stoke our vitality.

◆ When in doubt, it's better to have control over our decisions than to have our wishes fulfilled. The control over our own fate is for most of us an absolute condition for happiness and satisfaction. Helplessness is one of the least bearable of all feelings. People—and animals—respond to it with serious mental and physical deficits. When a wish is fulfilled only at the price of dependence (going into debt, for example), one usually does better by choosing freedom.

But what is most important of all for well-being is our relationship to other people. It is no exaggeration to equate happiness with friendship and love. The attention we pay to those close to us redounds to our own happiness.

These basic principles are valid for all people, since our emotions and many of our behaviors are a legacy from evolution. Nonetheless, within this framework we all make our own choices and have our own needs and preferences. For this reason, the recommendations in this book, even if they are based on modern science and the experience of many thousands of people, are only meant as suggestions. The choice has to be yours.

Therefore, the most important task in the search for happiness is to know yourself. This doesn't require anything particularly elaborate or special. It's enough to pay attention to your reactions to daily stimuli and to experiment a bit with settled habits. In this way, we get better and better at knowing what works for us. We will all discover our own answers. We are six billion people, and there are six billion paths to happiness.

NOTES

Introduction

1. Ramachandran describes his research in his excellent book *Phantoms in the Brain: Probing the Mysteries of the Human Mind* (New York, 1998).

2. There is one word designated for the happiness that gives one a pleasant feeling (*sukha*), another for the satisfaction one gets from an accomplishment (*krtarthata*), others yet for joy (*ananda*) and for the pleasant physical feeling after yoga exercises (*sampad*). There's even a word for the excited happiness one experiences after the fear that comes from having seen the Divinity.

3. The experiment was conducted by the American cultural psychologist Paul Rozin. He used the classical Indian treatise on dramaturgy, the *Natyashashtra*. Written more than 2000 years ago, it contains the oldest transmitted discussion of acting and feelings in drama. While the negative feelings described in the *Natyashashtra* largely correspond to our own, the Indian text contains many more kinds of happiness than exist in Western culture. See Hejmadi, Davidson and Rozin 2000.

4. These are conservative estimates. See Kessler et al. 2005 and references cited therein.

5. The fewest number of reported suicides are in South America, Africa and some Asian countries. Argentina, for example, has, relative to the size of its population, half as many suicides as Germany. In some countries like Egypt, there are hardly any suicides at all. See *Demographic Yearbook of the United Nations*, editions from 1981 to 1997.

6. The risk that a Parisian, for example, who was born between 1945 and 1954 suffered a serious depression before the age of 15 was barely 4 percent. For those born in the following ten years, the risk increased to 12 percent. The figures for American cities are similar. See Cross-National Collaborative Group, "The Changing Rate of Major Depression," *JAMA* 268 (v. 21), pp. 3,098–3,105 (1992).

7. No one knows just what it is that causes this psychological suffering.

Possible reasons: urbanization, work-related stress, divorce rates, or the decline of physical labor. One thing, however, is certain: the alarming increase in depression cannot be explained simply by asserting that more people are seeking and receiving psychological help earlier.

8. Currently the consequences of serious depression (major unipolar depression) rank fourth on the World Health Organization's list of leading causes of disability worldwide. See Murray and Lopez 1997.
9. Isen 1987; Isen and Daubmann 1984; Murray et al. 1990; Frederickson 1998.
10. Isen 2001; Basso 1996; Baron 1987; Myers 1987.

260

Chapter 1: The Secret of Smiling

1. There are good summaries of Ekman's studies in Ekman 1999, Ekman 1993.
2. Ito and Cacioppo 2000.
3. Ekman et al 1990.
4. Duchenne 1991.
5. Birnbaumer and Schmidt 1999.
6. Damasio 1995.
7. Bechera et al. 1997.
8. Pascal 1980.
9. An extensive discussion of the differences between feelings and emotion is found in Damasio 2000.
10. Damasio et al. 2000.
11. Damasio 2000.
12. Critchley, Mathias and Dolan 2001; Damasio 2000.
13. Tatarkiewicz 1976.
14. Ekman and Davidson 1993.

Chapter 2: Positive Feelings as a Compass

1. Damasio 1995.
2. Bechara et al. 1994.
3. Ito et al. 1998; Crites et al. 1995.
4. Aristotle 1998.

Chapter 3: The Happiness System

1. Birnbaumer and Schmidt 1999.
2. Ramachandran 2001.
3. Right hemispheric neurons that respond to unpleasant stimuli: Kawasaki H. et al. 2001. On left hemispheric counterparts see Damasio 2001.
4. Davidson et al. 2000.
5. Fox and Davidson 1984.
6. This applies to right-handed people. Because there are fewer left-handed people, they are almost never considered in this kind of study. So we don't know what the effects of right brain dominance (left-handedness) are

on the processing of feelings. But there are indications that a somewhat higher frequency of emotional troubles occurs among left-handers than in the general population.

7. Damasio 1995.
8. Ekman 1990.
9. For the underlying neurobiology, see Zieglgänsberger and Spanagel 1999.
10. See, for example, Horn 1998, Russell 1946.
11. PET scans and functional MRIs show that the activity in the left prefrontal cortex is in inverse relation to the activity in the amygdala. As activity in the left prefrontal cortex increases, activity decreases in the amygdala, and vice versa. See Abercrombie et al. 1996.
12. Jackson et al. 2000.
13. Mallick and McCandless 1966; Travis 1989.
14. Wheeler, Davidson and Tomarken 1993; Davidson and Tomarken 1993.
15. R. Davidson, personal communication with the author; Davidson et al. 1999.
16. Davidson and Fox 1989.
17. Lykken and Tellegen 1996.
18. Lykken 1999.
19. Francis et al. 2000.
20. R. Davidson: personal communication.

Chapter 4: The Malleable Brain

1. Naj 1992.
2. For summaries see Rozin 1990; Bayens at al. 1996; Stevenson and Yeomans 1995.
3. Rozin 1990.
4. Kleist 1985.
5. Klein 2000.
6. Cited in Horn 1998.
7. Horn 1998.
8. O'Craven and Kanwisher 2000.
9. Ovid: Metamorphoses, XV, 147–151.
10. Bonhoeffer used a so-called two-photon fluorescence microscope, which enables one to see the changes in the neurons three-dimensionally and in real time.
11. Engert and Bonheoffer 1999.
12. This description is fundamentally correct, but somewhat simplified. The direct connection between stimulus and emotional reaction is due primarily to the connection between the subcortical regions, which release the emotions, and the prefrontal cortex, which suppresses the formation of strong emotions.
13. There are good reasons why the plasticity of the areas of the cerebrum that are responsible for perception and the body's movement have been studied more than other parts of the brain. The so-called somatosensory cortex

("soma" is classical Greek for "body") is immediately beneath the top of the skull and can therefore be viewed relatively easily with probes and scanners. But it's very likely that similar neuroplastic processes (as researchers in gray-cell reprogramming call them) occur in many other regions. Since these changes in the brain have been studied only relatively recently, much research still needs to be done.

14. Pascual-Leone and Torres 1993; Pascual-Leone et al. 1995.
15. Similar observations were made in cellists, whose brain areas for the fingers of the left hand, which plays on the fingerboard, are clearly larger than those of the right hand, which simply holds the bow. When neurologists examined the brains of secretaries and mechanics with fine-motor skills, they found an unusually large number of neuron branches for the sense of touch and finger control. Ebert et al 1995; Scheibel et al. 1990.

16. Maguire et al. 2000.
17. The molecular processes of short and long-term potentiation are described extensively in Kandel et al. 1996.
18. Cohen-Cory and Fraser 1995; McAllister et al. 1995.
19. Duman, Heninger and Nestler 1997.
20. Bailey and Chen 1983.
21. A change of this kind could not be found in a comparison group that was not treated. Baxter et al. 1992; Schwartz et al. 1996.
22. Brody et al. 2001.
23. Bench et al. 1995.
24. Kandel, Schwartz and Jessell 1995.
25. Wurtz and Goldberg 1989.
26. Radhakrishnan 2000.
27. Flor 2002.
28. Thich Nhat Hanh 1995.
29. Dalai Lama and Cutler 1998.

Chapter 5: Origins in the Animal Kingdom

1. LeDoux 1996.
2. de Waal 1996.
3. Nesse and Berridge 1997.
4. Pedersen et al. 1982.
5. Blaffer Hrdy 1999.
6. Descartes 1984.

Chapter 6: Desire

1. All citations are taken from Sacks 1973, which also includes a detailed report of Leonard's illness.
2. More precisely, L-Dopa is the precursor substance that the brain itself naturally transforms into dopamine. There would be little sense in giving dopamine directly to a patient: since it can't pass the blood-brain barrier, it would be filtered out of the blood on its way to the brain.

3. The recipients of the flow of dopamine are the centers of the cerebral cortex that are responsible for our pursuing our goals, as well as controlling the voluntary muscles. Other dopamine branches reach the *nucleus accumbens* in the prefrontal cortex, which plays an important role in the memory of good experiences, and the amygdala, which releases emotions and stores them in memory. As one goes through this listing, it's notable how many parts of the brain receive dopamine signals. That is why this transmitter has such an impact on the functioning of the brain, influencing our thoughts and feelings, how we see the world and act in it.

4. People suffering from Parkinson's disease, who also suffer from dopamine deficiency, now receive L-Dopa regularly. There are side effects, but they're minor. Nonetheless, L-Dopa (also called Lovodopa) and similar medications are not a cure-all for Parkinson's. Their effectiveness diminishes over time because increasing numbers of cells in the *substantia negra* degenerate.

5. Dopamine can also have an inhibiting effect on some neurons. See Zieglgänsberger and Spanagel 1999.

6. Wickelgren 1997.

7. Schultz, Apicella and Ljungberg 1992 and 1993; Schultz, Dayan and Montague 1997; Wickelgren 1997.

8. Schultz 2000.

9. Montague, Dayan, Person and Sejnowski 1995.

10. This process has been shown to occur in living rats' brains. After ten minutes, the coupling strength of the neurons in the midbrain, which control behavior, changed.

11. This does not mean, however, that the bees experience something similar to human pleasure when they discover an especially rich blossom. A bee doesn't need feelings, which serve to steer complex beings through their intricate lives. A bee lives only in the present. Unlike humans, it can't mentally juggle the possibilities presented by the future and ask itself, for example, whether it wouldn't rather watch television than go out and gather honey.

12. Elliott, Friston and Dolan 2000.

13. Koepp et al. 1998.

14. Fiorino, Coury and Phillips 1997.

15. Rodriguez-Manzo and Fernandez-Guasti 1994; 1995.

16. Rolls 1999; Hamer 1998.

17. Baker and Bellis 1995.

18. Marina Maria Morsini, the daughter of one of Venice's foremost patrician families, is identified in Casanova's memoirs only as M.M. But there is no question as to her identity. See Casanova 1964.

19. Vincent 1990.

20. Aristotle 1998.

21. Turning off curiosity is difficult and requires strong measures. People who suffer from schizophrenia can temporarily lose their curiosity when

doctors give them halperidol, a drug that blocks dopamine's natural effect. Sometimes there's no alternative but to give a strong dose of this medication to patients suffering from major attacks in order to protect them from their own fantasies. Halperidol moderates the insanity, but it also hampers one's ability to move, and it diminishes desire and curiosity. It's sad to see such people shuffling stiffly in hospital corridors as if they were automatons, interested in nothing.

22. It's different with aspects of one's personality such as fearfulness or being prone to anger, when the particular circumstances are much more important in determining how someone responds. It's usually not justifiable to label someone "fearful" or "anger-prone"—but there are certainly people who are innately more curious, or less so. See Spielberger 1975; Panskepp 1990.

23. Blum 1996.
24. In the Berlin edition of 1964.
25. Isen, personal communication, and Isen et al. 1991.
26. Ashby et al. 2001; Ashby et al. 1999.
27. The particular impact of dopamine on the *gyrus cinguli* is noteworthy. Parkinson patients, who suffer from dopamine deficiency, can retain new impressions and control their attention only with difficulty.
28. On dopamine and schizophrenia, see Feldman et al. 1997.

Chapter 7: Enjoyment

1. McInerney, 2000.
2. Breiter conducted his experiments on addicts taking cocaine—a particularly drastic example.
3. Murphy et al. 1990.
4. Pfeiffer 1996.
5. Cromwell and Berridge 1993.
6. Cooper and Kirkham 1993.
8. This is shown by the example of rat mothers who were willing to care for completely unknown rat babies when opiates were artificially released in their brains. See Thompson and Kristal, 1996.
8. *Odyssey*, 1996
9. Lewin 1964.
10. Loomis et al. 1898, cited in Panksepp 1998.
11. In a letter to Theodor Storm, cited in Randow 2001.
12. Montmayeur et al. 2001; Max et al. 2001.
13. Vincent 1996.
14. Kurihara and Kashiwayanagi 1998; Rolls 1999.
15. Kerverne et al. 1989.
16. Panksepp et al. 1980.
17. Panksepp 1998.
18. Herz and Spanagel 1995.
19. Nuñez et al. 1998.

20. Sapolsky 1998.
21. Namely in the hypothalamus and the striatum, two centers under the cerebral cortex that are responsible for arousal, movement, and desire. See Persky 1987; Panksepp 1998.
22. Kohelet 2; 11, 17.

Chapter 8: The Dark Side of Desire

1. Olds and Milner 1954; Olds 1977.
2. Reynolds et al. 2001.
3. Reynolds et al. 2001.
4. Smith 1971.
5. Breiter et al. 2001.
6. Zeiglgänsberger and Spanagel 1999.
7. Sell et al. 1999.
8. This is especially valid for addiction to alcohol and nicotine addictions, by far the most widespread of dependencies. By contrast, many people (and, it seems, also lab animals) perceive cocaine and heroine as pleasant the first time they take it.
9. Linsky et al. 1985.
10. Grinspoon and Bakalar 1986.
11. Marlatt et al. 1975.
12. Charles O'Brien, University of Pennsylvania, personal communication with the author.
13. Piazza et al. 1989.
14. Thanos et al. 2001.
15. Wecker 1998.
16. "Die Kokain-Gesellschaft." In: *Der Spiegel* 44/2000.

Chapter 9: Love

1. Moss 1978; Vincent 1996.
2. Ferguson et al. 2000; 2001.
3. Young et al. 1999.
4. Insel and Young 2000.
5. Insel and Young 2001.
6. Imperato-McGinley 1974.
7. Kandel et al. 1996.
8. Carter 1998.
9. Oomura et al. 1988.
10. Nonetheless, these mechanisms of sexual desire utilize the all-purpose system for desire, as described in chapters 6 and 8. In animal experiments, if dopamine's effect is blocked, sexual desire vanishes entirely.
11. LeVay 1993.
12. LeVay 1991.
13. Kandel 1996.
14. Murphy et al. 1987.

15. Landgraf et al. 1992.
16. This was demonstrated in a strain of rats in which a genetic defect caused a vasopressin deficiency. Panskepp 1998.
17. Sodersten et al. 1983.
18. Carmichael et al. 1994.
19. Goldfoot et al. 1980.
20. Bartels and Zeki 2001.
21. Panksepp 1998.
22. Krican et al. 1995.
23. Lorberbaum et al. 1999.
24. McCarthy 1990.
25. Insel and Young 2001.
26. Uvnäs-Mosberg et al. 1990.
27. Argyle 1987.
28. Kobrin and Hendershot 1977.
29. *Psychologie Heute* 03/2001.

Chapter 10: Friendship

1. Sapolsky et al. 1997.
2. Sapolsky 2001.
3. Argyle and Lu 1990; Okun et al. 1984.
4. House et al. 1989; Argyle 2000.
5. Spiegel et al. 1989; Spiegel 1991.
6. For comprehensive, current and clearly presented information, see the homepages of the National Cancer Institute (http://www.cancer.gov), the University of Pennsylvania's OncoLink (http://www.oncolink.upenn.edu), and the American Cancer Society (http://www.cancer.org).
7. Berkman 1983; House et al. 1988.
8. Sapolsky 2000.
9. Kiecolt-Glaser et al. 1984.
10. Coe et al. 1989.
11. Riley 1981.
12. Rosengren et al. 1993.
13. Panskepp 1998.
14. Panskepp 1998.
15. Field et al. 1986.
16. The medieval chronicler Salimbene of Parma, quoted in Montagu 1974.
17. Winslow and Insel 1991.
18. Surprisingly, addictive drugs calm restlessness caused by loneliness better than standard tranquilizers, which are otherwise effective against anxiety. Panskepp sees this as further proof for his thesis that we have a dedicated brain circuit that causes people in isolation to panic, and therefore makes us seek closeness to others. If fear of spiders and elevators is treated most effectively with Valium and similar medications (so-called benzodiazepines), and loneliness, on the other hand, with opiates, so these two

variants of fear must be fundamentally different and come about in different ways. See Panskepp 1998.

19. Cocteau 1998.
20. On ecstasy and dopamine, see, for example, Liechti and Vollenweider 2000, Obradovic et al. 1996.
21. A. Shulgin: personal communication with the author. This passage should not be misunderstood as a recommendation to take Ecstasy. Although this drug probably does not result in addiction, there are indications that it damages the brain when used repeatedly. Furthermore, the pills that are normally available are almost never pure Ecstasy (chemically MDMA) but almost always a mixture that includes other substances. This makes it difficult to predict its effect on the user and thus riskier. But in spite of the danger of misuse, the effects of drugs have brought valuable insights to science.
22. de Waal 1997.
23. de Waal and Berger 2000.
24. de Waal 1997.
25. Damasio 2000.

Chapter 11: Passion—A User's Manual

1. For further information, see chapter 14.
2. Biddle and Mutrie 1991.
3. Scully et al. 1998.
4. Biddle and Mutrie 1991.
5. Moses et al. 1989.
6. Rolls 1999; O'Doherty et al. 2000.
7. Tagore 1976.
8. Zajonc 1968; Frederick and Loewenstein 2000.
9. Naipaul 1991.
10. Kiecolt-Glaser et al. 1987; Kiecolt-Glaser et al. 1994.
11. Kiecolt-Glaser et al. 1994.
12. Montaigne 2001.
13. The experiments that Jaak Panksepp undertook on young rats are interesting in this connection. Playful fighting is their primary expression of social contact. Rats that are given a small dose of morphium win these fights. Apparently a kind of social confidence is enhanced that enables the animal to easily win the upper hand. See Panskepp et al. 1985.
14. Meyers 1992.
15. Robins and Rieger 1991.
16. House et al. 1988. Corresponding differences are evident even in mortality rates. The life expectancy of people who live alone is much lower in all age brackets than among people who live with a partner or in a family. See Stroebe and Stroebe 1991.
17. Argyle 2000. A relationship with a long-term partner gives life stability. This seems to be another explanation for the greater well-being of people

who are in such relationships. Happiness and health force us to look after ourselves, even if it's sometimes inconvenient, and our partners make sure we stick with it. Thus, the lack of freedom in a committed relationship has its advantages.

18. Panksepp 1998.

Chapter 12: Conquering Our Shadows

1. According to the internationally recognized DSM-IV criteria, a suspicion of serious depression is warranted when on every day (or almost every day) within two weeks a person experiences at least five of the following symptoms: sadness; a sharply diminished interest, or no interest, in all or almost all activities; significant weight loss or weight gain, or decreased or increased appetite; sleeplessness or too much sleep; physical restlessness; tiredness or loss of energy; feelings of worthlessness or guilt; recurring thoughts of death or suicide.

   Further information and resources can be found at the Institute of Mental Health, http://www.nimh.nih.gov/publicat/depression.cfm.
2. Lindner 1968.
3. Hiroto 1974.
4. Bench et al. 1995. Rogers et al. 1998 give an overview of the many brain scan studies on depression.
5. Henriques and Davidson 2000.
6. Baker et al. 1997.
7. Wenzlaff 1993.
8. Matt et al. 1992.
9. Sapolsky 1998.
10. Solomon 2001 gives an impressive firsthand account in conjunction with research results and a literature review.
11. Rogers et al. 1998.
12. Vogel 2000.
13. Rajkowska 2000.
14. Wayne Drevets, a University of Pittsburgh psychiatrist, found certain parts of the prefrontal cortex diminished by 40 percent. Not only the neurons but the so-called glia cells, which support and clean the actual nerve cells, also atrophy.

    That depression has an effect on the brain structure is a new discovery, though it's not yet universally accepted. It has been found that depression change brain structure not only in humans but also in monkeys and rats. See Duman et al. 2000.
15. Vogel 2000.
16. Lopez et al. 1999; Lopez et al. 1998.
17. Malberg et al. 2000.
18. Duman et al. 1997.
19. Baker et al. 1997.
20. R. Davidson, personal communication; Robbins 2000.

21. Kempermann et al. 1997.
22. Chaouloff 1997.
23. Blumental et al. 1999; Babyak et al. 2000; Steptoe et al. 1996.
24. Elkin et al. 1989.
25. Comer 2001.
26. Berk and Efran 1983; Svartberg and Stiles 1991.
27. For recommended guides to this method see Seligman 1991; Schwartz 1998.

Chapter 13: The Power of Perspective

1. Brickman, Coates and Janoff-Bulman 1978. 11 paraplegics, 18 quadraplegics and 22 lottery winners were interviewed. Subsequent studies, in which several hundred patients were interviewed, produced the same results.
2. Frederick and Loewenstein 2000.
3. N. Schwarz, personal communication with the author.
4. Kahneman 2000.
5. Medvec et al. 1995.
6. Parducci 1968.
7. Seligman 1991 gives a good overview.
8. Smith, Diener and Garonzik 1990.
9. Montaigne 2001.
10. Schwarz et al. 1988.
11. Strack et al. 1990.
12. Russell 1977.
13. Brown 1978.
14. Epictetus 1995.
15. Diener 1985.
16. Löwer 2000.
17. Diener et al. 1993; Haring et al. 1984.
18. Brickman and Campbell 1971.
19. Schmuck et al. 2000; Kasser and Ryan 1996; Kasser and Ryan 1993; Ryan et al. 1999.
20. The effects were similar to those in a standard cognitive behavioral therapy. Fava et al. 1998; Fava 1999.

Chapter 14: Rapturous Moments

1. Luxemburg 2000.
2. Matthew 14: 28–31.
3. Rees et al. 1997.
4. Although the primate researcher Jane Goodall reports observing chimpanzees in the wild dancing joyfully under waterfalls, other primatologists are skeptical of an interpretation according to which the chimps' happiness derives from their perception of water as a life-giving force. It's much more likely that they simply enjoyed playing in the water.
5. Konsalik and Goetsche 1998.
6. Czikszentmihalyi 1992.

7. Lavie 1995.
8. Caplan et al. 1975.
9. Further research is required to confirm this theory. It would be expensive but absolutely doable with current techniques. One could, for example, experimentally give people who are engaged in intellectually demanding activities medication that blocks particular neurotransmitters. Another possibility would be to use scanning to observe the brains of experimental subjects while they're engaged in a given activity.
10. Durstewitz et al. 1999.
11. Wallace and Benson 1972.
12. Begley 2001.
13. Acts 9: 4.
14. On the mystical experiences of historical figures see Engel 1989; LaPlante 1993.
15. Newberg et al. 2001; Saver and Rabin 1997.
16. The firsthand accounts are reported in Begley 2001.
17. Newberg's findings are consistent with other studies. See Lazar et al. 2000.
18. Cook and Persinger 1997.

Chapter 15: The Magic Triangle

1. Incomes have risen about eightfold since the 1950s, and purchasing power is at least three times what it was. The difference in the two figures is a result of inflation.
2. Brecht 1979.
3. In the United States, the average purchasing power has increased enormously in the past fifty years, while the proportion of the population that describes itself as happy remains stubbornly at 33 percent. See Myers and Diener 1995.
4. This relationship still holds when one removes the formerly communist countries, which have undergone a difficult political and social transformation, from consideration.
5. Diener and Suhk 2000.
6. Sen 1999.
7. Wilkinson 1996.
8. Adler 2001.
9. Source: OECD-Document DEELSA/ELSA/WD (2000) 3.
10. Kawachi et al. 1997; Kaplan et al. 1996.
11. Measured against the proportion of total income earned by the poorest 20 percent of the population. Source: Economic Policy Institute, Center on Budget and Policy Priorities. There are other indicators for income distribution, but the correlation between inequality of income and mortality remains independent of whatever indicator is used. See Kennedy, Kawachi and Prothrow-Stith 1996; Kawachi and Kennedy 1997.
12. Wilkinson 1996.
13. For a good overview, see the World Bank: www.worldbank.org/poverty/inequality/intro.htm.

14. Kopp 2000; Kopp et al. 2000; WHO Regional Office for Europe: Atlas of Mortality in Europe 1980/81 and 1990/91. WHO Regional Publications, European Series, No. 75. Copenhagen 1997

15. Egolf et al. 1992; Bruhn and Wolf 1979

16. On the relation between cancer and the mind, see chapter 10, including endnote 6.

17. One of the earliest and still one of the best studies is the so-called Alameda Study, in which social researchers followed the lives of the inhabitants of Alameda County, California, in minute detail for a decade. See Berkman and Syme 1979. An analysis of the development of life expectations in England during the two world wars shows the enormous significance of an equitable distribution of goods, a sense of community, and a shared interest in society. From the worker up to the Peers of the Realm, food rationing was at the same low level across the board. Although economic productivity fell, from 1914 to 1918 and from 1940 to 1945, life expectancy in England was much higher than in the decades before or afterward. See Wilkinson 1996; Sen 1999.

18. The thesis that the egalitarian society of the Netherlands can be traced back to the constant threats from the sea stems from the English social historian Simon Schama. Cf. Shermer 2000.

19. All these quotations can be found in Blomberg 2001. The quotation from Perelman also comes from this book.

20. Argyle 1996.

21. Putnam 1993.

22. Putnam 2000; Kawachi et al. 1997; Kawachi and Kennedy 1997; Kaplan et al. 1996.

23. Frey 2001.

24. Clark and Oswald 2002.

25. Argyle 2000; Frey 2001; Argyle 1989; Ingelhart 1990; Lahelma 1989.

26. Kahlweit 2002.

27. B. McEwen: Stree and Health. Lecture at the annual conference of the American Association for the Advancement of Science, February 12, 2001, San Francisco.

28. Sapolsky 2000; Sapolsky 1998; Sapolsky 1993.

29. Oettingen and Seligman 1990.

30. The lower the government employees were on the social ladder, the greater was the negative effect on resistance to insulin and clotting factors in the blood. Resistance to insulin can have an impact on obesity and heart and circulatory problems. Too many clotting factors in the blood increase the risk of stroke. Both values deteriorate when someone is subject to constant stress. See Marmot et al. 1997; Brunner 1997; Marmot et al. 1991.

31. Sapolsky 1998.

32. Rodin 1986; Rowe and Kahn 1987.

33. Frey and Stutzer 2002; Frey 2001.

34. As the social psychologist Ed Diener determined, the countries whose

citizens are at the top of the life satisfaction rankings all have long democratic traditions. These countries have enjoyed free elections, freedom of the press, and the rule of law since at least 1920, interrupted only by German occupation. On the other hand, the citizens in all industrial countries whose current democracies were founded only after World War II or later (e.g., Germany, Poland, Spain) are less satisfied than in the traditionally democratic countries. It seems that the "civic sense" takes several generations to establish itself. Democracy has to seep into the mind.

35. Sen 1999; Sen 1982.
36. Sen 1999. On education's effect on well-being see Frey 2001; Ostrove et al. 2000.

BIBLIOGRAPHY

Abercrombie, H. C., et al.: Medial prefrontal and amygdalar glucose metabolism. In: *Psychophysiology* 33, p. 17, 1996.

Adler, N.: *Stress and Health: Biology, Behaviour and the Social Environment.* Lecture at the 167th Annual Conference of the American Association for the Advancement of Science in San Francisco, February 15–20, 2001.

Allman, J.: *Evolving Brains.* New York 2000.

Argyle, M.: *The Psychology of Happiness.* London, New York 1987.

———: *The Social Psychology of Work.* London 1989.

———: *The Social Psychology of Leisure.* London 1996.

———: Causes and correlates of happiness. In: Kahneman, D., et al. (ed.): *Well-Being: The Foundations of Hedonic Psychology.* New York 2000.

Argyle, M., and Lu, L.: The happiness of extraverts. In: *Personality and Individual Differences* 11, pp. 1,011–1,017, 1990.

Aristotle: *Nikomachische Ethik.* Frankfurt a.M. 1998.

Ashby, F., et al.: A neuropsychological theory of positive affect and its influence on cognition. In: *Psychological Review*, 106, pp. 529–550, 1999.

———: The effects of positive affect and arousal on working memory and executive attention. In: Moore, S., and Oaksford, M. (ed.): *Emotional Cognition. From Brain to Behaviour.* Amsterdam 2001.

Babyak, M., et al.: Exercise treatment for major depression: Maintenance of therapeutic benefit at 10 months. In: *Psychosomatic Medicine*, September/October 2000.

Bailey, C. H., and Chen, M.: Morphological basis of long-term habituation and sensitization in Aplysia. In: *Science* 220, pp. 91–93, 1983.

Baker, R., and Bellis, M.: *Human Sperm-Competition: Copulation, Competition and Infidelity.* London 1995.

Baker, S., et al.: The interaction between mood and cognitive function studied with PET. In: *Psychological Medicine* 27, pp. 565–576, 1997.

Baron, R.: Interviewer's mood and the reaction to job applicants: The influence of affective states on applied social judgements. In: *Journal of Applied Social Psychology*, 17, pp. 911–926, 1987.

Bartels, A., and Zeki, S.: The neural basis of romantic love. In: *NeuroReport* 11, pp. 3,829–3,834, 2001.

Basso, M., et al.: Mood and global-local visual processing. In: *Journal of the International Neuropsychological Society*, 2, pp. 249–255, 1996.

Baudelaire, C.: *Baudelaire.* Translated and edited by Laurence Lerner. London, 1999.

Baxter, L.R., et al.: Caudate glucose metabolic rate changes with both drug and behavior therapy for obsessive-compulsive disorder. In: *Archives of General Psychiatry* 49, pp. 681–689, 1992.

Bayens, F., et al.: Observational evaluative conditioning of an embedded stimulus element. In: *European Journal of Social Psychology* 26, pp. 15–28, 1996.

Bechara, A., et al.: Insensitivity to future consequences following damage to human prefrontal cortex. In: *Cognition* 50, pp. 7–12, 1994.

——: Deciding advantageously before knowing the advantageous strategy. In: *Science* 275, pp. 1,293–1,295, 1997.

Begley, S., and Underwood, A.: Religion and the Brain. In: *Newsweek*, May 7, 2001.

Bench, C.J., et al.: Changes in regional cerebral blood flow on recovery from depression. In: *Psychological Medicine* 25, pp. 247–251, 1995.

Berk, S., and Efran, J.: Some recent developments in the treatment of neurosis. In: Walker, C., et al. (ed.): *The Handbook of Clinical Psychology.* Homewood, Illinois 1983.

Berkman, L.: *Health and Ways of Living: Findings from the Alameda County Study.* New York 1983.

Berkman, L., and Syme, S.: Social networks, host resistance and mortality. A nine-year-follow-up study of Alameda County residents. In: *American Journal of Epidemiology* 109, pp. 186–204, 1979.

Berridge, K.: Pleasure, pain, desire and dread: Hidden core processes of emotion. In: Kahneman, D., Diener, E., and Schwarz, N.(ed.): *Well-Being: The Foundations of Hedonic Psychology.* New York 2000.

Biddle, S., and Mutrie, N.: *Psychology of Physical Activity and Exercise.* London 1991.

Billig, A.: *Ermittlung des ökologischen Problembewusstseins der Bevölkerung. Umweltbundesamt.* Berlin 1994.

Birnbaumer, N., and Schmidt, R.: *Biologische Psychologie.* Heidelberg, Berlin 1999.

Blaffer Hrdy, S.: *Mother Nature.* New York, 1999.

Blomberg, A. v.: *Der Lust-Quotient.* Reinbek 2001.

Blum, K., et al.: Reward deficiency syndrome. In: *American Scientist* 84, pp. 132–146, 1996.

Blumenthal, J., et al.: Effects of exercise training on older patients with major depression. In: *Archives of Internal Medicine*, October 25, 1999.

Brecht, B. *Collected Plays*, vol. 2. Ed. and trans. J. Willett and R. Manheim. London 1979.

Breiter, H., et al.: Acute effects of cocaine on human brain activity and emotion. In: *Neuron* 19, pp. 591–611, 1997.

———: Functional imaging of neural responses to expectancy and experience of monetary gains and losses. In: *Neuron* 30, pp. 619–639, 2001.

Brickman, P., and Campbell, D.: Hedonic relativism and planning the good society. In: Appley, M.(ed.): *Adaptation-Level Theory*. New York 1971.

Brickman, P., Coates, D., and Janoff-Bulman, R.: Lottery winners and accident victims: Is happiness relative? In: *Journal of Personality and Social Psychology*, 36, pp. 917–927, 1978.

Brody, A. L., et al.: Regional brain metabolic changes in patients with major depression treated with either paroxetine or interpersonal therapy. In: *Archives of General Psychiatry* 58, pp. 631–640, 2001.

Brown, R.: Divided we fall. In: Tajfel, H. (ed.): *Differentiation between Social Groups*. London 1978.

Bruhn, J., and Wolf, S.: *The Roseto Story*. Norman, Oklahoma 1979.

Brunner, E.J.: Stress and the biology of inequality. In: *British Medical Journal* 314, pp. 1,472–1,476, 1997.

Caplan, R., et al.: *Job Demands and Worker Health*. US Department of Health, Education and Welfare 1975.

Carmichael, M., et al.: Relationships among cardiovascular, muscular and oxytocin response during human sexual activity. In: *Arch. Sex. Behav.* 23, pp. 59–79, 1994.

Carter, R.: *Mapping the Brain*. Berkeley 1998.

Casanova, G.: *Geschichte meines Lebens*. Vol. 1. Berlin 1964

Chaouloff, F.: Effects of acute physical exercise on central serotonergic systems. In: *Medical Science of Sports and Exercise* 29, pp. 58–62, 1997.

Clark, A., and Oswald, A.: *A statistical method for measuring how life events affect happiness*. University of Warwick, Unpublished manuscript, 2002.

Cocteau, J.: *Opium. Ein Tagebuch*. Munich 1968.

Coe, C., et al.: Immunological consequences of maternal separation in infant primates. In: Levis, M., and Worobey, J. (ed.): *Infant Stress and Coping*. San Francisco 1989.

Cohen-Cory, S., and Fraser, S.E.: Effects of brain-derived neurotrophic factor on the optic axon branching and remodelling in vivo. In: *Nature* 378, pp. 192–196, 1995.

Comer, R.: *Abnormal Psychology*. New York, 2003.

Cook, C., and Persinger, M.: Experimental induction of the "sensed presence" in normal subjects and an exceptional subject. In: *Percept. Mot. Skills* 85, pp. 683–693, 1997.

Cooper, S., and Kirkham, T.: Opioid mechanims in the control of food consumption and taste preference. In: Herz, A., et al. (ed.): *Handbook of Experimental Pharmacology*. Vol. 104/2. Berlin 1993.

Critchley, H., Mathias, C., and Dolan, R.: Neuroanatomical basis for first- and second-order representations of bodily states. In: *Nature Neuroscience* 4, No. 2, pp. 207–212, 2001.

Crites, S., et al.: Bioelectrical echoes from evaluative categorisations. In: *Journal of Personality and Social Psychology* 68, pp. 997–1,013, 1995.

Cromwell, H., and Berridge, K.: Where does damage lead to food aversion? In: *Brain Research* 624, pp. 1–10, 1993.

Czikszentmihalyi, M.: *Flow: The Psychology of Optimal Experience.* New York, 1990.

Dalai Lama and Cutler, H.: *The Art of Happiness.* New York, 1998.

Damasio, A.: *Descartes' Error.* New York, 2005.

———: *The Feeling of What Happens*, 1999.

———: A neurobiology for emotion and feeling. Proceedings of the Symposium "Feelings and Emotions," Amsterdam, June 13–16, 2001.

Damasio, A., et al.: Subcortical and cortical brain activity during the feeling of self-generated emotions. In: *Nature Neuroscience* 3, No. 10, pp. 1,049–1,056, 2000.

Davidson, R., et al.: Individual differences in prefrontal activation asymmetry predict natural kill cell activity. In: *Brain, Behaviour and Immunity* 13, pp. 93–108, 1999.

Davidson, R., and Fox, N.: Frontal brain asymmetry predicts infants' response to maternal separation. In: *Journal of Abnormal Psychology* 98, pp. 127–131, 1989.

Davidson, R. J., et al.: While a phobic waits. In: *Biological Psychiatry* 47, pp. 85–95, 2000.

Davidson, R. J., Tomarken, A. J., and Henriques, J. B.: Resting frontal asymmetry predicts affective response to films. In: *Journal of Personal and Social Psychology* 59, pp. 791–801, 1990.

de Waal, F.: *Good Natured.* Cambridge, MA, 1996.

de Waal, F., and Berger, M.: Payment for labor in monkeys. In: *Nature* 404, p. 563, 2000.

Descartes, R.: *Die Leidenschaften der Seele.* Hamburg 1984.

Defoe, D.: *Robinson Crusoe and Other Writings.* New York 1997.

Diener, E., and Sukh, E. S.: National differences in subjective well-being. In: Kahneman, D., Diener, E., and Schwarz, N. (eds.): *Well-Being: The Foundations of Hedonic Psychology.* New York 2000.

Diener, E., et al.: Happiness of the very wealthy. In: *Social Indicators Research* 16, pp. 263–274, 1985.

———: The relationship between income and subjective well-being: Relative or absolute. In: *Social Indicators Research* 28, pp. 195–223, 1993.

———: *Norms for Affect: National Comparisons.* Lecture, 9th Conference at the International Society for Research on Emotions, Toronto, August 13–17, 1996.

Duchenne, B.: *The Mechanism of Human Facial Expression or an Electro-Physiological Analysis of the Expression of the Emotions.* New York 1991.

Duman, R., et al.: A molecular and cellular theory of depression. In: *Archives of General Psychiatry* 54, pp. 597–606, 1997.

———: Neuronal plasticity and survival in mood disorders. In: *Biol. Psychiatry* 48, pp. 732–739, 2000.

Duman, R., Heninger, G., and Nestler, E.: A molecular and cellular theory of depression. In: *Archives of General Psychiatry* 54, pp. 597–606, 1997.

Durstewitz, D., et al.: A neurocomputational theory of the dopaminergic modulation of working memory functions. In: *Journal of Neuroscience* 19, pp. 2,807–2,822, 1999.

Egolf, B., et al.: The Roseto effect: A 50-year comparison of mortality rates. In: *American Journal of Public Health* 82, pp. 1,089–1,092, 1992.

Ekman, P.: Facial Expression and Emotion. In: *American Psychologist* 48, 4, pp. 384–392, 1993.

———: Facial Expressions. In: Dalgleish, T., and Power, M.: *Handbook of Cognition and Emotion*. New York 1999.

Ekman, P., et al.: The Duchenne Smile: Emotional expression and brain physiology II. In: *Journal of Personality and Social Psychology* 58, 2, pp. 342–353, 1990.

Ekman, P., and Davidson, R.: Voluntary smiling changes regional brain activity. In: *Psychological Science* 4, pp. 342–345, 1993.

Elbert, T., et al.: Increased cortical representation of the fingers in the left hand of string players. In: *Science* 270, pp. 305–307, 1995.

Elkin, I., et al.: National Institute of Mental Health treatment of depression collaborative research program: General effectiveness of treatments. In: *Archives of General Psychiatry* 46, pp. 971–982, 1989.

Elliott, R., Friston, K., and Dolan, R.: Dissociable neural responses in human reward systems. In: *Journal of Neuroscience* 20, pp. 6,159–6,165, 2000.

Engel, J.: *Seizures and Epilepsy*. Philadelphia 1989.

Engert, F., and Bonhoeffer, T.: Dendritic spine changes associated with hippocampal long-term synaptic plasticity. In: *Nature* 399, pp. 66–70, 1999.

Epictetus: *Wege zum glücklichen Handeln*. Frankfurt a. M. 1995.

Fava, G.: Well-Being Therapy: Conceptual and technical issues. In: *Psychotherapy and Psychosomatics* 68, pp. 171–179, 1999.

Fava, G., et al.: Well-being therapy: A novel psychotherapeutic approach for residual symptoms of affective disorders. In: *Psychological Medicine*, 28, pp. 475–480, 1998.

Feldman, R., et al.: *Principles of Neuropsychopharmacology*. Sunderland MA 1997.

Ferguson, J., et al.: Social amnesia in mice lacking the oxytocin gene. In: *Nature Genetics* 25, pp. 284–288, 2000.

———: Oxytocin in the medial amygdala is essential for social recognition in the mouse. In: *Journal of Neuroscience* 21, pp. 8,278–8,285, 2001.

Field, T., et al.: Tactile/kinetic stimulation effects on preterm neonates. In: *Pediatrics* 77, p. 654, 1986.

Fiorino, D. F., Coury, A., and Phillips, A. G.: Dynamic changes in nucleus accumbens dopamine efflux during the Coolidge effect in male rats. In: *Journal of Neuroscience* 17, pp. 4,849–4,855, 1997.

Flor, H.: *Spouses and Chronic Pain*. Lecture, Annual Meeting of the Society of Neuroscience, Orlando, November 3, 2002.

Fogel, R., and Egermann, S.: *Time on the Cross: The Economics of American Negro Slavery*. 1974, cited in Sen, A.: *Development as Freedom*: New York 1999.

Fox, N. A., and Davidson, R. J. (ed.): *The Psychobiology of Affective Development*. Hillsdale 1984.

Francis, D., et al.: Nongenomic transmission across generations of maternal behavior and stress responses in the rat. In: *Science* 286, pp. 1,155–1,158, 1999.

Frederick, S., and Loewenstein, G.: Hedonic adaptation. In: Kahneman, D., Diener, E., and Schwarz, N. (ed.): *Well-Being: The Foundations of Hedonic Psychology*. New York 2000.

Frederickson, B.: What good are positive emotions? In: *Review of General Psychology* 2, No. 3, pp. 300–319, 1998.

Frey, B.: Glück und Nationalökonomie. Walter-Adolf-Jöhr-Vorlesung an der Universität St. Gallen 2001. St. Gallen: *Forschungsgemeinschaft für Nationalökonomie* 2001.

Frey, B., and Stutzer, A.: *Happiness and Economics: How the Economy and Institutions Affect Human Well-Being*. Princeton 2002.

Goel, V., and Dolan, R.: The functional anatomy of humor. In: *Nature Neuroscience* 4, pp. 237–238, 2001.

Goldfoot, D., et al.: Behavioural and physiological evidence of a sexual climax in female stump-tailed macaque. In: *Science* 208, pp. 1,477–1,479, 1980.

Grastyan, E., et al.: Rebound, reinforcement, and self-stimulation. In: *Commun. Behav. Biol.* 2, pp. 235–266, 1968.

Grinspoon, L., and Bakalar, J.: Can drugs be used to enhance the psychotherapeutic process? In: *American Journal of Psychotherapy* 40, pp. 393–404, 1986.

Hamer, D.: D4 dopamine receptor genes and promiscuity. Lecture at the annual conference of the American Association for the Advancement of Science, Philadelphia, February 1998.

Haring, J. M., et al.: A research synthesis of literature on work status and subjective well-being. In: *Journal of Vocational Behaviour* 25, pp. 316–324, 1984.

Hejmadi, A., Davidson, R., and Rozin, P.: Exploring Hindu Indian Emotion Expressions. In: *Psychological Science* 11 pp. 183–187, 2000.

Henriques, J., and Davidson, R.: Decreased responsiviness to reward in depression. In: *Cognition and Emotion* 14, pp. 711–714, 2000.

Herz, A., and Spanagel, R.: Endogenous Opioids and Addiction. In: Tseng, L. S.: *The Pharmacology of Opioid Peptides*. Amsterdam 1995.

Hiroto, D.: Locus of control and learned helplessness. In: *Journal of Experimental Psychology*, 20, pp. 301–312, 1974.

Horn, C.: *Antike Lebenskunst*. Munich 1998.

House, J., et al.: Social relationship and health. In: *Science* 241, pp. 540–544, 1988.

Imperato-McGinley, J.: Steroid 5 alpha-reductase deficiency in man: an inherited form of male pseudohermaphroditism. In: *Science* 186, pp. 1,213–1,215, 1974.

Ingelhart, R.: *Culture Shift in Advanced Industrial Societies*. Princeton 1990.

Ingelhart, R., and Klingemann, H. D.: Genes, Culture, Democracy, and Happiness. In: Diener, E., and Sukh, E. S. (ed.): *Culture and Subjective Well-Being*. Cambridge 2000

Insel, T., and Young, L.: Neuropeptides and the evolution of social behaviour. In:

Current Opinion in Neurobiology 10, pp. 784–789, 2000.

Insel, T., and Young, L.: The neurobiology of attachment. In: *Nature Reviews Neuroscience* 2, pp. 129–136, 2001.

Insel, T., et al.: Oxytocin, Vasopressin, and Autism. In: *Biological Psychiatry* 45, pp. 145–157, 1999.

Isen, A.: Positive affect, cognitive processes, and social behaviour. In: *Advances in Experimental Social Psychology*, 20, pp. 203–253, 1987.

———: Positive affect facilitates thinking and problem solving. Proceedings of the Symposium "Feelings and Emotions." Amsterdam, June 13–16, 2001.

Isen, A., et al.: Positive affect facilitates creative problem solving. In: *Journal of Personality and Social Psychology* 52, pp. 1,122–1,131, 1987.

———: The influence of positive affect on clinical problem solving. In: *Medical Decision Making* 11, pp. 221–227, 1991.

Isen, A., and Daubmann, K.: The influence of affect on categorization. In: *Journal of Personality and Social Psychology* 47, pp. 1,206–1,217, 1984.

Ito, T., and Cacioppo, J.: The Psychophysiology of Utility Appraisals. In: Kahneman, D., Diener, E., and Schwarz, N. (ed.): *Well-Being: The Foundations of Hedonic Psychology*. New York 2000.

Ito, T., et al.: Negative information weighs more heavily on the brain. In: *Journal of Personality and Social Psychology* 75, pp. 887–900, 1998.

Jackson, D., et al.: Supression and enhancement of emotional responses to unpleasant pictures. In: *Psychobiology* 73, pp. 515–522, 2000.

Jahoda, M., Lazarsfeld, P., and Zeisel, H.: *Die Arbeitslosen von Marienthal. Ein soziographischer Versuch über die Wirkungen langdauernder Arbeitslosigkeit.* Frankfurt a. M. 1975.

Jugendwerk der Deutschen Shell (ed.): Jugend 2000. 13. *Shell Jugendstudie.* Opladen 1997.

Kahlweit, C.: Vor den Geranien winkt der Job. In: *Süddeutsche Zeitung*, March 26, 2002.

Kahneman, D.: Experienced utility and objective happiness: A moment-based approach. In: Kahneman, D., and Tversky, A. (ed.): *Choices, Values and Frames*. New York 2000.

Kandel, E., et al.: *Essentials of Neural Sciences and Behavior*. Norwalk, CT 1995.

Kaplan, G., et al.: Inequality in income and mortality in the United States. In: *British Medical Journal* 312, pp. 1,004–1,007, 1996.

Kasser, T., and Ryan, R. M.: A dark side of the American dream: Correlates of financial success as a central life aspiration. In: *Journal of Personality and Social Psychology* 63, pp. 410–422, 1993.

Kasser, T., and Ryan, R. M.: Further examining the American dream: Differential correlates of intrinsic and extrinsic goals. In: *Personality and Social Psychology Bulletin* 22, pp. 280–287, 1996.

Kawachi, I., et al.: Social capital, income inequality, and mortality. In: *American Journal of Public Health* 87, pp. 1,491–1,498, 1997.

Kawachi, I., and Kennedy, B.: Health and social cohesion. In: *British Medical Journal* 314, pp. 1,037–1,040, 1997.

———: The relationship of income inequality to mortality—does the choice of indicator matter? In: *Social Science & Medicine* 45, pp. 1,121–1,127, 1997.

Kawasaki, H., et al.: Single-neuron responses to emotional visual stimuli recorded in human prefrontal cortex. In: *Nature Neuroscience* 4, pp. 15–16, 2001.

Kempermann, G., et al.: More hippocampal neurons in adult mice living in an enriched environment. In: *Nature* 386, pp. 493–495, 1997.

Kennedy, B., Kawachi, I., and Prothrow-Stith, D.: Income distribution and mortality: cross sectional ecological study of the Robin Hood index in the United States. In: *British Medical Journal* 312, pp. 1,004–1,007, 1996.

Kerverne, E., et al.: Beta-Endorphin concentrations in CSF of monkeys are influenced by grooming relationships. In: *Psychoneuroendocrinology* 14, pp. 155–161, 1989.

Kessler R et al. Lifetime prevalence and age-of-onset distributions of DSM-IV disorders in the National Comorbidity Survey Replication. In: *Archives General Psychiatry* 62, pp. 593–602. 2005.

Kiecolt-Glaser, J., et al.: Psychosocial modifiers of immunocompetence in medical students. In: *Psychosomatic Medicine* 46, p. 6, 1984.

———: Marital quality, marital disruption and immune function. In: *Psychosomatic Medicine* 49, pp. 13–34, 1987.

———: Stressful relationships: Endocrine and Immune Function. In: Glaser, R., Kiecolt-Glaser, J. (ed.): *Handbook of Human Stress and Immunity*. San Diego 1994, pp. 321–339.

Klein, S.: *Die Tagebücher der Schöpfung*. Munich 2000.

Kleist, H. v.: Aufsatz, den sicheren Weg des Glücks zu finden. In: *Sämtl. Werke u. Briefe*, Vol. 2. Munich 1985.

Kobrin, F., and Hendershot, G.: Do family ties reduce mortality? Evidence from the United States. In: *Journal of Marriage and the Family* 39, pp. 737–745, 1977.

Koepp, M. J., et al.: Evidence for striatal dopamine release during a video game. In: *Nature* 39, pp. 266–268, 1998.

Konsalik, H., and Goetsche, M.: "Ich träume nicht, ich schreibe." In: *Deutsches Allgemeines Sonntagsblatt*, 39/1998.

Kopp, M.: Cultural Transition. In: Fink, G. (ed.): *Encyclopedia of Stress*. Vol. I. San Diego 2000.

Kopp, M., et al.: Psychosocial and traditional risk factors, inequality and self-rated morbidity in a changing society. In: Weidner, G., Kopp, M., and Kristenson, M. (ed.): *Heart Disease: Environment, Stress and Gender*. NATO Publications, Amsterdam 2000.

Krican, M., et al.: Oxytocin blocks the development of heroin-fetanyl cross-tolerance in mice. In: *Pharmacol. Biochem. Behav.* 52, pp. 591–594, 1995.

Kurihara, K., and Kashiwayanagi, M.: Introductory remarks on umami taste. In: *Annals of the New York Academy of Science* 855, pp. 393–397, 1998.

Lahelma, E.: *Unemployment, Re-Employment and Mental Well-Being*. Dissertation, University of Helsinki, 1989.

Landgraf, R., et al.: Push-pull perfusion and microdialysis studies of central oxytocin and vasopressin release in freely moving rats during pregnancy, parturition, and lactation. In: *Annals of the New York Academy of Sciences* 625, pp. 326–329, 1992.

LaPlante, E.: Seized. New York 1993.

Lavie, N.: Perceptual load as a necessary condition for selective attention. In: *Journal of Experimental Psychology: Human Perception and Performance* 21, pp. 451–468, 1995

Lazar, S., et al.: Functional brain mapping of the relaxation response and meditation. In: *NeuroReport* 11, pp. 1–5, 2000.

LeDoux, J.: *The Emotional Brain*. New York 1996.

LeVay, S.: A difference in hypothalamic structure between heterosexual and homosexual men. In: *Science* 253, pp. 1,034–1,037, 1991.

———: *The Sexual Brain*. Cambridge 1993.

Lewin, L.: *Phantastica: Narcotic and Stimulating Drugs*. London 1964.

Liechti, M., and Vollenweider, F.: Acute psychological and physiological effects of MDMA ("Ecstasy") after haloperidol pretreatment in healthy humans. In: *European Neuropsychopharmacology* 10, pp. 289–295, 2000.

Lindner, M.: *Hereditary and environmental influences upon resistance to stress*. Dissertation University of Pennsylvania 1968.

Linsky, A., et al.: Stressful events, stressful conditions and alcohol problems in the United States: A partial test of Bale's theory. In: *J. Stud. Alc.* 46, pp. 72–80, 1985.

Loomis, A. L., et al.: A System of Practical Medicine by American Authors. New York 1898. Quoted in: Panksepp, J.: *Affective Neuroscience*. Oxford 1998.

Lopez, J., et al: Regulation of the 5-HT1A receptor, glucocorticoid and mineralcorticoid receptor in rat and human hippocampus. Implications for the neurobiology of depression. In: *Biological Psychiatry* 42, pp. 547–573, 1998.

———: Neural circuits mediating stress. In: *Biological Psychiatry* 46, pp. 1,461–1,471, 1999.

Lorberbaum, J., et al.: Feasibility of using fMRI to study mothers responding to infant cries. In: *Depression and Anxiety* 10, pp. 99–104, 1999.

Löwer, C.: Die Selbst AG. In: *Der Spiegel* 36/2000.

Luxemburg, R.: *Briefe aus dem Gefängnis*. Berlin 2000.

Lykken, D.: Happiness: *What Studies on Twins Show Us about Nature, Nurture and the Happiness Set Point*. New York 1999.

Lykken, D., and Tellegen, A.: Happiness is a stochastic phenomenon. In: *Psychol. Science* 7, pp. 186–189, 1996.

Maguire, E. A., et al.: Knowing where and getting there. A human navigation network. In: *Science* 280, pp. 921–924, 1998.

———: Navigation-related structural change in the hippocampi of taxi drivers. In: *Proceedings of the National Academy of Sciences* 11, pp. 4,398–4,403, 2000.

Malberg, J., et al.: Chronic antidepressant treatment increases neurogenesis in adult rat hippocampus. In: *Journal of Neuroscience* 20, pp. 9,104–9,110, 2000.

Mallick, S. K., and McCandless, B. R.: A study of catharsis aggression. In: *Journal of Personality and Social Psychology* 4, pp. 591–596, 1966.

Marlatt, G., et al.: Provocation to anger and opportunity for retaliation as determinants of alcohol consumption in social drinkers. In: *Journal of Abnormal Psychology* 84, pp. 652–659, 1975.

Marmot, M., et al.: Contribution of job control and other risk factors to social variations in coronary heart disease incidence. In: *Lancet* 350, pp. 235–239, 1997.

Marmot, M., et al.: Health Inequalities among British Civil Servants: The Whitehall II study. In: *Lancet* 337, pp. 1,387–1,393, 1991.

Matt, G., et al.: Mood-congruent recall of affectively toned stimuli. In: *Clinical Psychology Review* 12, pp. 227–255, 1992.

Max, M., et al.: Tas1r3, encoding a new candidate taste receptor, is allelic to sweet responsiviness locus Sac. In: *Nature Genetics*, May 28 (1), pp. 58–63, 2001.

McAllister, A. K., et al.: Neurotrophins regulate dendritic growth in developing visual cortex. In: *Neuron* 15, pp. 791–803, 1995.

McCarthy, M.: Oxytocin inhibits infanticide in wild female house mice. In: *Horm. Behav.* 24, pp. 365–375, 1990.

McInerney, J. *How It Ended*. London, 2000.

Medvec, V., et al.: When less is more: Counterfactual thinking and satisfaction among Olympic medalists. In: *Journal of Personality and Social Psychology* 69, pp. 603–610, 1995.

Montagu, A.: *Touching: The Human Significance of the Skin*. New York, 1978.

Montague, P., Dayan, P., and Sejnowski, T.: Bee foraging in uncertain environments using predictive Hebbian learning. In: *Nature* 376, pp. 725–728, 1995.

Montaigne: *Essais*. Frankfurt a. M. 2001.

Montmayeur, J., et al.: A candidate taste receptor gene near a sweet taste locus. In: *Nature Neuroscience* 4 (5), pp. 492–498, 2001.

Moses, J., et al.: The effects of exercise training on mental well-being in the normal population: a controlled trial. In: *Journal of Psychosomatic Research* 33, pp. 47–61, 1989.

Moss, R.: Effects of hypothalamic peptides on sex behaviour in animal and man. In: Lipton, M., et al. (ed.): *Psychopharmacology*. New York 1978.

Murphy, M., et al.: Changes in oxytocin and vasopressin secretion during sexual activity in men. In: *J. Clin. Endocrinol. Metab.* 65, pp. 738–741, 1987.

———: Naloxone inhibits oxytocin release at orgasm in man. In: *J. Clin. Endocrinol. Metab.* 71, pp. 1,056–1,058, 1990.

Murray, C., and Lopez, A.: Global mortality, disability, and the contribution of risk factors: Global burden of disease study. In: *Lancet* 349, pp. 1,436–1,442, 1997.

Murray, C., et al.: The influence of mood on categorization. In: *Journal of Personality and Social Psychology*, 59, pp. 411–425, 1990.

Myers, D.: *Social psychology*. New York 1987.

———: *The Pursuit of Happiness*. New York 1992.

Myers, D., and Diener, E.: Who is happy? In: *Psychological Science* 6, 10–19, 1995.

Naipaul, V. S.: *India—A Million Mutinies Now*. London 1991.

Naj, A.: *Peppers. A Story of Hot Pursuits*. New York 1992.

Navratil, L.: *Schizophrenie und Sprache*. Munich 1966.

Nesse, R., and Berridge, K.: Psychoactive drug use in evolutionary perspective. In: *Science* 278, pp. 63–66, 1997.

Newberg, A., et al.: The measurement of regional cerebral blood flow during the complex cognitive task of meditation: a preliminary SPECT study. In: *Psychiatry Research: Neuroimaging Section* 106, pp. 113–122, 2001.

Nuñez, J., et al.: Alarm pheromone induces stress analgesia via opioid system in the honeybee. In: *Physiol. Behav.* 63, pp. 75–80, 1998.

Obradovic, T., et al.: Methylenedioxymethamphetamine-induced inhibition of neuronal firing in the nucleus accumbens is mediated by both serotonin and dopamine. In: *Neuroscience* 74, pp. 469–481, 1996.

O'Craven, K., and Kanwisher, M.: Mental imagery of faces and places activates stimulus-specific brain regions. In: *Journal of Cognitive Neuroscience* 12, pp. 1,013–1,023, 2000.

O'Doherty, J., et al.: Sensory-specific satiety-related olyfactory activation of the human orbitofrontal cortex. In: *NeuroReport* 11, pp. 893–897, 2000.

Odyssey. R. Fagles, trans. New York 1996.

Oettingen, G., and Seligman, M.: Pessimism and behavioural signs of depression in East versus West Berlin. In: *European Journal of Social Psychology* 20, pp. 207–220, 1990.

Okun, M., et al.: The social activity/subjective well-being relation: A quantitative synthesis. In: *Research on Aging* 6, pp. 45–65, 1984.

Olds, J.: *Drives and Reinforcement: Behavioral Studies of Hypothalamic Functions.* New York 1977.

Olds, J., and Milner, P.: Positive reinforcement produced by electrical stimulation of septal and other regions of the rat brain. In: *Journal of Comparative Physiological Psychology* 47, pp. 419–427, 1954.

Oomura, Y., et al.: Central control of sexual behaviour. In: *Brain Research Bulletin* 20, pp. 863–870, 1988.

Ostrove, J., et al.: Objective and subjective assessments of socioeconomic stature and their relationship to self-rated health in an ethically diverse sample of pregnant women. In: *Health Psychology* 19, pp. 613–618, 2000.

Ovid: *Metamorphosen.* Munich 1997.

Panksepp, J.: *Affective Neuroscience: The Foundations of Human and Animal Emotions.* Oxford 1998.

Panksepp, J., et al.: Opioid blockade and social comfort in chickens. In: *Pharmacol. Biochem. Behav.* 13, pp. 673–683, 1980.

———: Opiates and play dominance in juvenile rats. In: *Behavioural Neuroscience* 99, pp. 441–453, 1985.

Parducci, A.: The relativism of absolute judgments. In: *Scientific American* 219, pp. 84–90, 1968.

Pascal, B.: *Gedanken.* Munich 1980.

Pascual-Leone, A., and Torres, E.: Plasticity of the sensorimotor cortex representations of the reading finger in Braille readers. In: *Brain* 116, pp. 39–52, 1993.

283

Pascual-Leone, A., et al.: The role of reading activity on the modulation of motor cortical outputs to the reading hand in Braille readers. In: *Annals of Neurology* 38, pp. 910–915, 1995.

Pedersen, C., et al.: Oxytocin induces maternal behaviour in virgin female rats. In: *Science* 216, pp. 648–650, 1982.

Persky, H. (ed.): *Sexual Medicine*, Vol. 6: Psychoendocrinology of human sexual behaviour. Westport 1987.

Pfeiffer, A., et al.: Psychotomimesis mediated by opiate receptors. In: *Science* 239, pp. 774–776, 1986.

Piazza, V., et al.: Neuroactive steroids: mechanisms of action. In: *Science* 245, pp. 1,511, 1989.

Pinker, S.: How the Mind Works. New York 1997.

Putnam, R.: *Making Democracy Work*. Princeton 1993.

———: *Bowling Alone. The Collapse and Revival of American Community*. New York 2000.

Radhakrishnan, S.: *Indian Philosophy*. Oxford, 6th ed. 2000.

Rajkowska, G.: Postmortem Studies in mood disorders indicate altered numbers of neurones and glial cells. In: *Biological Psychiatry* 48, pp. 766–777, 2000.

Ramachandran, V. S.: *Phantoms in the Brain*. New York 1998.

Randow, G. von: *Genießen*. Hamburg 2001.

Rees, G., et al.: Modulating irrelevant motion perception by varying attentional load in an unrelated task. In: *Science* 278, pp. 1,616–1,619, 1997.

Reynolds, J., et al.: A cellular mechanism of reward-related learning. In: *Nature* 413, pp. 67–70, 2001.

Riley, V.: Psychoneuroendocrine influences on immunocompetence and neoplasia. In: *Science* 212, p. 1,100, 1981.

Robbins, J.: Wired for sadness. In: *Discover* 4/2000, p. 77.

Robins, L., and Rieger, D.: Psychiatric Disorders in America. New York 1991.

Rodin, J.: Aging and health. Effects of the sense of control. In: *Science* 233, p. 1,271, 1986.

Rodriguez-Manzo, G., and Fernandez-Guasti, A.: Reversal of sexual exhaustion by serotonergic and noradrenergic agents. In: *Behav. Brain Res.* 62, pp. 127–134, 1994.

———: Opioid antagonists and the sexual satiation phenomenon. In: *Psychopharmacol.* 122, pp. 131–136, 1995.

———: Participation of the central noradrenergic system in the reestablishment of copulatory behavior of sexually exhausted rats by yohimbine, naloxone, and 8-OH-DPAT. In: *Brain Research Bulletin* 38, pp. 399–404, 1995.

Rogers, M., et al.: Frontostriatal deficits in unipolar major depression. In: *Brain Research Bulletin* 47, pp. 297–301, 1998.

Rolls, E.: *The Brain and Emotion*. Oxford 1999.

Rosengren, A., et al.: Stressful life events, social support and mortality in men born in 1933. In: *British Medical Journal* 307, pp. 1,102–1,105, 1993.

Rowe, J., and Kahn, R.: Human aging: Usual and successful. In: *Science* 237, p. 143, 1987.

Rozin, P.: Getting to like the burn of chili pepper. In: Green, B. G., et al. (ed.): *Chemical Irritation in the Nose and Mouth*. New York 1990.

Russell, B.: *History of Western Philosophy*. London 1946.

———: *The Conquest of Happiness*. New York 1930.

Ryan, R. M., et al.: The American dream in Russia: Extrinsic aspirations and well-being in two cultures. In: *Personality and Social Psychology Bulletin 25*, pp. 1,509–1,524, 1999.

Sacks, O.: *Awakenings*. London 1973.

Sapolsky, R.: Endocrinology al fresco: Psychoendocrine studies of wild baboons. In: *Recent Progress in Hormone Research 48*, pp. 437–459, 1993.

———: *Why Zebras Don't Get Ulcers*, 3rd ed. New York 2004.

———: *A Primate's Memoir*. New York 2001.

———: The Physiology and Pathophysiology of Unhappiness. In: Kahneman, D., Diener, E., and Schwarz, N. (eds.): *Well Being: The Foundations of Hedonic Psychology*. New York 2000.

Sapolsky, R., et al.: Hypercortisolism associated with social isolation among wild baboons. In: *Archives of General Psychiatry 54*, pp. 1,137–1,143, 1997.

Saver, J. L., and Rabin, J.: The neural substrates of religious experience. In: *J. Neuropsychiatry 9*, pp. 498–510, 1997.

Scheibel, A. B., et al.: A quantitative study of dendrite complexity in selected areas of the human cerebral cortex. In: *Brain and Cognition 12*, pp. 85–101, 1990.

Schmuck, P., et al.: Intrinsic and extrinsic goals: Their structure and relationship to well-being in German and US college students. In: *Social Indicators Research 50*, pp. 225–241, 2000.

Schultz, W.: Multiple reward signals in the brain. In: *Nature Reviews Neuroscience 1*, pp. 199–207, 2000.

Schultz, W., Apicella, P., and Ljungberg, T.: Responses of monkey dopamine neurons during learning of behavioral reactions. In: *J. Neurophysiology 67*, pp. 145–163, 1992.

———: Responses of monkey dopamine neurons to reward and conditioned stimuli during steps of learning a delayed response task. In: *J. Neuroscience 13* (3), pp. 900–913, 1993.

Schultz, W., Dayan, P., and Montague, P.: A neural substrate of prediction and reward. In: *Science 275*, pp. 1,593–1,599, 1997.

Schwartz, D.: *Vernunft and Emotion*. Dortmund 1998.

Schwartz, J. M., et al.: Systematic changes in cerebral glucose metabolic rate after successful behavior modification treatment of obsessive-compulsive disorder. In: *Archives of General Psychiatry 53*, pp. 109–113, 1996.

Schwarz, N., et al.: Soccer, rooms and the quality of your life: Mood effects on judgments of satisfaction with life in general and with specific domains. In: *European Journal of Social Psychology 17*, pp. 69–79, 1987.

———: Judgments of relationship satisfaction: Inter- and intraindividual comparison strategies as a function of questionnaire structure. In: *European Journal of Social Psychology 18*, pp. 485–96, 1988.

Scully, D., et al.: Physical exercise and psychological well being: a critical review. In: *British Journal of Sports Medicine*, 32 (2), 111–120, 1998.

Seligman, M.: *Learned Optimism*. New York 1991.

Sell, A., et al.: Activation of reward circuitry in human opiate addicts. In: *European Journal of Neuroscience*, 11, pp. 1,042–1,048, 1999.

Sen, A.: *Choice, Welfare and Measurement*. Oxford 1982.

———: *Development as Freedom*. New York 1999.

Shermer, M.: The pundit of primate politics. In: *Sceptic* 8, pp. 29–35, 2000.

Smith, D. A.: Lateral hypothalamic stimulation: Experience and deprivation as factors in rat's licking of empty drinking tubes. In: *Psychological Science* 23, pp. 329–331, 1971.

Smith, R., Diener, E., and Garonzik, R.: The roles of outcome satisfaction and comparison alternatives in envy. In: *British Journal of Social Psychology* 29, pp. 247–255, 1990.

Sodersten, P., et al.: Vasopressin alters female sexual behaviour by acting on the brain independently of alterations in blood pressure. In: *Nature* 301, pp. 608–610, 1983.

Solomon, A.: *Noonday Demon: An Atlas of Depression*. New York 2001.

Spiegel, D.: A psychosocial intervention and the survival time of patients with metastatic breast cancer. In: *Advances* 7, p. 10, 1991.

Spiegel, D., et al.: Effect of psychosocial treatment on survival of patients with metastasic breast cancer. In: *Lancet* 2, pp. 888–891, 1989.

Spielberger, C. D.: The measurement of state and trait anxiety: Conceptual and methodological issues. In: Levi, L. (ed.): *Emotions: Their Parameters and Measurement*. New York 1975.

Steptoe, A., et al.: Exercise and the experience and appraisal of daily stressors. In: *Journal of Behavioural Medicine* 21, pp. 363–374, 1996.

Stevenson, R. J., and Yeomans, M. R.: Does exposure enhance liking for the chili burn? In: *Appetite* 24, pp. 107–120, 1995.

Storm, T.: Cited in Randow, G. v.: *Genießen*. Hamburg 2001.

Strack, F., et al.: The salience of comparison standards and the activation of social norms: Consequences for judgments of happiness and their communication. In: *British Journal of Social Psychology* 18, pp. 429–442, 1990.

Stroebe, W., and Stroebe, M.: Partnerschaft, Familie und Wohlbefinden. In: Aberle, A., and Becher, P. (ed.): *Wohlbefinden*. Weinheim 1991.

Svartberg, M., and Stiles, T.: Comparative effects of short-term psychodynamic psychotherapy: A meta-analysis. In: *J. Cons. Clin. Psychol.* 59, pp. 704–714, 1991.

Tagore, R.: *Later Poems*. Translated by A. Bose. Delhi 1976.

Tatarkiewicz, W.: *Analysis of Happiness*. Warsaw 1976.

Thanos, P., et al.: Overexpression of dopamine D2 receptors reduces alcohol self-administration. In: *Journal of Neurochemistry* 78, pp. 1,094–1,103, 2001.

Thich Nhat Hanh: *Die Kunst, einen Baum zu umarmen*. Munich 1995.

Thompson, A., and Kristal, M.: Opioid stimulation in the ventral tegmental area facilitates the onset of maternal behavior in rats. In: *Brain Research* 743, pp. 184–201, 1996.

Travis, C.: Anger: *The Misunderstood Emotion*. New York 1989.

Uvnäs-Mosberg, K., et al.: Personality traits in women 4 days post partum and their correlation with plasma levels of oxytocin and prolactin. In: *Journal of Psychosomatics and Gynecology* 11, pp. 261–273, 1990.

Vincent, J. D.: *Casanova*. Paris 1990.

———: *The Biology of Emotions*. Cambridge, 1990.

Vogel, G.: New brain cells prompt new theory on depression. In: *Science* 290, pp. 258–259, 2000.

Wallace, R. K., and Benson, H.: The Physiology of Meditation. In: *Scientific American* 226 (2), pp. 84–90, 1972.

Wecker, K.: "Ich liebte meinen Dealer." In: *Der Spiegel* 25/1998.

Wenzlaff, R.: The mental control of depression. In: Wegner, D., and Pennebaker, J. (ed.): *Handbook of Mental Control*. Englewood Cliffs NJ 1993.

Wheeler, R. E., Davidson, R. J., and Tomarken, A. J.: Frontal brain asymmetry and emotional reactivity: a biological substrate of affective style. In: *Psychophysiologie* 30, pp. 547–558, 1993.

Wickelgren, I.: Getting the brain's attention. In: *Science* 278, pp. 35–37, 1997

Wilkinson, R.: *Unhealthy Societies*. London 1996.

Winslow, J., and Insel, T.: Endogenous opioids: Do they modulate the rat pup's response to social isolation? In: *Behavioural Neuroscience* 105, pp. 253–263, 1991.

Wittchen, H. U.: Die Studie "Depression 2000." In: *Fortschritte der Medizin Sonderheft* I/2000.

Wurtz, R. H., and Goldberg, M. E. (ed.): The neurobiology of saccadic eye movements. In: *Reviews of Oculomotor Research*, Vol. 3. Amsterdam 1989.

Young, L., et al.: Increased affilative response to vasopressin in mice expressing the V1a receptor from a monogamous vole. In: *Nature* 400, pp. 766–768, 1999.

Zajonc, R.: Attitudinal effects of mere exposure. In: *Journal of Personality and Social Psychology Monographs* 9, pp. 1–32, 1968.

Zieglgänsberger, W., and Spanagel, R.: Molekularbiologie der Sucht. In: Ganten, D., and Ruckpaul, K. (ed.): *Handbuch der molekularen Medizin*, Bd. 5. Berlin–Heidelberg 1999.

ACKNOWLEDGMENTS

I have been fortunate in getting to know many of the leading researchers in the study of the brain and emotions, and they have been generous with their time and insights. For this I thank Nancy Adler, Ralph Adolphs, Patricia Churchland, Antonio Damasio, Richard Davidson, Raymond Dolan, Paul Ekman, Chris Frith, Fritz Henn, Steven Hyman, Tom Insel, Ravi Kapur, Charles O'Brien, Detlev Ploog, Jaak Panksepp, Signe Preuschoft, V. S. Ramachandran, Carol Ryff, Wolfram Schultz, Terrence Sejnowski, Alexander Shulgin, Frans de Waal, and Walter Zieglgänsberger.

I owe a special debt to those scientists who not only answered my questions but also read parts or all of the manuscript: Udo Becker and Isabella Heuser of the Free University of Berlin's Psychiatrisches Klinikum Benjamin Franklin, Volker Gerhardt of the Philosophische Fakultät of Berlin's Humboldt University, Rainer Landgard of the Max-Planck-Institut für Psychiatrie in Munich, Norbert Schwarz of the University of Michigan in Ann Arbor, and Rainer Spanagel of the Zentralinstitut für Seelische Gesundheit in Mannheim. Their friendly criticisms were enormously helpful in bringing me closer to my goal of writing not only as clearly but as precisely as possible. Responsibility for any errors are, of course, mine alone.

My assistants Jana Binder, Christoph Leischwitz and Martina Kienow have gathered and gone through a huge amount of material. Without them I would not have been able to manage the preliminary work of this project in such a relatively short time. Monika Klein not only browsed the Internet and spent hours in the library but copyedited the manuscript and helped me prepare the notes and bibliography.

My friends Joerg Altekruse, Ulrich Bahnsen, Stefan Bauer, Hildegard Diehl-Bode, Volker Foertsch, Margitta Holler, and Wolfgang Schneider repeatedly took the time to review the concept and the manuscript in its various versions from the reader's perspective. Their praise and blame were most stimulating and helpful, and thanks to them I was spared the loneliness that is endemic to writers.

When questions arose, Uwe Naumann of the Rowohlt Verlag was always open to my wishes and advice. Ursula Nussbaum managed the publicity and worked on the book's behalf with care and engagement. Eva Ninnemann and Elektra Rigos designed the successful website (www.stefanklein.info). And Matthias Landwehr, my agent, was enthusiastic about this project from the beginning and then skillful in representing it.

My wife, Alexandra Rigos, accompanied this book in all phases of its development, from vague idea to completed page proofs. It owes an infinite debt to her keen judgment, sensitivity, and feeling for language. To whom else should I dedicate a book on happiness?

—*Stefan Klein, PhD*

My thanks to Elizabeth Lewis and Carol Sabersky for their patient and invaluable help with the translation.

—*Stephen Lehmann,*
Philadelphia, December 2005

289

INDEX